D1294116

RESEARCH WITH HIGH-RISK POPULATIONS

RESEARCH WITH HIGH-RISK POPULATIONS

Balancing Science, Ethics, and Law

Edited by
David Buchanan,
Celia B. Fisher,
and Lance Gable

American Psychological Association • Washington, DC

Published by
American Psychological Association
750 First Street, NE
Washington, DC 20002
www.apa.org

To order
APA Order Department
P.O. Box 92984
Washington, DC 20090-2984
Tel: (800) 374-2721; Direct: (202) 336-5510
Fax: (202) 336-5502; TDD/TTY: (202) 336-6123
Online: www.apa.org/books/
E-mail: order@apa.org

In the U.K., Europe, Africa, and the Middle East, copies may be ordered from
American Psychological Association
3 Henrietta Street
Covent Garden, London
WC2E 8LU England

Typeset in Goudy by Stephen McDougal, Mechanicsville, MD

Printer: Book-Mart Press, Inc., North Bergen, NJ
Cover Designer: Mercury Publishing Services, Rockville, MD
Technical/Production Editor: Emily Welsh

Library of Congress Cataloging-in-Publication Data

Research with high-risk populations : balancing science, ethics, and law / edited by David Buchanan, Celia B. Fisher, and Lance Gable. -- 1st ed.
p. cm.
Includes bibliographical references and index.
ISBN-13: 978-1-4338-0424-3
ISBN-10: 1-4338-0424-7
1. Psychology—Research—Moral and ethical aspects. I. Buchanan, David A. II. Fisher, Celia B. III. Gable, Lance.

BF76.5.R467 2009
616.89'027—dc22 2008040490

British Library Cataloguing-in-Publication Data
A CIP record is available from the British Library.

Printed in the United States of America
First Edition

CONTENTS

CONTRIBUTORS

David Buchanan, DrPH, School of Public Health & Health Sciences University of Massachusetts, Amherst

Jennifer J. Cercone, PhD, Charlie Norwood VA Medical Center, Augusta, GA

Catherine Cerulli, JD, PhD, Laboratory of Interpersonal Violence and Victimization, Rochester, NY

Li-Shiun Chen, MD, MPH, ScD, Washington University School of Medicine, St. Louis, MO

Carla Kmett Danielson, PhD, Department of Psychiatry & Behavioral Sciences, Medical University of South Carolina, Charleston

Eloise Dunlap, PhD, National Development and Research Institutes, Inc., New York

Celia B. Fisher, PhD, Department of Psychology, Fordham University, New York

Lance Gable, JD, MPH, Wayne State University Law School, Detroit, MI

Sabrina J. Goodman, MA, Department of Psychology, Fordham University, New York

Debbie Green, MA, Department of Psychology, Fordham University, New York

Ashley Hughes Haden, MSW, Department of Psychiatry, Washington University School of Medicine, St. Louis, MO

G. Derrick Hodge, PhD, Mount Sinai School of Medicine, New York

Bruce D. Johnson, PhD, National Development and Research Institutes, Inc., New York

Dean G. Kilpatrick, PhD, Department of Psychiatry & Behavioral Sciences, Medical University of South Carolina, Charleston

David M. Ledgerwood, PhD, Wayne State School of Medicine, Detroit, MI

Jacqueline V. Lerner, PhD, Lynch School of Education, Boston College, Boston, MA
Richard M. Lerner, PhD, Institute for Applied Research in Youth Development, Tufts University, Medford, MA
Collins E. Lewis, MD, Washington University School of Medicine, St. Louis, MO
Lang Ma, MD, PhD, Half the Sky Foundation, Beijing, The People's Republic of China
Meena Mahadevan, PhD, Department of Psychology, Fordham University, New York
Gregory Mirhej, BA, Center for Community Health Research, Hispanic Health Council, Hartford, CT
Matthew Oransky, MA, Department of Psychology, Fordham University, New York
Erin Phelps, EdD, Institute for Applied Research in Youth Development, Tufts University, Medford, MA
Rumi Kato Price, PhD, MPE, Washington University School of Medicine, St. Louis, MO
Doris Randolph, MA, National Development and Research Institutes, Inc., New York
Nathan K. Risk, MA, St. Louis, MO
Barry Rosenfeld, PhD, ABPP, Department of Psychology, Fordham University, New York
Kenneth J. Ruggiero, PhD, Department of Psychiatry & Behavioral Sciences, Medical University of South Carolina, Charleston
Merrill Singer, PhD, Professor of Anthropology, University of Connecticut, Storrs
Christopher D. Thomas, JD, Nixon Peabody LLP, Rochester, NY
Gregory A. Widner, MSW, Washington University School of Medicine, St. Louis, MO

RESEARCH WITH HIGH-RISK POPULATIONS

INTRODUCTION

DAVID R. BUCHANAN, CELIA B. FISHER, AND LANCE GABLE

These are complicated times for researchers and institutional review boards (IRBs) with respect to the protection of human subjects. On the one hand, many people believe that research involving human subjects is not being given sufficient scrutiny and oversight (Brown, 1998; Emanuel, 2002; Emanuel, Wood, et al., 2004). On the other hand, many researchers complain that IRBs have overreached their mandate and have become overly cautious to the point of stifling important research that holds virtually no risk to the safety and well-being of the participants (Cohen, 2007). In focusing on descriptive research with high-risk populations, this book examines the middle ground between these polar positions. In research with high-risk populations, study participants are defined as more likely than average to be suicidal, to commit acts of violence, or to have been traumatized by child abuse or battering.

Social scientists often encounter the following sorts of situations. In a list of items on future intentions (e.g., to smoke marijuana in the next month), an adolescent crosses out one of the items and writes in "commit suicide" on a confidential but nonanonymous questionnaire (with coded individual identifiers). During the course of an ethnographic field study of HIV risk among injection drug users, the researcher observes a couple, whose HIV status is known through prior confidential interviews to be discordant, about to share a needle. In a longitudinal study of the health of Vietnam veterans, a participant expresses progressively despondent depressive symptoms and suicide ideation over time in follow-up interviews. In a research interview on contraceptive practices, a male participant exclaims that he is going to beat his partner the next time he sees her because of her suspected infidelity. What should researchers do in these situations? How should IRBs assess the threat of harm to the participants, and other third parties, in these types of studies? What are the obligations of research institutions, both to the participants and to society, in confronting such dilemmas?

This book focuses on descriptive research, which by definition does not expose participants to experimental interventions. Hence, the type of research examined here is categorically distinct from clinical medical trials, in which patients are exposed to novel pharmacological, radiological, or surgical treatments with unknown risks and for which the most widely recognized ethical standards for conducting research with human subjects have been developed. Yet, unlike, for example, studies of voting preferences, investigators who conduct research with high-risk populations must be prepared for the possibility of harm befalling the participants themselves or noninvolved third parties during the course of the research.

In the 35 years since the inception of the field of bioethics, the predominant focus of the field has been clinical settings (e.g., end-of-life bedside counseling) and clinical trials (e.g., testing new drugs to treat cancer). There is now an extensive literature on the ethical and legal responsibilities of researchers conducting randomized controlled trials, in which participants must be protected from undue harm associated with an experimental intervention (e.g., the side effects of new pharmaceutical agents). Relatively little attention, however, has been paid to the distinct ethical and legal challenges that may arise in the course of conducting descriptive, nonexperimental research, especially in the context of potential threat of harm from the research participants themselves, in cases of suicide, or when it falls on third parties not directly involved in the research, in cases of domestic violence and child abuse.

The deaths of two subjects in two separate clinical trials—Jesse Gelsinger in a gene therapy trial in 1999 and Ellen Roche, a healthy volunteer who was administered a drug designed to induce a mild asthma attack, in 2001—have dramatically altered the climate surrounding IRB reviews (Savulescu, 2001; Savulescu & Spriggs, 2002; Somia & Verma, 2000; Steinbrook, 2002). Even though both studies involved medical experiments, they have had a palpable effect on ethical reviews of social scientific research. The two incidents, close on the heels of one another, generated widespread media attention and heightened public concern about whether IRBs pay sufficient attention to protecting research participants from harm, relative to the weight given to the presumed benefits of conducting health research. IRBs have reacted to the backlash generated by these two experiments by becoming increasingly risk aversive and reluctant to approve research that has any inherent possibility of significant harm befalling the participants. Fears of litigation and liability have reinforced a conservative approach to IRB review (Mello, Studdert, & Brennan, 2003; Resnik, 2004).

In light of these developments, it is critically important to identify and address legal and ethical issues unique to descriptive research on high-risk behaviors. This book seeks to map out an appropriate balance between protecting human subjects from harm and generating new scientific knowledge, knowledge that could potentially benefit countless numbers of research participants and others who may face harm from suicide, abuse, and violence in the future.

PURPOSE

Research With High-Risk Populations: Balancing Science, Ethics, and Law provides in-depth analyses and guidance to social scientists regarding ethical and legal responsibilities that may arise in the course of conducting research with high-risk populations and in responding appropriately to threats of suicide, child abuse, and violence that may arise during the course of data collection. These discussions offer valuable lessons both for researchers who are planning to investigate the etiology of these particular problems and for researchers who may be confronted with similar threats of harm while investigating other health concerns such as HIV/AIDS or substance abuse.

Because of the paucity of informed analyses of this critical topic area, researchers now find themselves caught between contradictory assumptions about the nature of the risks involved in descriptive research with populations at risk of violence and other harms. On the one hand, the traditional view has been that descriptive research poses minimal risk, as it is completely unlike medical experiments in which participants are exposed to novel experimental treatments. One common view is that if the research involves merely asking people questions, then the ethical risk of such research is limited to the harms that could emerge if confidential information were to be inadvertently disclosed. On the other hand, research with high-risk populations raises acute and appropriate questions for investigators, IRBs, and other interested parties about a duty to protect: When or at what point does the threat of harm, such as suicide, child abuse, or violence, warrant overriding confidentiality protections?

The chapters that follow present the experiences and analyses of leading researchers, ethicists, lawyers, and IRB members from across the country who have wrestled with these issues for years. They illuminate the complexities of the issues involved and provide model standards for researchers and IRB members with respect to critical ethical and legal considerations in conducting research with high-risk populations. On the basis of case studies from ongoing research projects, this collection of ethical and legal analyses examines both the challenges of conducting research designed to gain a better understanding of the etiology of these serious health problems responsibly and the moral and legal obligations of researchers who learn of threats of violence in the course of pursuing the primary objectives of the research. (For more chapter details, see the section "Organization and Overview of the Book" at the end of this chapter.)

Ethical considerations in the case studies presented here address issues of confidentiality and disclosure: When does the threat of harm, such as suicide, child abuse, or violence, justify disclosing information offered under assurances of protecting the participant's confidentiality? Contributors consider the distinct issues involved in informed consent documents for studies of suicide, child abuse, and domestic violence: How does one identify and adequately communicate to participants the limits of confidentiality protections? How does one address the tensions between subject recruitment and warnings about the investigators' obligation to disclose behaviors that may be the focus of the research? The chapters on legal issues describe and analyze federal, state, and local laws that either mandate or prohibit researchers from responding in situations that threaten violence, child abuse, and suicide; provide investigators protection from subpoenas of their confidential records; highlight distinctions between ethical and legal requirements; and outline evolving case law regarding the legal liability of institutions that sponsor such research.

HISTORICAL BACKGROUND

Debates about the safety of research participation and the adequacy of human subjects protections have undergone major shifts over the past century of medical research, with periodic pendulum swings in the level of public anxieties. It is important to situate current controversies in this larger context. Walter Reed's use of informed consent in his yellow fever experiments in Cuba in 1900 is generally recognized as one of the earliest well-documented examples of the systematic application of ethical standards in health research (Berg, Appelbaum, Lidz, & Parker, 2001; Levine, 1986). There can be little question, however, that it was the horror of the Holocaust and the so-called Doctors Trial at the Nuremberg War Crimes Tribunal that marked the emergence of serious public, political, and intellectual attention to the potential for harm and suffering that could be inflicted in the name of health research. In the aftermath of the brutal Nazi experiments involving concentration camp inmates, the Nuremberg Code placed great weight on the principle of respect for human autonomy and, consequently, stringent mandates for informed consent and voluntary participation. These principles were subsequently reaffirmed by the World Medical Association in the Declaration of Helsinki in 1964 (World Medical Association, 1997).

Yet, despite these documents, it took newspaper reports in the early 1970s revealing the ongoing U.S. Public Health Service Syphilis Study at Tuskegee—research that began in the 1930s—to provoke sufficient public outrage to force the U.S. Congress to address for the first time the ethics of publicly funded health research in a major national public forum (Jonsen, 2000). In response to the egregious misconduct by researchers at Tuskegee (and other controversies surrounding the notorious Milgram obedience experiments and the covert ethnographic "tearoom trade" study of homosexual behaviors conducted without the participants' consent; Beecher, 1966; Humphreys, 1970), the National Commission for the Protection of Human Subjects of Biomedical and Behavioral Research was convened by Congress in 1974 and their landmark Belmont Report issued in 1978 (National Commission, 1979). The Belmont Report provided guidelines for the ethical conduct of health research and still stands as one of the most articulate expositions of the rationale, warrants, and ethical principles that should guide the conduct of health research.

In the climate of the times, the Belmont Report (National Commission, 1979) focused primarily on protecting potential research participants from harm and exploitation, in lieu of other possible ethical concerns. The recommendations of the National Commission were incorporated into detailed regulations governing research involving human subjects funded by the U.S. government. These regulations, known as the Common Rule (Protection of Human Subjects, 2005), specify the requirements for independent prospective review by IRBs, reasonable estimates of foreseeable risks and benefits, and strict adherence to written voluntary and informed consent. These regulations also enumerate the conditions in which children and adults incapable of providing their own competent consent can be enrolled in research and the conditions for which informed consent requirements can be waived (Protection of Human Subjects, 2005).

As investigators and IRBs gained experience in conducting clinical medical trials under these regulations, the weight of public moral concerns began to shift, from a preoccupation with the risks of participating in research to an appreciation of the potential benefits that research could provide society (Kahn, Mastroianni, & Sugarman, 1998; McCarthy, 1998; Powers, 1998). As the Belmont Report noted, both the risks and the benefits of research must be distributed fairly, in accordance with principles of justice (National Commission, 1979). Throughout the 1980s, heart disease studies, for example, excluded women from participation on the questionable grounds that the research posed unreasonable risks to the reproductive, child-bearing capacities of women. However, as a result, the effects of new drugs and new medical procedures on the distinct female biology and physiology were not investigated. Not only were women being denied access to new and potentially life-saving therapies in the trials themselves, but also, outside of the trials, women as a class were being denied information on the risks and benefits of new therapeutic interventions. With the onset of the AIDS epidemic, the dire need for effective treatments led many people to view research participation not as a burden, but as an opportunity to obtain the most scientifically advanced therapies possible (Melton, Levine, Koocher, Rosenthal, & Thompson, 1988). In 2001, the National Institute of Mental Health, the American Foundation for Suicide Prevention, and the National Institutes of Health Office of Rare Diseases organized a meeting to address the tensions between the public's growing need for research on the causes of and effective prevention strategies for suicide and IRB concerns about the absence of specific regulatory guidance on protections for this vulnerable population (Fisher, Pearson, Kim, & Reynolds, 2002). This change in public attitudes shifted the focus of public debates about participation in health research from concerns about the threat of harms to issues of access and concerns for the inclusion of traditionally excluded groups, such as women, minorities, and children. The inclusion of these groups is now seen to be ethically and legally mandatory so that they too can benefit from publicly funded research, both directly through their participation and indirectly as members of distinct social groups who stand to gain from advances in health research (Fisher, Hoagwood, et al., 2002; Trimble & Fisher, 2006).

While public attitudes toward medical research were growing more benign, there were simultaneous countercurrents with respect to the conduct of social scientific research. In a line of thinking that can be traced back to the Hippocratic Oath, there has long been concern about the need to protect the confidentiality of patients—and likewise that of research participants—in which one major threat of harm lies in the embarrassment or stigma to the individual that may result from disclosure of personal information. Thus, the principle of respect for individual autonomy, and protecting confidentiality accordingly (granting individuals the right to decide whether they want the information to be revealed), has been well established for centuries. The legal salience of privacy protections increased further as a result of a series of U.S. Supreme Court decisions in the 1960s and 1970s that recognized a constitutional right to privacy. Moreover, many states enacted privacy and confidentiality protections for research participants and patients in the clinical setting. An individual's right to privacy, however, did not mean that one could prevent the disclosure of identifiable data in all circumstances. A California court recognized an important exception to confidentiality in the seminal case of *Tarasoff v. the Regents of the University of California* in 1974 and reaffirmed it in 1976.

Tarasoff was based on the murder of Tatiana Tarasoff by a graduate student receiving services at the counseling center of the University of California, Berkeley. After the student revealed his intent to murder Tarasoff during a counseling session, the therapist and his supervisors asked the university police to detain the student for involuntary hospitalization and assessment. The police did not detain him, and he failed to return for treatment. Two months later, he killed Tarasoff. The victim's family sued, and in 1976 the California Supreme Court established the precedent of a duty to protect, ruling that the "privilege of confidentiality ends where public peril begins" (*Tarasoff v. Regents of the University of California*, 1976). The need to prevent harm to an identified third party outweighed the obligation to protect the patient's confidentiality, justifying the disclosure of personal information without consent.

Over the past 30 years, interpretations of the duty to protect by the courts and state legislatures have also undergone a pendulum swing, characterized by Felthous (2001) as expansion, diversification, and retreat. Because of the current generally poor ability to predict violent outbreaks and the lack of effective methods to prevent their occurrence, the general trend by legislatures and courts has been toward limiting the circumstances in which a duty to protect would attach in *Tarasoff*-like situations in more recent legal rulings and state statutes (Walcott, Cerundolo, & Beck, 2001).

One notable exception to the trend toward limiting Tarasoff (among other examples, see Perlin, 2006–2007) is the Kennedy Krieger Lead Paint Abatement Project. The Kennedy Krieger Institute at Johns Hopkins University conducted research on low-cost, partial lead abatement procedures to prevent lead poisoning in children living in public housing in inner city Baltimore. When the research was being conceived, an estimated 95% of low-income housing in identified neighborhoods in Baltimore was contaminated with lead-based paint (Pollak, 2002). Studies at the time showed that 40% to 50% of the predominantly African American children living in these high-risk neighborhoods had elevated blood lead levels of more than 20 micrograms per deciliter, deemed "moderate" blood lead elevation by contemporary Centers for Disease Control and Prevention standards. However, because of the high costs of implementing the recommended total lead abatement procedure (approximately $20,000 per house), little was being done about the problem (Barltrop, 1974; Needleman, 1998; Satcher, 2000).

In the late 1980s, the Kennedy Krieger Institute tested several alternative, less-expensive lead reduction methods in empty properties and demonstrated that these techniques reduced ambient lead paint dust by 80% or more (Farfel & Chisolm, 1991; Farfel, Chisolm, & Rohde, 1994). They then proposed a follow-up study to determine whether the reduction in lead paint dust in housing would result in lower blood lead levels in children living in houses so treated. Overall, the results of the research showed significant reductions in lead dust in all study conditions and in the blood lead levels of children residing in the treated homes, although there were a few cases of increases (Chisolm, 2001; Environmental Protection Agency, 1997).

Two families later sued the Kennedy Krieger Institute, however, stating that they were not fully informed of the risks of participation for their children and that the institute failed to inform them in a timely manner of test results. In *Grimes v. Kennedy Krieger Institute* (2001), the Court of Appeals

(Maryland's highest court) overturned a lower court's initial ruling to dismiss and reinstated the families' lawsuits. In August 2001, the Court of Appeals issued a scathing 96-page ruling comparing the research to the Tuskegee syphilis study and Nazi research on prisoners (*Grimes v. Kennedy Krieger Institute*, 2001). The judges characterized the research as a callous scientific experiment that put children in harm's way and used them merely as "measuring tools." The court's remand focused on three issues: (a) informed consent, declaring that parents cannot give consent for their children to enroll in "nontherapeutic" research (p. 7); (b) a duty to protect because of the "special relationship" (p. 7) between the researchers and participants; and (c) the inadequacies of the IRB's review, referring to the Johns Hopkins IRB as "in-house organs" (p. 11) who were not "as sufficiently concerned with ethicality of the research as they were with the success of the experiment" (p. 7). The timing of the court's ruling was calamitous for Johns Hopkins, coming at the same time as the healthy volunteer, Ellen Roche, died in the hexamethonium experiment. The court's ruling touched off waves of controversy among researchers and sent chills down the spines of IRB members across the nation. In the aftermath of these events, the federal government has mandated that all researchers who receive federal funding provide documentation that they have received training in the ethical standards governing the conduct of research and protection of human subjects (National Institutes of Health, 2001). These training programs are widely available online; they provide assurance that researchers have at least a minimal level of knowledge about historical abuses and current federal regulations. Unfortunately, because of the limitations of the medium, they cannot possibly cover the full range and complexity of issues involved in research involving human subjects. This book takes up where these programs leave off. As these standards are frequently referenced in the chapters that follow, we provide a brief capsule summary of them here.

EIGHT ETHICAL STANDARDS

The goal of health research is to generate new scientific knowledge toward the aim of improving the diagnosis, treatment, and prevention of disease and other health problems. Because such research often involves the participation of human beings as subjects, there is an inherent tension between pursuing rigorous science and protecting human subjects. In a major review of the most significant historical documents and ethical codes to date, Emanuel, Wendler, and Grady (2000) and Emanuel, Wendler, et al. (2004) distilled a set of eight ethical standards for health research from these documents. According to the authors, these eight requirements, when upheld, make research ethical: (a) social value, (b) scientific validity, (c) fair subject selection, (d) favorable risk–benefit ratio, (e) independent review, (f) informed consent, (g) respect for enrolled subjects; and (h) community collaboration. Taken together, these eight principles provide the ethical foundation for justifying the participation of human subjects in research. Each principle provides particular safeguards, and collectively they specify how research can be conducted successfully such that it respects human autonomy, avoids exploitation (using people as a means to an end), minimizes the potential for harm, and maximizes its social benefits (Buchanan & Miller, 2007).

Social Value

To be of benefit, an "experiment should be such as to yield fruitful results for the good of society" (Nuremberg Code, 1946, Principle 2). In general, most psychological research is designed to answer scientific questions about the etiology, treatment, and prevention of mental health and social problems. Without a socially valuable question or hypothesis, a study is not worth conducting. The risks to volunteers in studies lacking societal value cannot be justified, making such research unethical. To meet this ethical standard, as the risks of a study increase, the value of the science should become proportionately more compelling. Nevertheless, the fact that a study has great potential for producing social value does not justify imposing grave risks on research subjects. When conducting research with populations at risk of violent actions or victimization, investigators must ask themselves, who benefits? Will the knowledge generated by the research be of value to the populations represented by the participants, or will it be used to support societal prejudices and autonomy-restricting rather than health-promoting policies (Fisher, 1999; Fisher & Wallace, 2000)?

Scientific Validity

To achieve the potential value of the research, studies must be designed with sufficient methodological rigor to provide scientifically valid answers to the research questions and thus contribute to generalizable knowledge (Freedman, 1987). If the study design lacks methodological rigor, such that it cannot produce interpretable results or valid data, then it is not worth conducting. The risks to human participants in poorly designed research cannot be justified. Tensions between methodological rigor and other ethical requirements give rise to many challenging ethical issues. For example, what is the cost to scientific validity when investigators in the course of conducting descriptive longitudinal research on victimization believe it is their moral obligation to refer for services an individual who appears traumatized by his or her experience?

Fair Subject Selection

Concerns about fairness in subject selection typically focus on groups of human subjects regarded as "vulnerable." Certain types of people are considered vulnerable because their characteristics or situation appear to render them less than fully capable of making voluntary, informed decisions about research participation (Fisher, 1999, 2003; Levine, 1986). Vulnerable populations include children or adults with mental disabilities, because they are dependent on others and legally incapable of giving informed consent; prisoners, owing to the coercive environment of penal institutions; and economically disadvantaged individuals, who may be subject to undue inducement deriving from payment for research participation.

As a rule, subjects who are vulnerable to exploitation or undue influence should not be targeted for research unless their participation is necessary to answer valuable scientific questions. Fair subject selection, however, also demands not arbitrarily excluding people from research participation. For example, concern about undue inducement of economically disadvantaged individuals, especially when researching violence in disadvantaged drug-abusing populations, should be balanced against concern for avoiding discrimination and depriving research participants of the opportunity to receive due compensation for their time and contributions to the research (Buchanan, Shaw, Stopka, Khooshnood, & Singer, 2002; Fisher, 2004; Pace, Miller, & Danis, 2003).

Favorable Risk–Benefit Ratio

Risk–benefit assessment is ethically required to evaluate whether the risks to which participants are exposed are justified by the benefits anticipated from the proposed research. Three dimensions of risk are relevant to risk–benefit assessment: probability, magnitude, and duration of harm. Thus, three questions must be addressed in assessing the level of risks posed by a study. First, what are the chances that the research will result in harms to the participants? Second, how serious is the potential harm? Third, how long is the potential harm expected to last if it occurs?

Achieving a favorable risk–benefit ratio requires research risks to be minimized as much as possible. The Nuremberg Code (1946) states, "The experiment should be so conducted as to avoid all unnecessary physical and mental suffering and injury" (Annas & Grodin, 1992). The requirement to minimize risks does not mean that risks must be eliminated, for that would make almost all research impossible to conduct. Rather, risks must be minimized with respect to the task of answering valuable scientific questions by means of scientifically valid methods (illustrating the point that the ethical requirements of clinical research must operate in tandem). Investigators and IRBs should evaluate study designs to determine whether they could be modified to pose less risk to participants without compromising the validity of the study data.

A critical component of risk–benefit assessment is the capability to ascertain when the risks of a proposed study are too high, regardless of the potential scientific value. The U.S. federal regulations governing research with human subjects, however, provide little guidance with respect to judgments of acceptable risk (Protection of Human Subjects, 2005). The Nuremberg Code (1946) states, "No experiment should be conducted where there is an *a priori* reason to believe that death or disabling injury will occur" (p. 1060). Yet, how can investigators or IRBs determine whether the potential value of knowledge to be gained from a given study can justify the risks posed to healthy volunteers? There are no ready formulas available, especially in research involving violent behaviors. For example, when might recruitment of a victim of spousal abuse for research on the consequences of her spouse's behaviors increase the possibility of further abuse if her spouse discovers she is participating in the research? These types of assessments call for carefully considered and well-deliberated judgments by research sponsors, investigators, and IRBs.

Independent Review

The revelations in the 1960s of abuses of research subjects indicated that self-regulation by investigators was no longer sufficient. In response to these circumstances, the U.S. federal government mandated prospective independent review of research protocols by IRBs (Faden & Beauchamp, 1986). Independent review establishes a key procedural safeguard for protecting research participants from the inherent potential of research to compromise the rights or welfare of subjects. Independent review also provides public accountability for research that exposes participants to risks for the good of society. The task of the IRB is to apply the other substantive ethical requirements in their review, modification, approval, and oversight of research protocols. However, the extent to which independent review provides subject protections may be limited or enhanced by the degree to which IRB members are familiar with the living situations, relationships, behaviors, and other circumstances pertaining to the individuals who will be recruited for participation. For example, IRB members with no familiarity with street drug culture may overestimate the risks of providing drug users with monetary incentives or underestimate the extent to which speaking with participants in public might place participants in danger.

Informed Consent

Obtaining informed consent ensures that research participation reflects the free choice and self-determination of those who enroll in research. This requirement includes three basic components: Consent must be informed, consent must be voluntary, and a rationale for the study must be provided to the subject (Freedman, 1975). The investigator must ensure that prospective research participants both are informed about and understand what their participation entails: the goal of the study, the methods to be used, the risks and potential benefits (if any), alternatives to participation at any time, and the right to decline or withdraw participation without penalty. Subjects must voluntarily agree to participate under those conditions. Individuals who are engaged in or victims of violence often have comorbidities or other characteristics associated with these problems that might compromise their ability to understand consent information. Suicidality, for example, is often associated with depression and cognitive deficits that compromise consent comprehension. Similarly, the impulsivity and distractedness of drug abusers who are in withdrawal or high may impair consent.

Respect for Enrolled Subjects

Social research must be conducted with adequate safeguards to protect the welfare and rights of participants during the course of research. These safeguards include implementing procedures to protect privacy and confidentiality, monitoring the condition of the research subjects to ensure their safety, terminating study participation in the case of adverse events, and informing enrolled subjects about risks and benefits discovered in the course of research or new information reported in the literature. IRBs must review and approve written plans to monitor the condition of research participants. Adverse event reports must be prepared by investigators and submitted to IRBs in a timely fashion so that determinations can be made about whether to modify the study design, change informed consent documents, notify enrolled subjects, or stop the research study. Data safety management protocols have been developed for medical models that define safety in terms of research-associated medical or psychiatric symptoms. However, federal regulations offer little guidance on responsible monitoring of violent behaviors in descriptive studies and what actions by the investigator would be required in such situations.

Community Collaboration

Emanuel, Wendler, et al. (2004) later added an eighth requirement of community collaboration, in particular to address concerns about the potential for exploitation in international research conducted in developing countries. According to this ethical standard, researchers should develop a partnership with the host community (inclusive of but not limited to the participants). Community partners should be empowered to share responsibilities for determining the importance of the health problems to be investigated; assessing the value of the research; planning, conducting, and overseeing the research; and integrating the study findings into the health care system. A collaborative process also entails respect for the community's values, culture, traditions, and social practices and assurances that the participants will receive benefits from the conduct and results of the research (Fisher, Hoagwood, et al., 2002; Fisher & Wallace, 2000; Trimble & Fisher, 2006). For example, when suicide or violent crime is studied in an identified ethnic minority community, community members may feel that dissemination of the results will unfairly stigmatize their community, potentially depriving them of needed public funds or societal respect.

ORGANIZATION AND OVERVIEW OF THE BOOK

Our book is organized into four parts. The first section, regarding the ethical and legal issues entailed in conducting research with high-risk populations, provides essential information that places the chapters that follow in a broad theoretical context. The second section presents a range of different research methodologies that may enable researchers to conduct research on sensitive topics in ways that minimize harm while gathering valuable, scientifically valid data. The case studies in this section underscore that there is no perfect research method. There are inherent tradeoffs between inescapable risks or serious limitations in collecting data by any method that must be carefully balanced in identifying the optimal research design for research questions of interest. These chapters extend appreciation of different approaches and increase awareness of potential pitfalls that can be avoided with careful advance planning. The third section consists of four chapters that grapple with responding appropriately to immediate threats of violence, in light of the researchers' ethical and legal obligations. These case studies make an important contribution to the growing body of literature that promotes casuistical (case-based) reasoning, highlighting the irreducible element of judgment involved in responding appropriately to the complex and unique circumstances of the situation at hand. The fourth and final section presents a summary of the key issues identified in the preceding chapters and a synthesis of the major lessons learned.

Part I: Historical, Theoretical, and Legal Perspectives

Following this Introduction, Celia B. Fisher and Sabrina J. Goodman present the most theoretically well-developed model available in the field at this time, the goodness-of-fit ethics model, which provides investigators with sorely needed context-specific guidance for responsibly conducting research with high-risk populations. The goodness-of-fit model outlines a decision-making tool for identifying and resolving ethical challenges when research involves populations who are at greater risk of perpetrating or becoming victims of violence. The goodness-of-fit model conceptualizes research vulnerability as the product of the interaction between participant characteristics and research context. From this perspective, harms produced by participant–research interactions can be minimized by applying ethical procedures appropriately suited to participant susceptibility to or resilience against research harms.

Chapter 2, by Lance Gable, sets the key issues addressed in this book in their legal context, describing and analyzing the three main ways in which the law has an impact on descriptive, nonintervention research with high-risk populations. As Gable notes, first, the various pertinent laws create the structure within which research is conducted; they set standards of conduct for research, protect the privacy of research participants and the confidentiality of their information, and impose penalties on those who fail to enforce these protections. Second, the law often provides researchers with direction to resolve complicated issues, delineating legal standards of care, prospectively establishing processes for addressing foreseeable threats of harm (as in mandated reporting), and providing strong legal protections for researchers (e.g., with Certificates of Confidentiality). Finally, although distinct from the moral obligations of researchers, the law complements and supports ethical analyses, codifying norms of conduct in which high degrees of societal consensus exist.

Part II: Conducting Research Ethically

The second section, focusing on research methodologies, begins with chapter 3, by Jennifer J. Cercone, Carla Kmett Danielson, Kenneth J. Ruggiero, and Dean G. Kilpatrick, which examines the many advantages of anonymous telephone interviews in research on sensitive topics. Their chapter not only describes the feasibility, reliability, and validity of telephone surveys but also discusses the risks, safeguards, and benefits associated with telephone-based research. A case study of the National Survey of Adolescents, a telephone survey conducted with a large, nationally representative sample of adolescents, illustrates their thoughtful analysis of the critical issues involved in this type of research.

Chapter 4, by Lang Ma, Erin Phelps, Jacqueline V. Lerner, and Richard M. Lerner, focuses on the challenges of conducting naturalistic longitudinal research with adolescents in investigating factors associated with bullying. Longitudinal research presents particularly salient ethical concerns because the researchers know who specifically has been involved in bullying in the past, and hence they are in the weighty position of being better able to predict who may either perpetuate or be the victim of such violence in the future. On the basis of their case analysis of the 4-H Study of Positive Youth Development, the authors provide important recommendations for instituting, before the initiation of the research, ethical procedures with respect to referrals and informed consent that are consistent with protecting the integrity of the research.

Rumi Kato Price and her team then present a prospective cohort study of Vietnam veterans in chapter 5, focusing on the long-term sequelae of combat exposure. In their research, the suicide of one of their participants forced the authors to consider modification of their research protocol and to develop training, assessment, and intervention strategies to respond to participants who exhibited suicidal ideation. Their case study provides important lessons about the need to anticipate the possibility of serious or lethal events during the course of a research study.

In the final chapter in this section, Catherine Cerulli and Christopher D. Thomas present an eye-opening account of the potential for using existing state laws to gain access to court documents and other legal materials. These documents, which are often publicly available, provide a rich and unique opportunity to study the dynamics of domestic violence. This chapter makes a valuable contribution, alerting social scientists to the ways in which the law can be used to their advantage in enabling significant research on this important topic.

Part III: Responding to Threats of Violence

David R. Buchanan opens the third section with his analysis of significant yet unanticipated ethical dilemmas encountered in the course of conducting ethnographic field research with injection drug users on HIV/AIDS risk. The chapter describes three major ethical concerns that arose during the process of data collection: (a) novel problems in failing to protect confidentiality, (b) novel and unanticipated potential harms to participants, and (c) potential harms to third parties. He concludes with recommendations for setting standards for classifying the severity of collateral risks (analogous to the cancer research classification system Common Toxicity Criteria). He also suggests the development of advanced training programs to enhance researchers' sensitivity to the complex dynamics of field research and to strengthen capacity for more fully informed judgments about the best course of action in such situations.

Barry Rosenfeld and Debbie Green address ethical and legal issues that can arise in conducting mental health treatment research with potentially violent persons, including risks to third parties and research personnel. More important, they highlight the steps that can be used to minimize these risks, such as conducting risk assessment, defining appropriate inclusion and exclusion criteria, requiring mandatory safety training for research personnel, and identifying an appropriate research setting.

Chapter 9 advances the ethical values of community consultation. Celia B. Fisher and her coauthors present empirical data on the perspectives and recommendations of illicit drug users themselves regarding when researchers should feel obligated to invoke their duty to protect. Readers may find this community's perspectives surprisingly well informed, nuanced, and thoughtful, clearly positioning research investigators as moral agents whose duties include intervening to prevent harmful activities perpetrated by those participating in their studies.

Chapter 10 examines research with ethnic minority populations. Eloise Dunlap, Bruce D. Johnson, and Doris Randolph describe their poignant and gripping ethnographic research, spanning five different research projects, focusing on the intersecting epidemics of child abuse, sexual abuse, drug abuse, and murder. Their chapter is a powerful firsthand account of the wrenching emotional strains of complex ethical dilemmas with high stakes and no easy answers.

Part IV: Concluding Thoughts

The final chapter, by the volume editors, offers readers a synthesis of and more fully informed perspective on the ethical and legal issues involved in conducting research with high-risk populations. The ensuing debate highlights the new issues that arise as frameworks for thinking about the ethical and legal matters involved in research with high-risk populations evolve. The final value of this book may be found in enabling researchers and IRB members to become more knowledgeable and informed about different ways of allowing valuable research to go forward while minimizing the potential for harm and protecting all parties involved from undue harm and exploitation.

REFERENCES

Annas, G. J., & Grodin, M. A. (1992). *The Nazi doctors and the Nuremberg Code*. New York: Oxford University Press.

Barltrop, D. (1974). Children and lead. *American Journal of Diseases of Children, 127*, 165–166.

Beecher, H. K. (1966). Ethics and clinical research. *New England Journal of Medicine, 274*, 1354–1360.

Berg, J. W., Appelbaum, P., Lidz, C., & Parker, L. (2001). *Informed consent: Legal theory and clinical practice* (2nd ed.). New York: Oxford University Press.

Brown, J. G. (1998). *Institutional review boards: The emergence of independent boards* (OEI-01-97-00192). Washington, DC: Office of Inspector General, Department of Health & Human Services. Retrieved October 19, 2007, from http://www.oig.hhs.gov/oei/reports/oei-01-97-00192.pdf

Buchanan, D., & Miller, F. G. (2007). Justice in research on human subjects. In R. Rhodes, L. Francis, & A. Silvers (Eds.), *The Blackwell guide to medical ethics* (pp. 309-341). New York: Blackwell.

Buchanan, D., Shaw, S., Stopka, T., Khooshnood, K., & Singer, M. (2002). Ethical dilemmas created by the criminalization of status behaviors: Case examples from ethnographic research with injection drug users. *Health Education and Behavior, 29*(1), 30–42.

Chisolm, J. J. (2001). The road to primary prevention of lead toxicity in children. *Pediatrics, 107*, 581–583.

Cohen, P. (2007, February 28). As ethics panels expand grip, no field is off limits. *New York Times*, p. A1.

Emanuel, E. (2002, October 17). Institutional review board reform. *New England Journal of Medicine, 347*, 1285–1286.

Emanuel, E. J., Wendler, D., & Grady, C. (2000, May 24). What makes clinical research ethical. *JAMA, 283*, 2701–2711.

Emanuel, E. J., Wendler, D., Killen, J., & Grady, C. (2004). What makes clinical research in developing countries ethical? The benchmarks of ethical research. *Journal of Infectious Diseases, 189*(5), 764–765.

Emanuel, E. J., Wood, A., Fleischman, A., Bowen, A., Hammerschmidt, D. E., Getz, K. A., et al. (2004). Oversight of human participants research: Identifying problems to evaluate reform proposals. *Annals of Internal Medicine, 141*, 282–291.

Environmental Protection Agency. (1997). *Lead-based paint abatement and repair and maintenance study in Baltimore: Findings based on two years of follow-up* (EPA Report No. 747-R-97-005). Washington, DC: Author.

Faden, R. R., & Beauchamp, T. L. (1986). *A history and theory of informed consent.* New York: Oxford University Press.

Farfel, M. R., & Chisolm, J. J. (1991). An evaluation of experimental practices for abatement of residential lead-based paint: Report on a pilot project. *Environmental Research, 55*, 199–212.

Farfel, M. R., Chisolm, J. J., & Rohde, C. A. (1994). The longer-term effectiveness of residential lead paint abatement. *Environmental Research, 66*, 217–221.

Felthous, A. R. (2001). Introduction to this issue: The clinician's duty to warn or protect. *Behavioral Sciences & the Law, 19*, 321–324.

Fisher, C. B. (1999). Relational ethics and research with vulnerable populations. In *Research involving persons with mental disorders that may affect decision making capacity:* Vol. II. Commissioned papers by the National Bioethics Advisory Commission (pp. 29–49). Rockville, MD: National Bioethics Advisory Commission. Retrieved April 1, 2007, from http://www.bioethics.gov/reports/past_commissions/nbac_mental2.pdf

Fisher, C. B. (2003). A goodness-of-fit ethic for informed consent to research involving persons with mental retardation and developmental disabilities. *Mental Retardation and Developmental Disabilities Research Reviews*, 9, 27–31.

Fisher, C. B. (2004). Ethics in drug abuse and related HIV risk research. *Applied Developmental Science*, 8, 90–102.

Fisher, C. B., Hoagwood, K., Boyce, C., Duster, T., Frank, D. A., Grisso, T., et al. (2002). Research ethics for mental health science involving ethnic minority children and youth. *American Psychologist, 57*, 1024–1040.

Fisher, C. B., Pearson, J. L., Kim, S., & Reynolds, C. F. (2002). Ethical issues in including suicidal individuals in clinical research. *IRB: Ethics & Human Research, 24*, 1–6.

Fisher, C. B., & Wallace, S. A. (2000). Through the community looking glass: Re-evaluating the ethical and policy implications of research on adolescent risk and psychopathology. *Ethics & Behavior, 10*, 99–118.

Freedman, B. (1975). A moral theory of informed consent. *Hastings Center Report, 5*, 32–39.

Freedman, B. (1987). Scientific value and validity as ethical requirements for research: A proposed explication. *IRB: A Review of Human Subjects Research, 9*, 7–10.

Grimes v. Kennedy Krieger Institute, Inc., 366 Md. 29, 782A 2d 807 (2001). Retrieved September 30, 2008, from http://www.courts.state.md.us/opinions/coa/2001/128a00.pdf

Humphreys, L. (1970). *Tearoom trade: Impersonal sex in public places*. Chicago: Aldine.

Jonsen, A. (2000). *A short history of medical ethics*. New York: Oxford University Press.

Kahn, J., Mastroianni, A., & Sugarman, J. (1998). Changing claims about justice in research: An introduction and overview. In J. Kahn, A. Mastroianni, & J. Sugarman (Eds.), *Beyond consent: Seeking justice in research* (pp. 1–10). New York: Oxford University Press.

Levine, R. J. (1986). *Ethics and regulation of clinical research* (2nd ed.). New Haven, CT: Yale University Press.

McCarthy, C. (1998). The evolving story of justice in federal research policy. In J. Kahn, A. Mastroianni, & J. Sugarman (Eds.), *Beyond consent: Seeking justice in research* (pp. 11–31). New York: Oxford University Press.

Mello, M. M., Studdert, D. M., & Brennan, T. A. (2003). The rise of litigation in human subjects research. *Annals of Internal Medicine, 139*, 40–45.

Melton, G. B., Levine, R. J., Koocher, G. P., Rosenthal, R., & Thompson, W. C. (1988). Community consultation in socially sensitive research: Lessons from clinical trials of treatments for AIDS. *American Psychologist, 43*, 573–581.

National Commission for the Protection of Human Subjects of Biomedical and Behavioral Research. (1979). *The Belmont Report: Ethical principles and guidelines for the protection of human subjects of research.* Washington, DC: U.S. Government Printing Office.

National Institutes of Health. (2001). *Required education in the protection of human research participants*. Washington, DC: U.S. Government Printing Office. Available at http://grants.nih.gov/grants/guide/notice-files/NOT-OD-01-061.html

Needleman, H. L. (1998). Childhood lead poisoning: The promise and abandonment of primary prevention. *American Journal of Public Health, 88*, 1871–1877.

Nuremberg Code. (1946). *JAMA, 132*, 1090.

Pace, C., Miller, F. G., & Danis, M. (2003). Enrolling the uninsured in clinical trials: An ethical perspective. *Critical Care in Medicine, 31*, S121–S125.

Perlin, M. L. (2006–2007). "You got no secrets to conceal": Considering the application of the Tarasoff doctrine abroad. *University of Cincinnati Law Review, 75*, 611–629.

Pollak, J. (2002). The Lead-Based Paint Abatement Repair and Maintenance Study in Baltimore: Historic framework and study design. *Journal of Health Care Law & Policy*, 6, 89–108.

Powers, M. (1998). Theories of justice in the context of research. In J. Kahn, A. Mastroianni, & J. Sugarman (Eds.), *Beyond consent: Seeking justice in research* (pp. 147–165). New York: Oxford University Press.

Protection of Human Subjects, 45 C.F.R. § 46 (2005).

Resnik, D. B. (2004). Liability for institutional review boards. *Journal of Legal Medicine*, *25*, 131–184.

Satcher, D. (2000). The Surgeon General on the continuing tragedy of childhood lead poisoning. *Public Health Reports*, *115*, 579–580.

Savulescu, J. (2001). Harm, ethics committees, and the gene therapy death. *Journal of Medical Ethics*, *27*, 148–150.

Savulescu, J., & Spriggs, M. (2002). The hexamethonium asthma study and the death of a normal volunteer in research. *Journal of Medical Ethics*, *28*, 3–4.

Somia, N., & Verma, I. (2000). Gene therapy: Trials and tribulations. *Nature Reviews Genetics*, *1*, 91–99.

Steinbrook, R. (2002, February 28). Protecting research subjects—The crisis at Johns Hopkins. *New England Journal of Medicine*, *346*, 716–720.

Tarasoff v. Regents of the University of California, 17 California 3d 425, 551 P.2d 334, 131 Cal. Rptr. 14. (1976). Retrieved June 2008 from http://www.stanford.edu/group/psylawseminar/Tarsoff%20I.htm

Trimble, J. E., & Fisher, C. B. (Eds.). (2006). *The handbook of ethical research with ethnocultural populations and communities*. Thousand Oaks, CA: Sage.

Walcott, D. M., Cerundolo, P., & Beck, J. C. (2001). Current analysis of the Tarasoff duty: An evolution towards the limitation of the duty to protect. *Behavioral Sciences & the Law*, *19*, 325–343.

World Medical Association. (1997, March 19). Declaration of Helsinki. *JAMA*, *277*, 925–926.

I

HISTORICAL, THEORETICAL, AND LEGAL PERSPECTIVES

1

GOODNESS-OF-FIT ETHICS FOR NONINTERVENTION RESEARCH INVOLVING DANGEROUS AND ILLEGAL BEHAVIORS

CELIA B. FISHER AND SABRINA J. GOODMAN

Nonintervention research examining the correlates and sequelae of suicide, violence, and child abuse raises unique ethical challenges. Although federal regulations and professional guidelines for human research protections provide a general framework for research ethics decision making, investigators working with such high-risk populations need context-specific guidance for conducting research responsibly. To meet these demands, investigators typically rely on advice from colleagues, recommendations from institutional review boards (IRBs), and their own moral compass. However, reliance on professional logic or scientific inference alone is inadequate to help investigators working with populations who may be involved in illegal activities, whose lives may be in jeopardy, or who pose a threat to others navigate among multiple ethical challenges and choices. The goodness-of-fit

The writing of this chapter was partially supported by National Institute on Drug Abuse Grant 1 RO1 DA015649-01A1 to Celia B. Fisher.

approach to research ethics (Fisher, 2002a, 2003b; Fisher & Masty, 2006b; Fisher & Ragsdale, 2006; Masty & Fisher, 2008) provides a decision-making tool for identifying and resolving ethical challenges when research involves populations who are at greater risk of perpetrating or becoming a victim of violence. In this chapter, we closely examine the goodness-of-fit approach and its use of the colearning process to identify research challenges and ethical decision-making strategies involving informed consent and confidentiality. We also present a five-step approach to determining confidentiality and disclosure procedures.

THE SCIENTIST–CITIZEN DILEMMA

Many of the ethical challenges faced by researchers can be understood in terms of the "scientist–citizen dilemma" (Fisher & Rosendahl, 1990; Veatch, 1987). This dilemma arises from investigators' dual obligation to produce scientifically valid knowledge and at the same time protect the rights and welfare of research participants. The scientist–citizen dilemma frequently emerges in nonintervention research on potentially life-threatening behaviors. For example, how do investigators studying suicide, child abuse, or violent behaviors strike an appropriate balance between protecting the internal validity of a longitudinal survey study and protecting the welfare of research participants or of others whom experimental procedures reveal are in danger? Does the special expertise of scientists working with violent populations create a special obligation to help individuals who are or may become the victims of violence during the course of the research? Can investigators working with drug-using, child-abusing, or suicidal individuals obtain truly informed consent? How does one obtain consent to participate in socially sensitive research without jeopardizing the social or legal rights and welfare of prospective participants? How does an investigator determine fair and noncoercive research compensation for individuals who may be in desperate need of money to purchase basic goods or drugs? These are just some of the scientist–citizen dilemmas for which investigators are seeking adequate tools for ethical decision making. Fisher's goodness-of-fit ethics is one such tool (Fisher, 2002a, 2003b; Fisher & Masty, 2006b; Fisher & Ragsdale, 2006; Masty & Fisher, 2008).

Goodness-of-Fit Ethics and Research Risk

Goodness-of-fit ethics conceptualize research vulnerability as the joint product of participant characteristics and the research context. From this perspective, harms produced by participant–research interactions can be minimized by fitting ethical procedures to participant susceptibility to or resilience against research harms. Goodness-of-fit ethics involve dual attention to characteristics of participants and the research context that may conjointly create or exacerbate research vulnerability. Such analysis is followed by exploration of alternative approaches to shaping the research design and ethical procedures that will maximize scientific advancement and the protection of participant and social welfare (Fisher & Ragsdale, 2006). To identify and minimize risks emerging from the intersection of population and research characteristics, the goodness-of-fit approach encourages investigators to ask three questions: What special life circumstances may render participants more susceptible to risks that arise in this research design? What aspects of the methodology, implementation, or dissemination may create or exacerbate such research risks? And how can research procedures be fitted to participant characteristics to best minimize risk? (Fisher, 2003b; Masty & Fisher, 2008).

Colearning

Colearning is a goodness-of-fit process whereby perspectives from the prospective participant populations are used to help identify ethical issues and construct ethical procedures (Fisher, 1999, 2002b). It enables researchers to fit research methods and ethical procedures to the needs and values of the participant population (Fisher & Ragsdale, 2006) and assumes that ethical decision making is inadequate if it fails to consider the views of individuals or their representatives (Fisher, 1999, 2000, 2002a). A second substantive assumption of colearning is that researchers, participants, and participant communities have equally important but different expertise in areas that are essential to the conduct of responsible science. Although researchers have expertise in the extant research literature and the research methods that can be used to study public health concerns, prospective participants and their community representatives have expertise in what they think is important to study, how they will react to planned procedures, the subjective risk–benefit balance of the research, and the moral and cultural frameworks informing their perspectives (Fisher, 1997, 1999, 2000; Stiffman, Freedenthal, Brown, Ostmann, & Hibbeler, 2005). The sections that follow highlight the ways in which goodness-of-fit ethics can enhance identification of research risk, informed consent, and confidentiality and disclosure challenges intrinsic to research involving illegal, violent, or self-harming behaviors.

IDENTIFYING RESEARCH RISK

A hallmark of nonintervention research ethics decision making is determining that the risks of participation are minimized and outweighed by the prospective knowledge benefits to society. Although most descriptive and predictive social behavioral and public health research typically involves no greater than minimal risk procedures, conducting nonintervention research on life-threatening conditions with high-risk populations can create research vulnerabilities that are not common to other types of research. One component of research vulnerability stems from susceptibilities of the research participants themselves. For participants of research on suicide, child abuse, and violence, such vulnerabilities can include addiction, comorbid mental health disorders, illegal behaviors, poverty, social stigma, minority status, a dangerous social network, and other health risks. Yet from a goodness-of-fit perspective, the interactive effects of participant characteristics and the research context itself may mediate or exacerbate the ways in which participant characteristics would be considered research vulnerabilities. For example, there is no evidence that survey questions on socially sensitive topics such as adolescent drug use or sexual history are harmful to healthy adolescent populations living in safe environments (Becker-Blease & Freyd, 2006; Fisher, 2003a; Fisher & Wallace, 2000). However, such questions may trigger cravings in someone highly addicted to drugs or posttraumatic stress disorder or anxiety reactions in victims of sexual abuse. Similarly, standard procedures for protecting confidentiality in the publication of results may not be sufficient when the research involves small and unique populations such as high school students who are victims of a nationally publicized violent event.

Research Risks Involving Disadvantaged and Disenfranchised Populations

Researchers in the areas of violence, suicide, abuse, or drug use who work with less educated, disenfranchised, or impoverished populations may also discover unanticipated consequences created by an interaction between participant characteristics and the research methodology. For example, Clair, Singer, Huertas, and Weeks (2003) discovered that using saliva tests to assess for HIV in a street drug–using population inadvertently contributed to community misperceptions about the transmission of HIV (e.g., that it could be transmitted by kissing). The irresponsible conduct of research can also have unanticipated reverberations. Reverby (2001) described how revelations of participant exploitation in the 30-year Public Health Service–sponsored Tuskegee study has spawned a generation of suspicion of research and medical treatment within many African American communities. More recent research has suggested, for example, that some ethnic minority leaders have interpreted research on needle-exchange programs or the use of blinded seroprevalence studies as a form of genocidal neglect (Fairchild & Bayer, 1999). Others believe that the true intent of current seroprevalence research is to inflict rather than study the HIV virus (Fisher & Wallace, 2000). In these cases, the consequences of research distrust can create disparities in recruitment and responses to research methods, which can in turn undermine knowledge generated to understand and promote the welfare of disenfranchised populations.

Dissemination

Dissemination of research findings can be harmful to disenfranchised communities, especially when the focus of the study is to examine community members who engage in health-compromising or illegal behaviors. The Barrow Alaskan Native alcohol study provides an unfortunate example of such risks (Foulks, 1989). Researchers were initially invited by the tribe to study the rates and correlates of alcoholism. The tribe's intent was to obtain information that could inform community efforts to reduce drinking. However, when the investigators disseminated their findings, the resultant media exposure led to deeply felt public embarrassment and stigmatization of all tribe members. Unforeseen problems associated with dissemination of research on drugs and violence can also arise when the data are misused as actuarial predictors of dangerous or illegal behaviors. Investigators need to be sensitive to the possibility that large-scale epidemiological studies on violence can result in criminal profiling or judicial judgments based on group means rather than on individual behaviors (Melton, 1990). Risk can be minimized by clarifying in scientific reports the limits of application of the type of research being done.

Multiple Relationships and Third-Party Informants

Dunlap, Johnson, and Randolph (chap. 10, this volume) and Singer et al. (1999) have drawn much-needed attention to the risks involved in the blurring of scientific and personal boundaries that sometimes arises during ethnographic and field observation work with drug-using populations. Involvement in nonintervention research can benefit participants by creating a social support network and access to otherwise unavailable information about health care and social services. It may also heighten participant self-esteem through a sense of altruism in sharing their knowledge and experience to help others. However, when investigators do not set or clarify limits to these relationships, blurring of boundaries can threaten the validity of the data collected and lead to reciprocal participant–investigator coercion, exploitation, or harm (Haverkamp, 2005). Participants may feel personally obligated to continue in a research project they find threatening, or investigators may feel pressured to yield to participant demands for involvement in illegal behaviors (e.g., holding or transporting drugs) or in behaviors for money or other resources beyond those directly tied to research participation (Singer et al., 1999).

Dignitary Risks

There are also dignitary risks that may arise from multiple relationships among field workers and participants from small ethnic, racial, or language minority populations. For example, investigators often hire indigenous field workers to go out into the community to recruit or interview participants. Although this practice can be helpful in understanding the issues being investigated and in presenting community members with a familiar face, using field workers can pose ethical challenges. For instance, if the field worker has a dual relationship with individuals in the community, participant confidentiality or voluntariness can be threatened (Fisher, Hoagwood, et al., 2002). In addition, the use of field workers to project a "face of color" on the project can be perceived as deceptive if it leads the community to wrongly believe that a minority scientist is directing and controlling the data collection (Fisher, Hoagwood, et al., 2002).

Traditional use of informants or collateral sources (e.g., family members, teachers, peers) to obtain information about violent or illegal behaviors may also be seen as harmful by participants. Fisher (2002b) found that parents and teenagers from diverse ethnic and economic communities believed that drawing on teacher opinions about the high-risk behaviors of student research participants could damage student–teacher relationships and lead to student distrust, and in many instances had little validity (and therefore little research benefit). Although investigators typically inform participants during informed consent that collateral data will be collected, in some communities local values pertinent to the principle of respect may require that the person serving as the source obtain permission from the participant before sharing information with the experimenter.

Physical and Social Risks

However, including all participants in a joint consent procedure can lead to harm in other research contexts. For instance, in a project submitted for IRB review, an investigator studying the behaviors of men who had been incarcerated for domestic violence sought to supplement the men's survey responses with interviews of their current domestic partners. In this context, knowledge that their spouses had agreed to participate in the project might trigger violent reactions in the men against their partners. Among the factors that would be considered in arriving at a goodness-of-fit response to this dilemma are (a) empirical or other evidence of the validity of the assessment of threat to the spousal population if husbands were made aware that their wives would be interviewed; (b) dignitary, social, and legal risks to men participants posed by obtaining information from their spouses without their knowledge or permission; (c) whether the information provided by the spouses would add sufficiently to the knowledge benefits to justify the risks and evaluation of alternative procedures that could produce similar information; (d) whether spousal participation could in fact be kept "secret" from the men participants; (e) whether introducing such secrecy might have an iatrogenic effect on the spousal relationship; (f) whether wives would feel free or coerced into participating; and (g) legal constraints.

Research on Substance Abuse and Violence Involving Suicide Risk

Ninety percent of suicide victims have had a mental or substance abuse disorder (Rudd, 2000). Nonetheless, risk aversion among investigators and IRBs in studies focused on substance abuse, domestic violence, or child abuse often excludes individuals perceived to be at risk of suicidality from research participation initially or during the course of the study. One reason for this exclusion may be that investigators without prior training in suicidality may judge that the ability to identify and appropriately address immediate suicide risk during a research protocol would go beyond the boundaries of their current training competencies and those of their research staff. Fisher, Pearson, Kim, and Reynolds (2002) provided additional explanations for this state of affairs by noting that ethical evaluation of research involving suicidal individuals has had "IRB-inequitable" consideration when compared with investigations of other life-threatening disorders. They suggested that two reasons why both IRBs and investigators may be risk averse when evaluating protocols that may include individuals at suicide risk. First, there is an empirically unsupported overestimation of suicide risk in response to surveys or interviews (Becker-Blease & Freyd, 2006). Second, there is an equally unsupported assumption that excluding such individuals from research increases their life expectancy, despite the fact that for most populations treatment efficacy for suicide has not been demonstrated. These perceptions have translated into few researchers being willing to conduct trials with individuals who evidence suicidal ideation because of perceived liability burdens to individual researchers and their institutions, which in turn has resulted in limited knowledge that can contribute to suicide reduction.

At present, for nonintervention suicide research to move forward, investigators need to construct research protocols that can include (a) assessment of suicide risk before and during research participation and (b) adequate staff training to identify and take adequate steps to assist or refer participants evidencing acute suicidal intention. Using the colearning process, participant perspectives can help inform these assessments. For example, in a series of studies examining the perspectives of adolescents and parents on the ethics of adolescent risk research, Fisher and her colleagues have repeatedly found that although the majority of teenagers and parents do not believe that survey questions on sexual activity or drug use will increase those behaviors, they do worry about the risks of asking teenagers questions about suicide in the absence of appropriate follow-up procedures (Fisher, 1994, 1999, 2000, 2002b; Fisher, Higgins-D'Alessandro, Rau, Kuther, & Belanger, 1996; O'Sullivan & Fisher, 1997). Investigators using surveys to better understand suicidality can also enhance identification of experimentally induced risk by empirically examining survey or interview participants' postexperimental reactions (Gould et al., 2005) or debriefing participants to address any distress evoked.

A GOODNESS-OF-FIT ETHIC FOR INFORMED CONSENT

A goodness-of-fit ethic looks at informed consent vulnerability as the joint product of individual and research characteristics that renders participants more susceptible to consent misunderstandings or coercion (Fisher, 2002a, 2003b; Fisher & Masty, 2006b; Fisher & Ragsdale, 2006; Masty & Fisher, 2008). Consent vulnerability is minimized by assessing how the research procedures can be fitted to the participant's consent capacities. Individual characteristics that make participants in research on suicide, child abuse, and violence vulnerable during consent decision making include cognitive vulnerabilities because of mental or medical disorders, intoxication and withdrawal symptoms, and immaturity or lack of experience (Fisher, 2004; McCrady & Bux, 1999). Characteristics of the consent procedure that increase consent vulnerability include technical language, language mismatched to participant education or cultural expectations, and the context in which the consent is obtained.

Mental Health and Consent Capacity

Investigators working with participants who are prone to violence or vulnerable to its effects are often seeking consent from individuals with impaired consent capacity because of long-term substance abuse, HIV/AIDS–related dementia, psychiatric disorders, or the experience of drug cravings or withdrawal (Adler, 1995; Cohen, 2002; Fisher, 2004; McCrady & Bux, 1999). Often, researchers working with high-risk adult populations minimize consent vulnerability by excluding those who are incapable of consenting properly. However, elimination of such individuals can compromise the external validity of the research if the phenomenon examined is largely exhibited in these populations.

Enhancing Consent

Better fitted approaches might include tailoring the consent language and procedures to the participants' level of understanding; educating participants about research procedures and their research rights; appointing a participant advocate to ensure consent is informed, rational, and voluntary; or encouraging joint decision making with a trusted family member or friend. Constructing language at a fifth-grade reading level and using video presentations, sequential single-unit disclosure (i.e., one consent element at a time), and a question-and-answer format can also increase understanding of consent information. Similarly, encouraging participants to review consent information at home, when they have time to carefully consider the personal consequences of participation and can obtain advice from friends and family members, can decrease participants' vulnerability and improve their ability to give meaningful consent. Finally, informing participants of their research rights can also be a useful tool. For instance, Bruzzese and Fisher (2003) found that brief exposure to a research participant's bill of rights improved understanding of research rights for both children and adults. Applying the colearning approach, investigators may construct other creative means of enhancing consent for unique populations (Palmer, Cassidy, Dunn, Spira, & Sheikh, 2008).

A Priori Assumptions

A priori assumptions of incapacity can also jeopardize individual autonomy and dignity. For example, some have suggested that the denial and impulsivity often associated with active substance abuse is evidence that such individuals lack the information or decision-making capacity to make an informed decision about research participation (Charland, 2002), whereas others have shown consent capacity in injection drug users (Harrison, Vlahov, Jones, Charron, & Clements, 1995). The principle of justice would appear to dictate that persons should not be judged consent incompetent simply on the basis of their addictions or mental status (Fisher, 1999, 2004; Lidz et al., 1984). Conversely, investigators should be aware that certain consent risk factors may be revealed during the course of a study that were not apparent during initial informed consent. For instance, suicidal ideation or thinking disorders may be revealed over the course of a clinical trial, not because the procedures elicited such responses but because the disorder was not reported or detected during an initial assessment or because the suicidal ideation fluctuates over time. This suggests that for populations with fluctuating cognitive capacity, consent must be conceptualized as an ongoing process that may be revisited during the course of the study.

Qualitative Research

The exploratory and open-ended nature of ethnographic research on or participant observation of violence-prone populations or those involved in illegal behaviors can also raise questions about whether truly informed consent for such research can be obtained (Marshall, 1992). In exploratory qualitative studies, it is often difficult to ensure fully informed consent at the start of a project because researchers do not know what type of information will emerge during the process of conducting the research (Haverkamp, 2005). One way to address this issue is to clarify in advance that if unanticipated and sensitive issues emerge during the course of observation or discussion, a mutually negotiated reconsent procedure will be implemented (Fisher, 2004; Haverkamp, 2005). This is especially important when investigators are required to report child abuse or have a legal duty to warn third parties but had not anticipated these issues would arise in the research.

Research Consent Vulnerability in Health or Social Services Contexts

Recruitment of individuals engaged in or victimized by violent behaviors often occurs within treatment centers, social service agencies or the penal system. In these settings, prospective participants may not distinguish between the role of the investigator to obtain voluntary participation in research and the role of professionals to provide services and evaluation or of those legally appointed to monitor their behaviors. In the former case, victims of child or domestic abuse or those with suicidal tendencies may fear that failure to consent will result in denial or discontinuation of services. Alternatively, they may transfer to the investigator their trust in the institution without understanding the difference between the investigator and the service provider roles. Persons who are on parole for violent acts may not be able to distinguish mandatory participation in services from voluntary participation in research. Language differences, lack of familiarity with research procedures, immigration status, and economic needs may further compound this confusion for racial and ethnic minority families. To ensure rational and voluntary participation, Fisher, Hoagwood, et al. (2002) recommended that informed consent procedures conducted in medical, social service, or legal settings should take extra steps to clarify (a) the roles of investigators and professional staff; (b) the relationship and obligations of the investigator to the institutional setting and to the participant; (c) the extent to which participation in the research is distinguishable from receipt of services, legal investigations, or child welfare evaluations; and (d) safeguards to ensure that prospective participants understand that research refusal or withdrawal does not result in termination of services or other negative consequences.

Informed Consent and Adolescent Risk Research

Informed consent for research involving adolescents engaged in violent behaviors or who have been identified as victims of child abuse presents its own set of challenges. Federal regulations (Protection of Human Subjects, 2005) and professional codes of ethics (American Psychological Association, 2002) require the permission of the parent or guardian when minors are involved in research for several reasons. With few exceptions, minors do not have the legal capacity to consent and, depending on their age and the complexity of the research context, may lack the cognitive capacity to comprehend the nature of the research and their research rights (Bruzzese & Fisher, 2003; Fisher, 2002b, 2003a). However, the high-risk physical and social conditions that are often of interest to researchers investigating violence, drug use, and abuse and neglect raise ethical concerns that seeking guardian permission may exacerbate such problems or place adolescent participants in danger or violate their rights to privacy (Brooks-Gunn & Rotheram-Borus, 1994; Fisher, 1993, 1994; Fisher, Hoagwood, & Jensen, 1996). For example,

Fisher and Wallace (2000) found that adolescents were often concerned that parental permission forms describing surveys on adolescent drug use or other risk behaviors would prompt parents to think their child had been recruited because he or she was known to be involved in these behaviors. Parental permission can also be a barrier to recruitment for research on stressors facing adolescent gay, lesbian, bisexual, and transgender youths if adolescents who have not come out to their families fear facing parental rejection or punishment if their sexual orientation becomes known. Federal guidelines also permit IRBs to waive this requirement to ensure that the child's best interests are served. According to Section 46.408c, guardian permission can be waived if there is serious doubt about whether the guardian's interests are reflective of the child or adolescent's interests or if permission cannot be reasonably obtained (Protection of Human Subjects, 2005). If these conditions are met and a parental waiver is not prohibited by state or local law, parental permission may be waived if an alternative procedure for protecting the rights and welfare of participants is in place (e.g., appointing an independent participant advocate).

Selecting the best approach to guardian permission policies is an ethically complex struggle between the scientist's obligations to ensure that waiver of parental permission does not take advantage of youths' decisional vulnerabilities and power inequities and that inflexible adherence to guardian permission policies does not deprive youths of participation in scientific studies that can generate knowledge on which effective risk prevention and treatment programs can be based (Fisher, 2002b; Fisher & Masty, 2006a). Compounding such decisions is the fact that state laws are often silent on how "mature minor" laws, designed to permit adolescent receipt of medical and mental health treatment in the absence of guardian permission, apply to research (Institute of Medicine, 2004). This is one reason why most IRBs do not frequently assert their right to waive guardian permission. Unfortunately, reluctance to waive parental permission often means that life-threatening social conditions of adolescence are not studied.

Investigators may help IRBs grant appropriate guardian permission waivers by providing information on the risk level of the research and its potential contribution to the adolescent empirical knowledge base, as well as an explanation of why alternative procedures or alternative populations would not be scientifically valid. If investigators believe guardian permission will expose the adolescent to harm or that guardians may not be competent to represent the adolescent's best interest, they should provide the IRB with credible evidence to back up this assumption. In deciding whether to request a waiver of guardian consent, researchers should also consider (a) the consequences of the waiver not only to the adolescent participants' physical welfare; (b) the norms of the parent–child relationship in the communities from which participants are recruited; (c) potential institutional biases regarding parental competence that might wrongly influence waiver decisions; and (d) what alternative protections are necessary (e.g., consent capacity of older adolescents, participant advocate) to ensure that adolescents' agreement to participate will be informed, rational, and voluntary (Fisher, 2002b, 2003a; Fisher, Higgins-D'Alessandro, et al., 1996). Guardian permission should never be waived simply as a matter of experimenter convenience or cost.

GOODNESS-OF-FIT AND CONFIDENTIALITY AND DISCLOSURE DECISIONS

Nonintervention studies are frequently designed to elicit sensitive information about personal problems and illegal behaviors. Such information is necessary to generate critical knowledge about the correlates, sequelae, and personal and social mediators of violence, child abuse, and suicide. Obtaining such information also raises unique confidentiality and disclosure concerns. First, the types of behaviors in which many of the participant populations are engaged (e.g., drug use, domestic conflict), if revealed, could place participants or their family members in social, physical, economic, or legal jeopardy. Second, such research often reveals information about serious psychological (e.g., suicidality, toxic drug dose administration), social (e.g., HIV serostatus), or legal (e.g., violation of child care laws) problems about which the subjects themselves were previously unaware. Finally, investigators often uncover aspects of subjects' behavior that pose a serious danger to known others, such as a planned gang hit, a violence-prone subject obtaining a gun, or keeping sexual partners naïve about their highly contagious sexually transmitted diseases.

The confidentiality risks and reporting obligations of nonintervention researchers working with such high-risk populations are less clear than the ethical obligations of those working in clinical settings in which assessment and intervention are expected. Consequently, for nonintervention research, the selection of ethically appropriate confidentiality procedures and guidelines for disclosing confidential information must be fitted to (a) the probability and the magnitude of harm if confidentiality is or is not protected, (b) the validity of the potential harm assessment, and (c) the availability of social, service, or legal systems to support the confidentiality or disclosure decision (Fisher, 1994, 2003a, 2002b; Fisher, Higgins-D'Alessandro, et al., 1996).

Confidentiality Risks

In the field settings in which research on violent or illegal behaviors often takes place, investigators frequently find that routine procedures for ensuring confidentiality (subject codes, secure storage and limited access, disposal of unnecessary information, supervision of research personnel, anonymous data collection) do not provide sufficient protections. For instance, risks of recruitment arise when an investigator known to be studying drug use or gang membership approaches an individual for research recruitment because this can alert police or other community members to the nature of the subject's behaviors. In some cases, the contact may lead to arrest or physical jeopardy if other drug users or gang members believe the subject is an informant. Similar concerns arise if studies involving domestic violence, child abuse, or HIV risk require prospective subjects to go to a testing site that is easily identified by other community members or when interviews are conducted in the community for ethnographic research (Fisher, 2004).

Protection of confidentiality may also be challenged because of the nature of the issues being studied. For example, data collected on the use or sale of illicit drugs or other illegal activities may be subject to subpoena stemming from criminal investigations or custody disputes. In these circumstances investigators can apply for a Certificate of Confidentiality under Section 301(d) of the Public Health Service Act (1988), providing immunity from any government or civil order to disclose identifying information contained in research records. The certificate does not, however, override state child abuse reporting laws (see Hoagwood, 1994; Melton, 1990), and this limitation should be made clear during informed consent.

Mandated or Voluntary Disclosure of Confidential Information

Research with high-risk populations often involves the discovery of unidentified problems or psychopathology, such as cognitive deficits, developmental delays, abuse, addictions, criminal activities, or other socially stigmatizing behaviors or characteristics (Fisher, 1993, 1994; Fisher & Rosendahl, 1990). Subsequently, another unique challenge of nonintervention research is whether to disclose information that researchers observe or learn about to the participant or to others. Scientists have typically been reluctant to disclose information about participants uncovered during nonintervention research because (a) assessments designed to evaluate differences between groups may lack diagnostic validity for individual participants; (b) taking action to help participants (e.g., making referrals for treatment) can threaten the internal validity of a research design (especially longitudinal designs), betray the trust of participants, or jeopardize recruitment; and (c) disclosing information can create harmful or stressful consequences for participants (Fisher, 1993; Fisher & Brennan, 1992; Fisher, Higgins-D'Alessandro, et al., 1996; Scott-Jones, 1994). For instance, if child protection agencies or school counselors react incompetently or punitively to reports of risky behaviors or if legal involvements and criminal proceedings result, the child or adolescent and his or her family might suffer from the disclosure. Accuracy of participant reports is another important consideration because harm can result if disclosed information consists of false accusations (e.g., of abuse; Fisher, 2002b).There are situations in which the decision to disclose is more clear-cut, such as when information is revealed that reporting laws (which vary by state) mandate investigators to disclose. However, other situations elicit difficult disclosure decisions, raising the scientist–citizen dilemma for researchers to navigate on their own. In the absence of explicit guidelines, investigators must determine whether protecting participant confidentiality is to the detriment of participant welfare or invalidates the scientific validity and social benefits of the study. In certain circumstances, failure to disclose may have iatrogenic effects. For instance, researchers may come across participants who need help but are unaware that they have a problem (e.g., participants who are taking an illegal substance known by the investigator to be highly toxic). Or a researcher may ask adolescents about high-risk behaviors but then not respond by helping them, and the adolescents may conclude that adults think their problems are unimportant, that no services are available, or that knowledgeable adults cannot be depended on to help children (Fisher, 1994, 1999, 2003a). Furthermore, there is evidence that some teens may want researchers to actively aid them in obtaining help for particular problems, such as suicide, and may expect help even when confidentiality has been promised (Fisher, 2002b, 2003a; Fisher, Higgins-D'Alessandro, et al., 1996; Fisher & Masty, 2006a; O'Sullivan & Fisher, 1997). Therefore, it is important for researchers to recognize that the decision to do nothing is itself an intervention and that failure to disclose may be harmful.

Steps for Determining Confidentiality and Disclosure Procedures

As mentioned earlier, investigators are often challenged to decide whether to disclose life-threatening information discovered while conducting nonintervention research. Goodness-of-fit ethics assume that (a) the nature and probability of disclosure challenges are a product of both participant risk characteristics and the type of information the research will elicit; (b) researchers have the expertise to anticipate disclosure challenges on the basis of their familiarity with extant literature and in many cases previous research experience with similar populations; (c) whenever possible, ethical challenges involving confidentiality should be anticipated and procedures to address the challenge developed before participant recruitment is initiated; (d) understanding the perspectives of prospective research participants is an essential element of fair and effective disclosure policies; (e) disclosure and confidentiality procedures should be explained to participants during informed consent and to all research staff during training; and (f) investigators should draw on feedback from participants and research team members to evaluate and modify, if necessary, ethical procedures that will best fit the participant population and research context.

Ethical confidentiality and disclosure policies are neither singular nor static. Every research project requires a series of decision points that build to the construction of best ethical practices for the particular population and research context. On the basis of these goodness-of-fit assumptions, we provide a multistep decision-making strategy for constructing responsible confidentiality and disclosure policies.

Step 1: Anticipate Disclosure Challenges

Investigators conducting research involving drug use, suicide, violence, and child abuse risk are in the best position to draw on empirical knowledge and experience to anticipate the types of behaviors or information that might require disclosure of confidential information. Analysis of appropriate disclosure procedures must also include deliberation about the validity of the observations or measures that will be relied on to make a risk assessment. For example, some instruments that are highly reliable for testing hypotheses about aggregate populations may not have sufficient predictive power to conclude that an individual is at high risk of harm to self or others. Specific actions investigators can take include

- drawing on empirical and experiential knowledge of the participant population to anticipate the types of disclosure challenges that are likely to emerge during the conduct of research;
- evaluating whether the observations or measurements used in the research are valid for assessment of individual risk behaviors for which disclosure decisions are anticipated; and
- if the measures are valid, identifing the referral/reporting criterion.

Step 2: Investigate Legal Responsibilities and Community Resources

Researchers must also investigate relevant state or local reporting laws that members of the research team may be mandated to follow, as well as the legal implications of maintaining confidentiality or disclosing information for participants and team members. In addition, exploration of legal and social services in the community is essential to developing appropriate reporting procedures and referral sources. Finally, in many instances the perspectives of the prospective participant population on the validity of risk identification and the value of referral sources in the community are quite different from those of the service providers or researchers themselves. Thus, stakeholder input is essential to responsible confidentiality and disclosure policy development.

- Investigate federal, state, and local reporting laws, including who on the research team may be a mandatory reporter for child abuse and neglect, knowledge of a crime that may be committed, or Tarasoff duty-to-warn laws (Appelbaum & Rosenbaum, 1989).
- Investigate community referral and treatment resources in advance to help maximize the probability that disclosures, if necessary, will result in harm reduction.

- Gather information from research stakeholders (prospective participants, community members) on their perceptions of the fairness and face validity of risk assessments that might be made and the value of the referral procedures contemplated.

Step 3: Generate Ethical Alternatives and Select a Disclosure Policy

Anticipating disclosure challenges and gathering facts about relevant laws, institutional contexts, and participant perspectives will generate several alternative ethical solutions to maximize the goodness of fit between participant characteristics and the nature of information that will be obtained during the study. There are no cookie-cutter solutions to disclosure policies, and each investigator needs to weigh the costs and benefits of each alternative policy because it will affect participants, research team members, the community, and in some cases the validity of the design. To accomplish this step, investigators can

- generate and evaluate alternative disclosure policies (including the decision not to disclose);
- provide feedback to and obtain feedback from consulted stakeholders on the disclosure policy adopted;
- on the basis of information gathered, select the confidentiality and disclosure policy that best fits the anticipated population risks, the nature and validity of risk information that will be obtained during the research, the availability and adequacy of reporting and referral resources, and stakeholder perspectives; and
- after the selection of a policy, establish appropriate relationships with identified reporting and referral resources.

Step 4: Communicate the Disclosure Policy to Research Team Members and Participants

The next step in the disclosure policy process is to specify how disclosure will be conducted, the criteria that will be used to determine whether a disclosure may be necessary, and persons to contact if such a determination is made. The investigator must then train the research team to become competent in implementing this policy. Also, participants need to be informed during consent about confidentiality and disclosure procedures, and whenever feasible participants should be advised when a disclosure will be made.

- Develop specific procedures for how research staff should identify, evaluate, and report information that may require disclosure, and appropriately train and supervise the staff.
- Clearly communicate the confidentiality and disclosure policy to prospective participants during informed consent.

- Whenever possible, inform participants when a disclosure decision has been made, and when feasible and appropriate engage their participation in the disclosure.

Step 5: Monitor the Implementation of the Policy and Make Modifications if Necessary

Well-informed ethical planning will reduce but not eliminate the confidentiality and disclosure challenges that will emerge during the course of research. As with supervision of research in general, principal investigators need to monitor the implementation of the policy to help ensure that research assistants are not under- or overestimating situations that may require disclosure. Errors in research assistant judgment may indicate a flawed disclosure policy or the need for enhanced training and supervision. The consequences to participants or affected third parties of decisions to withhold confidential information or to disclose must also be monitored and evaluated and procedures modified as needed. Specific actions that can be taken include

- monitoring staff for adherence to policy and encouraging staff to provide feedback on unanticipated problems;
- monitoring the procedure for its effect on participants, research team members, and the responsible conduct of the research design;
- when possible, gathering opinions from staff and participants who have been involved in a disclosure decision;
- modifying the policy if monitoring suggests more effective and beneficial approaches; and
- continuing to monitor, encouraging feedback, evaluating, and modifying as necessary.

CONCLUSION

Research designed to understand, describe, and predict the correlates of violence, suicide, and abuse often involves persons who are disenfranchised from society because of disadvantage, illness, illegal behaviors, or social prejudice. Such research is critical if society is to construct and evaluate fair and effective social policies that will ameliorate these problems and provide opportunities for personal growth and healthy lives. By definition, nonintervention research does not offer participants the probability of direct benefit. Rather, any benefit that might be derived from the knowledge generated will emerge through the application of that knowledge by policymakers, practitioners, or other health and social service professionals, and such benefits may only accrue to future populations. Thus, both investigator and participant are collaborating in a project that will ideally benefit others in the future.

The interrelatedness of participant and investigator also surfaces as a means of evaluating research risk and the ethical procedures that can minimize such risk. By conceptualizing research risk as the joint product of participant characteristics and the research context, ethical procedures can be appropriately fitted to the unique challenges that emerge when life-threatening and illegal behaviors are the focus of study. In goodness-of-fit ethics, research vulnerability is defined in terms of a susceptibility to research harms that is not solely determined by participant characteristics that society views as disadvantageous, but on the degree to which participant welfare is dependent on the specific actions of scientists within a specific experimental context (Fisher, 1999). From this perspective, protecting the "vulnerable" research participant is a moral obligation that emerges from the research design itself rather than a charitable inclination of scientists as moral agents to protect those who are intrinsically vulnerable (Fisher, 1999; Goodin, 1985).Goodness-of-fit ethics is essentially optimistic in its view that research vulnerability is not predetermined. It posits that even for persons whom society views as most vulnerable, research risks and harms can be minimized by understanding not only participants' problems but also their personal and social network strengths. This understanding of population resilience contributes to fitting research designs to maximize opportunities for participant autonomy and welfare. The translation of goodness-of-fit ethics into ethics-in-science practice is not, however, assumed to be achieved simply through a scientist's moral reflections or empirically based knowledge, but must be informed by the perspectives of those within the participant community. Consequently, although principles of beneficence, respect, and justice can and should guide research design and ethics-in-science practices, the investigator's interpretation of these principles should not stand in isolation from the values, fears, and hopes that participants bring to the research enterprise. Finally, as with all ethical endeavors, creating participant-fitted ethical practices provides scientists with opportunities for moral growth. It pushes us to envision research ethics as a process that draws on our knowledge as scientists of the human condition and our responsiveness to others as members of society to discover new means of resolving our obligations as scientists and citizens.

REFERENCES

Adler, M. W. (1995). College on problems of drug dependence, special report: Human subject issues in drug abuse research. *Drug and Alcohol Dependence, 37*, 165–175.

American Psychological Association Ethics Committee. (2002). Rules and procedures. *American Psychologist, 57*, 626–645.

Appelbaum, P. S., & Rosenbaum, A. (1989). Tarasoff and the researcher: Does the duty to protect apply in the research setting? *American Psychologist, 44*, 885–894.

Becker-Blease, K. A., & Freyd, J. J. (2006). Research participants telling the truth about their lives: The ethics of asking and not asking about abuse. *American Psychologist, 61*, 218–226.

Brooks-Gunn, J., & Rotheram-Borus, M. J. (1994). Rights to privacy in research: Adolescents versus parents. *Ethics & Behavior, 4*, 109–121.

Bruzzese, J. M., & Fisher, C. B. (2003). Assessing and enhancing the research consent capacity of children and youth. *Applied Developmental Science, 7*, 13–26.

Charland, L. C. (2002). Cynthia's dilemma: Consenting to heroin prescription. *American Journal of Bioethics, 2*, 37–47.

Clair, S., Singer, M., Huertas, E., & Weeks, M. (2003). Unintended consequences of using an oral HIV test on HIV knowledge. *AIDS Care—Psychological and Socio-Medical Aspects of AIDS/HIV, 15*, 575–580.

Cohen, P. J. (2002). Untreated addiction imposes an ethical bar to recruiting addicts for non-therapeutic studies of addictive drugs. *Journal of Law, Medicine & Ethics, 30*, 73–81.

Fairchild, A. L., & Bayer, R. (1999, May 7). Uses and abuses of Tuskegee. *Science, 284*, 919–921.

Fisher, C. B. (1993). Integrating science and ethics in research with high-risk children and youth. *SCRD Social Policy Report, 7*, 1–27.

Fisher, C. B. (1994). Reporting and referring research participants: Ethical challenges for investigators studying children and youth. *Ethics & Behavior, 4*, 87–95.

Fisher, C. B. (1997). A relational perspective on ethics-in-science decisionmaking for research with vulnerable populations. *IRB: A Review of Human Subjects Research, 19*(5), 1–4.

Fisher, C. B. (1999). Relational ethics and research with vulnerable populations. In *Reports on research involving persons with mental disorders that may affect decisionmaking capacity: Vol. II. Commissioned papers by the National Bioethics Advisory Commission* (pp. 29–49). Bethesda, MD: National Bioethics Advisory Commission. Retrieved March 21, 2006, from http://www.onlineethics.org/cms/9004.aspx

Fisher, C. B. (2000). Relational ethics in psychological research: One feminist's journey. In M. M. Brabeck (Ed.), *Practicing feminist ethics in psychology* (pp. 125–142). Washington, DC: American Psychological Association.

Fisher, C. B. (2002a). A goodness-of-fit ethic of informed consent. *Urban Law Journal, 30*, 159–171.

Fisher, C. B. (2002b). Participant consultation: Ethical insights into parental permission and confidentiality procedures for policy relevant research with youth. In R. M. Lerner, F. Jacobs, & D. Wertlieb (Eds.), *Handbook of applied developmental science* (Vol. 4, pp. 371–396). Thousand Oaks, CA: Sage.

Fisher, C. B. (2003a). Adolescent and parent perspectives on ethical issues in youth drug use and suicide survey research. *Ethics & Behavior, 13*, 302–331.

Fisher, C. B. (2003b). A goodness-of-fit ethic for informed consent to research involving persons with mental retardation and developmental disabilities. *Mental Retardation and Developmental Disabilities Research Reviews, 9*, 27–31.

Fisher, C. B. (2004). Ethics in drug abuse and related HIV risk research. *Applied Developmental Science, 8*, 90–102.

Fisher, C. B., & Brennan, M. (1992). Application and ethics in developmental psychology. In D. L. Featherman, R. M. Lerner, & M. Perlmutter (Eds.), *Life-span development and behavior* (pp. 189–219). Hillsdale, NJ: Erlbaum.

Fisher, C. B., Higgins-D'Alessandro, A., Rau, J. M. B., Kuther, R., & Belanger, S. (1996). Referring and reporting research participants at risk: Views from urban adolescents. *Child Development, 67*, 2086–2100.

Fisher, C. B., Hoagwood, K., Boyce, C., Duster, T., Frank, D. A., Grisso, T., et al. (2002). Research ethics for mental health science involving ethnic minority children and youth. *American Psychologist, 57*, 1024–1040.

Fisher, C. B., Hoagwood, K., & Jensen, P. S. (1996). Casebook on ethical issues in research with children and adolescents with mental disorders. In K. Hoagwood, P. S. Jensen, & C. B. Fisher (Eds.), *Ethical issues in research with children and adolescents with mental disorders* (pp. 135–238). Hillsdale, NJ: Erlbaum.

Fisher, C. B., & Masty, J. K. (2006a). Community perspectives on the ethics of adolescent risk research. In B. Leadbeater, T. Reicken, C. Benoit, M. Jansson, & A. Marshall (Eds.), *Research ethics in community-based and participatory action research with youth* (pp. 22–41). Toronto, Ontario, Canada: University of Toronto Press.

Fisher, C. B., & Masty, J. K. (2006b). A goodness-of-fit ethic for informed consent to pediatric cancer research. In R. T. Brown (Ed.), *Comprehensive handbook of childhood cancer and sickle cell disease* (pp. 205–217). New York: Oxford University Press.

Fisher, C. B., Pearson, J. L., Kim, S., & Reynolds, C. F. (2002). Ethical issues in including suicidal individuals in clinical research. *IRB: Ethics & Human Research, 24*(5), 9–14.

Fisher, C. B., & Ragsdale, K. (2006). Goodness-of-fit ethics for multicultural research. In J. E. Trimble & C. B. Fisher (Eds.), *The handbook of ethical research with ethnocultural populations and communities* (pp. 3–26). Thousand Oaks, CA: Sage.

Fisher, C. B., & Rosendahl, S. A. (1990). Psychological risks and remedies of research participation. In C. B. Fisher & W. W. Tryon (Eds.), *Ethics in applied developmental psychology: Emerging issues in an emerging field* (pp. 43–60). Norwood, NJ: Ablex.

Fisher, C. B., & Wallace, S. A. (2000). Through the community looking glass: Reevaluating the ethical and policy implications of research on adolescent risk and psychopathology. *Ethics & Behavior, 10*, 99–118.

Foulks, E. F. (1989). Misalliances in the Barrow Alcohol Study. *American Alaskan Native Mental Health Research, 2*, 2–17.

Goodin, R. E. (1985). *Protecting the vulnerable.* Chicago: University of Chicago Press.

Gould, M. S., Marroco, F. A., Kleinman, M., Thomas, J. G., Mostkoff, K., Cota, J., et al. (2005, April 6). Evaluating iatrogenic risk of youth suicide screening programs: A randomized controlled trial. *JAMA, 293*, 1635–1643.

Harrison, K., Vlahov, D., Jones, K., Charron, K., & Clements, M. L. (1995). Medical eligibility, comprehension of the consent process, and retention of injection drug users recruited for an HIV vaccine trial. *Journal of Acquired Immune Deficiency Syndromes and Human Retrovirology, 10*, 386–390.

Haverkamp, B. E. (2005). Ethical perspectives on qualitative research in applied psychology. *Journal of Counseling Psychology, 52*, 146–155.

Hoagwood, K. (1994). The Certificate of Confidentiality at the National Institute of Mental Health: Discretionary considerations in its applicability in research on child and adolescent mental disorders. *Ethics & Behavior, 4*, 123–131.

Institute of Medicine Committee on Clinical Research Involving Children, Field, M. J., & Behrman, R. E. (Eds.). (2004). *Ethical conduct of clinical research involving children*. Washington, DC: National Academies Press.

Lidz, C., Meisel, A., Zerubavel, E., Carter, M., Sestak, R., & Roth, L. (1984). *Informed consent: A study of decision-making in psychiatry*. New York: Guilford Press.

Marshall, P. A. (1992). Research ethics in applied anthropology. *IRB: A Review of Human Subjects Research, 14*(6), 1–5.

Masty, J., & Fisher, C. B. (2008). A goodness of fit approach to parent permission and child assent pediatric intervention research. *Ethics & Behavior, 18*, 139-160.

McCrady, B. S., & Bux, D. A. (1999). Ethical issues in informed consent with substance abusers. *Journal of Consulting and Clinical Psychology, 67*, 186–193.

Melton, G. B. (1990). Certificates of confidentiality under the Public Health Service Act: Strong protection but not enough. *Violence and Victims, 5*, 67–71.

O'Sullivan, C., & Fisher, C. B. (1997). The effect of confidentiality and reporting procedures on parent-child agreement to participate in adolescent risk research. *Applied Developmental Science, 1*, 185–197.

Palmer, B. W., Cassidy, E. L., Dunn, L. B., Spira, A. P., & Sheikh, J. I. (2008). Effective use of consent forms and interactive questions in the consent process. *IRB: Ethics & Human Research, 30*(2), 8–12.

Protection of Human Subjects, 45 C.F.R. § 46 (2005).

Public Health Service Act § 301(d), 42 U.S.C. 241(d), as amended by Pub. L. 100-607 § 163 (1988).

Reverby, S. M. (2001). More than fact and fiction: Cultural memory and the Tuskegee syphilis study. *Hastings Center Report, 31*, 22–28.

Rudd, M. D. (2000). Integrating science into the practice of clinical suicidology: A review of the psychotherapy literature and research agenda for the future. In R. W. Maris, S. S. Cannetto, J. L. McIntosh, & M. M. Silverman (Eds.), *Review of suicidology* (pp. 47–83). New York: Guilford Press.

Scott-Jones, D. (1994). Ethical issues in reporting and referring in research with low-income minority children. *Ethics & Behavior, 4*, 97–108.

Singer, M., Marshall, P. L., Trotter, R. T., II, Schensul, J. J., Weeks, M. R., Simmons, J. E., et al. (1999). Ethics, ethnography, drug use, and AIDS: Dilemmas and standards in federally funded research. In P. L. Marshall, M. Singer, & M. C. Clatts (Eds.), *Integrating cultural, observational, and epidemiological approaches in the prevention of drug abuse and HIV/AIDS* (National Institute on Drug Abuse, NIH Publication No. 99-4565, pp. 198–222). Rockville, MD: National Institute on Drug Abuse.

Stiffman, A. R., Freedenthal, S., Brown, E., Ostmann, E., & Hibbeler, P. (2005). Field research with underserved minorities: The ideal and the real. *Journal of Urban Health: Bulletin of the New York Academy of Medicine*, *82*(2, Suppl. 3), iii56–iii66.

Veatch, R. M. (1987). *The patient as partner*. Bloomington: Indiana University Press.

2

LEGAL CHALLENGES RAISED BY NONINTERVENTION RESEARCH CONDUCTED UNDER HIGH-RISK CIRCUMSTANCES

LANCE GABLE

Nonintervention research conducted under high-risk circumstances may raise difficult ethical and practical issues for researchers, research participants, and society more broadly. These issues, explored throughout this book, pose considerable challenges to researchers because of the unique context and distinct relationships created by nonintervention research. Often, researchers must find a balance between multiple obligations to protect their research participants, to protect members of the research team or third parties, and to conduct ethical and scientifically sound research within the contours of approved experimental protocols.

Law affects nonintervention research conducted under high-risk circumstances in at least three ways. Legal provisions (a) establish a framework that governs the conduct of research, (b) provide guidance for researchers to address difficult situations that may place research participants and others in high-risk circumstances, and (c) support ethical assessments of research conduct.

First, law creates the structure within which investigators conduct research. Law sets standards of conduct for research, protects the privacy of research participants and the confidentiality of their information, and imposes penalties on those who fail to enforce these protections. The legal framework seeks equilibrium between the interests of researchers and research participants by allowing researchers the flexibility to design innovative studies while preserving important protections for human research participants and others. Law may also impose responsibilities on researchers to protect participants and others from harm or to report threats to life or health that the researcher discovers during a study. Although some researchers may perceive law as an impediment to research (Fost & Levine, 2007), a robust legal framework is necessary to protect the safety and well-being of research participants. Moreover, well-designed legal provisions may actually facilitate good research.

Despite these general observations, when conflicts arise in the context of nonintervention research, existing law may or may not directly resolve them. For example, researchers confronted with threats of violence or suicide from their subjects may face contemporaneous and conflicting legal duties to maintain data confidentiality and to disclose data. Another type of conflict may occur when laws provide substantial protection for human research participants but limit efforts to protect others from harm.

Second, law provides researchers with guidance to resolve complicated issues. Legal requirements may assist researchers in finding the appropriate response to threats of harm—such as suicide, child abuse, and violence—that may arise during the course of conducting nonintervention research. Research protocols often incorporate legal standards of care and prospectively establish processes for addressing foreseeable threats of harm. Research protocols can benefit from strong legal protections—for example, Certificates of Confidentiality (Public Health Services Act, 1988)—that allow investigators significant control over access to the data they collect.

Third, law complements ethical considerations in the context of nonintervention research. Indeed, laws are often based on, and consistent with, ethical principles. Researchers must be guided not only by the law but also by ethical considerations. Legal principles, when used in concert with a robust understanding and application of ethical principles, inform researchers in resolving conflicts and alleviating potential risks of harm.

Nonintervention research encompasses several seemingly distinct fields of study, spanning social science, behavioral, observational, and ethnographic research, as well as research on conditions as varied as mental health, drug and alcohol abuse, suicidality, and violence. The common thread of these research studies is that although researchers in these studies collect and use data from human participants, they do not attempt to intervene in the lives of their research participants. Rather, nonintervention studies conducted among individuals or populations seek to obtain generalizable knowledge regarding certain social or health conditions without imposing therapies or otherwise intervening to address these conditions in the participants or populations being studied. As a result, the legal and ethical issues raised by these studies can differ markedly from traditional biomedical research.

The legal questions that arise in the context of nonintervention research are often distinct from other types of research with human participants. The noninterventionist nature of these research studies places the investigator in a different position relative to the participants and may affect the expectations created by the researcher–participant relationship. Many participants will agree to participate in the study only on the condition that the study involves no intervention. Because many of these studies involve behaviors that may be stigmatized, surreptitious, or illegal, maintaining trust and confidence, and often confidentiality, between researchers and participants is vital to success. The research participants in these types of studies, referred to collectively as *high-risk populations* elsewhere in this volume, may be more vulnerable to threats of suicide, abuse, neglect, and violence compared with other research populations.

The high-risk circumstances that arise during nonintervention research are characterized not only by the demographics of these often vulnerable populations but also by the context surrounding the research. Research participants may pose risks of harm to themselves or others and may directly affect the safety or well-being of researchers, study participants, or third parties. The release of identifiable data about a research participant may subject him or her to discrimination, embarrassment, or social opprobrium. Challenging legal questions abound. When does a particular risk of harm trigger legal protections or duties? When can researchers override confidentiality protections to protect a third party? How do researchers resolve conflicting obligations to maintain confidentiality and report certain behaviors? What happens when the risky behavior of a research participant endangers the participant? What happens when the risky behavior of a research participant endangers others? What happens when the risky behavior of a research participant endangers the success of the study? In each scenario, may a researcher conducting a nonintervention study take action to intervene and attempt to avert potential harm? And, perhaps more important, when should the researcher intervene?

The following sections present an overview of the major legal issues that face researchers engaged in nonintervention studies under high-risk circumstances. Rather than attempting to categorize all of the possible permutations of law in this diverse field, the sections that follow instead focus on broad legal issues that cut across many nonintervention studies and provide illustrative examples of how the law can affect these studies.

The first section of the chapter describes the three major categories of laws that pertain to nonintervention research: (a) laws governing the conduct of research with human subjects; (b) laws protecting the privacy and confidentiality of identifiable information related to research participants and others; and (c) laws that compel disclosure of information, including legal duties to warn or protect others from harm or to report certain behaviors or conditions that may affect life or health. This section outlines the applicable legal framework and highlights important legal concerns that may arise in the context of nonintervention research involving high-risk circumstances.

The second section discusses several unresolved legal questions that researchers, research participants, and review boards may face during the course of nonintervention studies. In addition, this section identifies the boundaries of law in addressing these situations. Existing legal provisions have some inherent limitations in addressing the full range of issues that arise in the context of nonintervention research studies. The law must be used in concert with other methods of assessment and decision making, including systems of ethics, risk–benefit balancing, and other practical considerations. This section also identifies several future areas of study that deserve the concerted attention of lawyers, scientists, and ethicists.

LAW AND NONINTERVENTION RESEARCH: AN OVERVIEW

Law fills several distinct and important roles for investigators conducting nonintervention research under high-risk circumstances. Legal rules and frameworks

- govern many of the acts undertaken by researchers;
- provide protections for human research participants, researchers, and third parties;
- impose requirements on researchers that set parameters on the scope of legitimate research activities; and
- in some instances, incorporate ethical norms into an enforceable legal structure.

Applying legal rules and identifying legal problems in a general way presents some difficulty in the context of nonintervention research. Nonintervention research involves multiple research methods, ranging from conducting personal interviews to collecting biological samples to examining epidemiological and archival data. These methods implicate differing legal concerns and may be subject to varying legal requirements. It may very well be impossible to suggest a unified legal framework sufficient to address all possible concerns in such a varied field. This section examines three primary categories of laws that may govern the actions of researchers engaged in nonintervention research under high-risk circumstances: (a) laws that regulate research with human participants, (b) laws providing privacy and confidentiality protections, and (c) legal duties that compel disclosure of data from researchers.

Laws Governing Research With Human Participants

The first category of relevant laws includes legal provisions that authorize and regulate research with human participants. These laws create a structure within which researchers may legally conduct their studies. Research using human participants in the United States is primarily conducted pursuant to requirements established by federal regulations. These federal requirements, known as the "Common Rule" because they have been adopted by 17 federal agencies, regulate all research involving human participants conducted by researchers and institutions receiving federal funding (Protection of Human Subjects, 2005). Federal regulations do not apply to research using human participants conducted by researchers and institutions not funded by the federal government, but such research may be subject to other regulations at the state level. The Common Rule regulations impose requirements and standards on research protocols designed to protect the safety, autonomy, and privacy of research participants and their communities, while simultaneously supporting the goals of research and scientific advancement. Significantly, the Common Rule defines human subjects research as including studies involving intervention or interaction with human research participants, as well as studies in which the researchers obtain private, identifiable information (Protection of Human Subjects, 2005, Section 46.102[f]). Research involving publicly available data or information that does not allow a person to be identified directly or through linked identifiers does not constitute human subjects research and does not require institutional review board (IRB) approval (Protection of Human Subjects, 2005, § 46.101[b][4]). Nevertheless, most nonintervention research studies conducted with federal funding are clearly within the ambit of these regulations, and researchers must comply accordingly.

Institutional Review Boards

The Common Rule (Protection of Human Subjects, 2005) establishes a critical oversight mechanism using IRBs to approve and monitor research protocols involving human participants. IRBs have the responsibility to assess whether research protocols are scientifically sound; to minimize risks to subjects and evaluate whether the risks are reasonable in relation to anticipated benefits; to ensure subject selection is equitable; and to provide for protections for informed consent, participant safety, subject privacy, and data confidentiality (Protection of Human Subjects, 2005, § 46.111[a]). Federal regulations authorize IRBs to impose special safeguards to protect the rights and welfare of vulnerable subjects such as children, prisoners, pregnant women, mentally disabled persons, or economically or educationally disadvantaged persons (Protection of Human Subjects, 2005, § 46.111[b]). IRBs play a vital role in the structure of research studies as independent gatekeepers, charged with vetting and monitoring research protocols and ensuring that sufficient provisions are in place to protect research participants from exploitation or harm.

Informed Consent

The law requires researchers to obtain informed consent from study participants. This requirement is premised on the ethical principle of respect for persons. Respect for persons demands that researchers enable study participants to make informed decisions about what shall or shall not happen to them (National Commission, 1979). The Common Rule (Protection of Human Subjects, 2005) codifies this concept in federal law as applied to research with human participants. Researchers must in most circumstances obtain informed consent from human participants before their participation in a research study. Informed consent requirements demand that researchers meet eight specific criteria, which include sharing with potential participants specific information regarding the foreseeable risks and potential benefits of participation in the study and the extent of confidentiality protections available (Protection of Human Subjects, 2005, § 46.116). Furthermore, informed consent must be obtained voluntarily while ensuring that participants have sufficient competence and understanding of the protocol to grant informed consent. Berg, Appelbaum, Lidz, and Parker (2001, p. 266) noted that the federal regulations do not provide much guidance on how to assess competency or understanding. Yet, the regulations make clear that the content of information provided to potential participants and the process for obtaining informed consent must be approved by an IRB.

The IRB retains broad discretion to alter informed consent requirements and may approve research using identifiable information in existing databases without specific informed consent if (a) the research involves no more than minimal risk; (b) the waiver of informed consent will not adversely affect the rights and welfare of the subjects; (c) the waiver is necessary to carry out the research; and (d) when appropriate, the subject will be informed after participation (Protection of Human Subjects, 2005, § 46.116[b]). These exceptions can facilitate retrospective records-based research, epidemiological studies, and other nonintervention studies by allowing researchers to proceed with these investigations without the onerous burden of obtaining individual consent to use each record in these databases.

State Laws Regulating Human Subjects Research

State laws may apply additional legal protections to research with human participants (Burris, Gable, Stone, & Lazzarini, 2003). The Common Rule explicitly does not override more stringent state-level protections for research participants (Protection of Human Subjects, 2005, § 101[f]). Only a few states, however, have enacted stronger protections for informed consent or independent review in the context of research studies (Schwartz, 2001). One example is Maryland, which in response to a high-profile case of unethical research conduct at a research university in the state has legislatively applied Common Rule standards to all research experiments conducted in the state, not only those funded with federal resources (Md. Stat. § 13-2002).

Law Addressing Privacy, Confidentiality, and Disclosure of Information

Privacy and confidentiality protections available for research participants and their identifiable health information make up the second category of relevant legal provisions. As the health information infrastructure in the United States continues to develop, laws that protect health information privacy have demanded additional scrutiny (Gostin, 1995; Gostin, Lazzarini, Neslund, & Osterholm, 1996). Efforts to further expand the use of electronic medical records will surely heighten privacy concerns and may demand the development of additional privacy protections for identifiable data. (U.S. General Accountability Office, 2007).

Although frequently used interchangeably, privacy and confidentiality are distinct concepts under the law (Goldman & Choy, 2001). Boruch and Cecil (1979a) described *privacy* as "the individual's control over whether and to what extent information about himself or herself will be shared with anyone else" (p. 23). By comparison, *confidentiality* "refers to the state of information" (Boruch & Cecil, 1979a, p. 25) and arises from the relationship between the researcher and research participant. Put another way,

> Privacy refers to an individual's unwillingness to disclose some personal information to anyone for any purpose. Confidentiality refers to the desire of an individual to restrict the recipients of personal information or the purposes to which it may be put. (Reiken, 1983, p. 4)

The persistent confusion between these two concepts in their Common Rule definitions and elsewhere in law has led some commentators to suggest amending existing laws to clarify this distinction (Boruch & Cecil, 1979a; Seiber, 2001).

The U.S. Supreme Court has recognized a limited right to informational privacy, finding that the accumulation of vast amounts of personal information in government databases poses an implicit threat to privacy (*Whalen v. Roe*, 1977). Courts have expressed great deference, however, to breaches of privacy by the government and others for purposes of recognizable public interest (Gostin, 1995; *United States v. Westinghouse Electric*, 1950). This deference is reflected in the multiple exceptions found in privacy and confidentiality laws that authorize and facilitate research. Legislative and regulatory provisions that protect privacy and confidentiality can affect a researcher's access to data, place limits on how a researcher can share or disclose data, or allow a researcher to keep data confidential from outside sources. The next sections discuss several areas of law that may pertain to the level of confidentiality afforded to identifiable data collected during research:

(a) the federal Privacy Act of 1974, (b) the Health Insurance Portability and Accountability Act (HIPAA) of 1996 privacy regulations, (c) the Freedom of Information Act of 1966, (d) federal Certificates of Confidentiality (Public Health Service Act, 1988), (e) state privacy laws, and (f) evidentiary privileges under statutory or common law.

Federal Privacy Act

The federal Privacy Act of 1974 establishes privacy protections applicable to federal agencies and institutions holding data pursuant to federal contracts. The act prohibits disclosure of identifiable information without first obtaining prior written consent of the individual whose information is contained in the record, subject to several exceptions. The scope of this privacy protection is limited, however, by two factors. First, these protections do not apply to data held outside of the federal government. Second, the act permits disclosure without consent for any purpose compatible with the purpose for which the data were originally collected. This exception has been interpreted broadly, effectively undermining privacy protections in numerous circumstances (Gostin, 1995).

HIPAA Privacy Rule

At the federal level, the most significant recent development in health information privacy law has been the health information privacy regulations (the "Privacy Rule"; Protection of Human Subjects, 2005, §§ 160, 164) adopted pursuant to HIPAA (1996). The Privacy Rule set a national standard limiting access to identifiable information (known under the Privacy Rule as protected health information, or PHI). These regulations recognize that identifiable health data demand protection from disclosure because of the sensitive content of such data and the privacy risks that may be created by unhindered disclosure.

The Privacy Rule may affect the acquisition and use of data by researchers in several ways. PHI generally may not be disclosed without the consent of the person identified in the data, but explicit exceptions allow disclosure without consent for research purposes with the approval of an IRB or privacy board (an IRB-like independent review board charged with specifically evaluating the risks to privacy that may result from disclosing PHI; Protection of Human Subjects, 2005, § 164.512[b]). These exceptions acknowledge the importance of giving researchers access to data while retaining safeguards to protect individual privacy. The Privacy Rule requires an IRB or privacy board to consider two additional factors when approving the use of PHI for research. The review body must determine that (a) the research does not impose more than a "minimal risk" to privacy rights and (b) these risks outweigh the anticipated benefits of the research (Protection of Human Subjects, 2005, § 164.512). These requirements have been criticized for being too vague and for unnecessarily imposing extra burdens on IRB review (Kulynych &

Korn, 2002). Others have called for the imposition of more stringent privacy protections during IRB review (Goldman & Choy, 2001).

Although the Privacy Rule (Protection of Human Subjects, 2005, §§ 160, 164) may limit researcher access to some data, or at least place additional restrictions on obtaining such data, in most cases the restrictions on disclosure will not impede researchers from using and sharing data they have legally obtained (National Institutes of Health [NIH], 2003). Most researchers are not "covered entities" or "business associates" under the Privacy Rule because they are not engaged in the provision of health care. Information generated through nonintervention research is particularly unlikely to fall within the Privacy Rule because of its inherent nature: Nonintervention research typically does not involve the provision of health care services.

The Privacy Rule does not preempt federal, state, or local statutes that require or permit disclosure of PHI for a specific purpose, including those state laws that grant heightened privacy protection above the national standards (Protection of Human Subjects, 2005, § 160.203[a]). Thus, researchers must still comply with state privacy laws and with laws that mandate reporting of diseases and abuse, as applicable (NIH, 2003). Other federal regulations, such as the Common Rule (Protection of Human Subjects, 2005), also continue to apply. Finally, the Privacy Rule requires certain entities that disclose PHI to account for these disclosures to affected individuals (Protection of Human Subjects, 2005, § 164.528). To the extent that disclosure and other requirements apply to researchers, they may impose additional logistical burdens. However, these potential burdens must be weighed against the goal of creating a system that enhances privacy protection for identifiable information.

Freedom of Information Act

The federal Freedom of Information Act of 1966 (FOIA) and similar state-level open records acts permit disclosure to the public of information held by the federal government under some circumstances. These provisions can be a boon to nonintervention researchers who engage in records-based research. FOIA disclosures may enable researchers to gain access to identifiable data in existing government databases that may be useful for conducting nonintervention studies (see chap. 3, this volume). Researchers who produce identifiable data directly for or under contract to the government have had success in defending the confidentiality of identifiable information and withholding records from public disclosures (Gostin, 1995). Several provisions of FOIA—including exemptions for personal and medical files that would constitute an invasion of privacy and for "privileged and confidential" data—allow agencies the discretion to decline disclosure. In addition, the U.S. Supreme Court has held that independent researchers need not disclose research data developed with federal funding (*Forsham v. Harris*, 1980). The 1999 enactment of the Shelby Amendment (Omnibus Consolidated & Emergency Supplemental Appropriations Act, 1999)—a measure designed to increase the validity and integrity of research data—required federal agencies to make raw research data available in some circumstances through FOIA. These changes, however, only apply in limited circumstances and are unlikely to affect identifiable or unpublished research data. Nevertheless, researchers and IRBs should continue to be aware of changes to FOIA and analogous state laws that may pose a threat to maintaining confidentiality of research information (Seiber, 2001).

Several more recent legislative and judicial developments have potentially complicated further issues related to access to research data. An Illinois court required the release of health information under state-level FOIAs after balancing the risk of harm from the disclosure with the public's interest in having access to the information (*Southern Illinoisan v. Illinois Department of Public Health*, 2004). Both the Patriot Act of 2001 and the Data Quality Act of 2001 authorize increased access to statistical data generated by federal research. The effect of these laws on the privacy of research data remains to be seen, particularly in light of the recently enacted Confidential Information Protection and Statistical Efficiency Act of 2002 (Singer, 2006).

Certificates of Confidentiality

The Secretary of the Department of Health and Human Services, or other federal agencies, may grant researchers Certificates of Confidentiality (NIH, 2003). Originally created to protect the confidentiality of research on the effects of drugs by the Comprehensive Drug Abuse Control and Prevention Act of 1970, legislation subsequently expanded the coverage of these certificates to protect the privacy of human research participants in other areas of research, including biomedical, behavioral, social, and observational research (Currie, 2005). The broad purpose of the certificate is to shield identifiable data from outside entities—such as law enforcement, litigating attorneys, or others—who may seek access to sensitive, private data collected by researchers.

Certificates of Confidentiality offer substantial confidential protection for information developed during research. The certificate authorizes

> persons engaged in biomedical, behavioral, clinical, or other research (including research on mental health, including research on the use and effect of alcohol and other psychoactive drugs), to protect the privacy of individuals who are the subject of such research by withholding from all persons not connected with the conduct of such research the names or other identifying characteristics of such individuals. Persons so authorized to protect the privacy of such individuals may not be compelled in any federal, state, or local civil, criminal, administrative, legislative, or other proceeding to identify such individuals. (Public Health Service Act, 1988)

The availability of certificates raises several noteworthy issues in the context of nonintervention research conducted under high-risk circumstances. First, the federal government may grant certificates for any research study that requires confidentiality to produce valid and reliable results (Currie, 2005), and specific NIH institutes may even recommend that investigators obtain a certificate as a condition of funding (Wolf, Zandecki, & Lo, 2004). This flexibility permits researchers engaged in a wide range of nonintervention studies to apply for and obtain certificates.

Second, authorized government officials can grant certificates to cover nonintervention studies regardless of the source of funding. Although any federal agency may issue certificates, the NIH approves the vast majority of those granted (Wolf et al., 2004). Agency officials, at their discretion, may grant certificates for any research that meets the agency's criteria and obtains official approval, regardless of whether the research is funded by the federal government. IRBs will require researchers intending to use a Certificate of Confidentiality to provide participants with specific information about the scope of coverage provided by this agreement (Wolf et al., 2004).

Once granted, the certificate can provide researchers and participants with strong protection against compelled disclosures of data related to research participants' identities. In many ways, the certificate establishes stronger and more extensive confidentiality protection than other privacy laws. For example, although PHI protected by the HIPAA (1996) Privacy Rule may be disclosed pursuant to a host of exceptions, including for judicial and administrative proceedings, the identity of research subjects may be withheld from similar requests under a certificate. Although the scope of protection afforded by a certificate has rarely been challenged in court, a New York court upheld the rights of a researcher with a certificate to refuse to release identifiable data about participants in a methadone study that were subpoenaed by police investigators (*People v. Newman*, 1973).

Certificates of Confidentiality have limits in their scope of protection. First, the certificate only covers the identifiable information of research subjects, not the data itself. If data can be deidentified, a court may still require it to be disclosed (Currie, 2005). Second, a certificate does not authorize researchers to protect sensitive information about third parties collected during the course of investigational research because confidentiality protections do not extend to nonsubjects (Margolin et al., 2005; Seiber, 2001). Disclosure of data and identifying information related to third parties may be compelled through a subpoena or other legal request. In addition, although researchers cannot be compelled to disclose identifiable information about research participants, researchers may voluntarily disclose such information (Currie, 2005; Gostin, 1995). Similarly, the certificate does not prevent participants from consenting to the release of their information. Researchers should inform research participants of reporting obligations in the consent form they sign at the start of the investigation (Wolf et al., 2004).

State Laws Related to Privacy and Confidentiality

All states provide some level of privacy protection for identifiable health data, but few have enacted comprehensive privacy laws (Solove & Rotenberg, 2003, pp. 207–210). The scope of privacy laws and the level of privacy protection afforded to health data in the possession of researchers vary across jurisdictions and may depend on the type of health data being used. Some states have opted for generally applicable privacy protections, and others have granted exceptional privacy protection to certain disease-specific information, such as information related to genetics (Gostin & Hodge, 1999) or HIV status (Bayer, 1991; Burris, 1994; Gostin & Hodge, 1998). Other state laws have placed specific limitations on sensitive data. For example, California requires that alcohol and drug abuse data may only be released for research without consent if the individual is not identifiable (Cal. Health & Safety Code § 11977).

Evidentiary Privileges

Evidentiary privileges, also referred to as privileged communications, have been established at the state level through statutory and case law and may provide confidentiality protection to information shared within commonly recognized relationships, such as physician–patient, psychotherapist–patient, attorney–client, spouses, and clergy–penitent. Although the law grants the privilege to the patient or client, either party engaged in a privileged relationship can assert this privilege to protect communications between the participants from judicial and other government proceedings (Solove & Rotenberg, 2003, p. 217). The U.S. Supreme Court held in *Jaffee v. Redmond* (1996) that "an asserted privilege must also 'serv[e] public ends.'" Evidentiary privileges have rarely extended confidentiality protection to information shared within the researcher–research participant relationship (O'Neill, 1996), but legal commentators have suggested that such a privilege should be recognized (Boness & Cordess, 1974; Valpariso Law Review, 1970).

Establishing a researcher–research participant privilege could bolster the confidentiality of research data and protect researchers from negative legal ramifications if the researcher does not comply with a subpoena or refuses to testify about research data (Traynor, 1970). In the context of nonintervention research conducted under high-risk circumstances, the recognition of a researcher–research participant privilege would extend confidentiality to much of the information generated during the course of research without the researcher having to obtain a Certificate of Confidentiality, although the confidentiality protection granted to research data would not be as broad under the privilege as compared with the certificate. The creation of an evidentiary privilege between researchers and research participants could also clarify the obligations of the researcher in light of conflicting legal and ethical duties with regard to reporting.

Compelled Disclosure of Research Data

The third subset of laws that affect the conduct of nonintervention research includes laws that compel disclosure of information. These laws make up three categories: (a) laws that require a researcher to report information to the state, (b) laws that require a researcher to disclose information to a third party or otherwise take steps to protect a third party from harm, or (c) laws that permit the government or another third party to demand research data.

State Reporting Requirements

Most states have enacted mandatory reporting laws that may require defined categories of persons to report information to the state on cases of child abuse, elder abuse, domestic violence, and communicable diseases and other health conditions. However, the applicability of and requirements imposed by these laws vary substantially from state to state. Reporting laws are grounded in the need for the state to have access to certain important information to advance state interests in protecting the public's health (e.g., disease reporting requirements) or in intervening to prevent harm to individuals at risk (e.g., child abuse, elder abuse, domestic violence). Although mandatory reporting laws serve an important government function, the effect of these laws on research can be substantial. In particular, these laws may decrease participation in studies in which potential subjects fear their information may be disclosed to government authorities or deter researchers from undertaking certain research studies that may require mandatory reporting.

Researchers may or may not have to comply with mandatory reporting laws. Many state requirements that compel infectious disease reporting apply only to specific conditions, thereby excluding any researchers who are not collecting those types of data. In addition, state reporting laws covering diseases and health conditions may only apply to clinical medical practitioners, such as physicians, and laboratories (Gostin, 2000). Therefore, only certain research data will be covered by these laws and only in some jurisdictions, which will allow most researchers to avoid reporting health conditions. Researchers who also have a clinical relationship with a research participant may be able to distinguish their clinical relationship from their researcher relationship and thus avoid reporting requirements with respect to research data.

Child abuse and elder abuse laws, to the extent that they exist in a particular state, may establish more expansive reporting obligations that may implicate researchers. For example, some states require all persons to report child abuse, and others have ambiguous requirements that do not exclude researchers as mandated reporters (Myers, 1998). Researchers who are covered by mandatory reporting requirements may have difficulty in determining the appropriate criteria for identifying abuse (Seiber, 2001) and should therefore seek guidance from knowledgeable experts regarding the scope of their responsibilities under the law.

There is some disagreement about the extent of protection provided when a Certificate of Confidentiality (Public Health Services Act, 1988) conflicts with state laws that require reporting of disease conditions or child abuse. Whether the confidentiality provisions granted by a certificate would trump reporting laws on child abuse and elder abuse would depend on whether such reporting requirements were deemed a "proceeding" shielded under the statute (Seiber, 2001). Although this question has not been tested in any reported court decisions, ethical considerations may dictate that researchers should comply with applicable reporting requirements regardless of the available legal protections (Fisher & Goodman, chap. 1, this volume). Researchers retain the discretion under the certificate to report abuse or to comply with other state reporting requirements.

Duties to Protect Third Parties

Another distinct legal and ethical question transpires when researchers have information that a third party may face a risk of harm from the actions or behaviors of a research participant. State laws may impose duties on certain professionals—typically psychotherapists and other mental health professionals—to protect others from harm or warn others against harm.

The duty of psychotherapists to protect third parties from harm stems from a 1976 California case, *Tarasoff v. Regents of the University of California*, discussed at length in the Introduction to this book. The therapist's duty to protect will only exist where three criteria have been met. First, the court must find that there is a special relationship between therapist and patient. Second, the therapist must have the ability to assess that the risk of harm is serious and foreseeable. Finally, the therapist must know the identity of the potential victim or category of victims. The therapist may satisfy the duty to protect by confining the patient if appropriate, warning the intended victim of the danger, alerting the police, or taking other reasonably necessary steps to protect the victim. In the aftermath of this decision, many other states soon followed this precedent and passed laws imposing a duty on psychotherapists and other mental health professionals to take reasonably necessary steps to protect a potential victim threatened by their patient (Appelbaum & Rosenbaum, 1989).

The duty to protect has not been legally extended through legislation or case law to researchers who are not therapists, although ethical duties may require a researcher to warn the person facing potential harm. Appelbaum and Rosenbaum (1989) suggested that if the duty to protect were to be applied to researchers, it would encompass researchers most similar to clinical mental health practitioners: those who have repeated contact with the research participants and some capability to assess their future risk of violence toward others. Thus, studies involving in-person interviews with participants who have a history of violent behavior would be more likely to implicate this duty than studies with little or no contact between researchers and participants (e.g., retrospective records analysis). The capacity of research investigators to effectively protect third parties is also questionable and may preclude a finding that a duty to protect exists in this context (Appelbaum & Rosenbaum, 1989).

The potential application to research of a duty to protect would have a significant impact on some types of nonintervention research. In addition to research involving violent behaviors and research with participants who may have the potential to commit violent acts against others, it is conceivable that a duty to protect could be extended to other types of research studies in which the researcher learns of behaviors that threaten the health of third parties. Fisher et al. describe in chapter 9 the ethical considerations related to a researcher's duty to warn implicit in an HIV research study. Moreover, legal duties requiring intervention to prevent patients from harming themselves could also be applied to researchers who encounter suicidal ideation and behaviors from research participants.

Laws That Permit the Government to Request Disclosure

The government may be authorized to compel disclosure of information in several other situations as well. Law enforcement officials, prosecutors, and judges can order the release of information related to a criminal investigation, a prosecution, or a civil proceeding. The U.S. Congress and state legislatures can subpoena information pursuant to their powers to investigate. Parties engaged in litigation may seek information through discovery authorized under the Federal Rules of Civil Procedure. Researchers faced with requests from the government or legal system to disclose information may be forced to comply unless contrary protections are available or they can successfully argue that the information requested is not relevant to the case (Goldman & Choy, 2001).

As described earlier, the government does not enjoy an unfettered ability to compel disclosure of identifiable research data. Rather, its powers are tempered by limitations on disclosure from Certificates of Confidentiality (Public Health Services Act, 1988) and other confidentiality provisions. Although requests for research data are rare, researchers who do not have a certificate in place may have greater difficulty successfully quashing a subpoena or avoiding contempt of court charges if they refuse to cooperate.

UNRESOLVED LEGAL CHALLENGES IN NONINTERVENTION RESEARCH

The framework of laws outlined presents a complex and perhaps daunting structure for researchers to navigate. The remainder of this chapter addresses how this legal framework fares in dealing with legal conflicts and ambiguities that may arise in the context of nonintervention research conducted under high-risk circumstances. Because existing legal provisions may foster or impede nonintervention research, additional guidance is needed to resolve several significant legal challenges:

- clarifying the legal framework applicable to nonintervention research,
- protecting research participants and others from harm,
- strengthening privacy and confidentiality protections for research participants,
- understanding the growing role of litigation related to research, and
- identifying the boundaries of law.

Clarifying the Legal Framework Applicable to Nonintervention Research

The first legal challenge is to understand and clarify the existing legal framework for nonintervention research conducted under high-risk circumstances. The existing legal structure combines a set of research regulations designed for biomedical research, a panoply of privacy and confidentiality protections enacted for a variety of purposes, and contrary duties and powers that may compel disclosure of research data in some circumstances. Assessing these disparate legal requirements is a substantial undertaking, and harmonizing them would likely be impossible. Nevertheless, efforts should be made to identify common legal concerns and to create specific legal guidance for IRBs and researchers engaged in nonintervention studies. This guidance should attempt to disentangle conflicting legal requirements, whether explicit (e.g., when reporting requirements and confidentiality protections do not align) or unintentional (e.g., when the law is ambiguous because of contradictions, bad drafting, or insufficient foresight). Legal guidance, once developed, can later be merged with complementary ethical guidance, yielding information that clarifies the law and allows IRBs and researchers to avoid or resolve complicated legal problems before they occur. This effort could also help incorporate procedures and protections consistent with the law into research protocols that anticipate likely high-risk circumstances and diminish the risk to participants, researchers, and third parties.

Once the existing legal framework is well understood, the next step should be to solidify a strong yet versatile legal framework for nonintervention research conducted under high-risk circumstances. Structural changes may be developed to adapt federal regulations to more directly address the concerns raised by nonintervention research. The capacity of IRBs to adequately evaluate and monitor nonintervention research protocols has been called into question by some commentators (National Research Council

[NRC], 2003; Seiber, 2001). Because the Common Rule (Protection of Human Subjects, 2005) was drafted primarily to deal with human participants in clinical and biomedical research protocols, the regulations do not provide much guidance for nonintervention studies that may pose different risks to participants (Goldman & Choy, 2001). For example, IRBs may not have sufficient expertise to evaluate the risks to participants' privacy and the ramifications of confidentiality violations in nonintervention studies (Barnes & Krauss, 2001). IRB membership requirements do not mandate inclusion of privacy experts (Currie, 2005). In addition, IRBs do not systematically consider risks to third parties during their assessment of the research protocol (Kimmelman, 2005).

In several important areas, federal regulations remain cursory and vague and could be improved. For example, the Common Rule (Protection of Human Subjects, 2005) could be amended to incorporate additional requirements for IRBs to explicitly weigh the risks to privacy and confidentiality inherent in nonintervention research. These requirements could be modeled on the disclosure provisions found in the HIPAA (1996) Privacy Rule, but should include more guidance to aid with implementation. Alternatively, these additional considerations could be offered as policy guidance rather than changes to federal regulations. Similarly, IRBs should develop methods to assess the competing risks among participants, research workers, and third parties, given the foreseeable risks to each group that may arise during nonintervention research conducted under high-risk circumstances. Increased transparency regarding IRB proceedings would also bolster this effort.

Additional consideration should be given to initiatives to provide legal and policy guidance to IRBs charged with assessing nonintervention studies that include vulnerable populations and involve high-risk circumstances. This guidance could come from the Office of Human Research Protection and the NIH, with specific input from researchers experienced with these issues and lawyers familiar with the applicable legal framework.

Protecting Research Participants and Others From Harm

IRBs faced with evaluating nonintervention research studies conducted under high-risk circumstances must consider a range of potential risks that will differ from those of traditional biomedical research. Although risks of harm resulting from breaches of privacy and confidentiality may occur in any research study, these harms may be accentuated in nonintervention studies that involve socially sensitive or stigmatized topics. Risks to subjects may include physical harms (e.g., retaliatory violence directed at participants by third parties on the basis of their participation in the study), psychological harms (e.g., depression, suicidality, embarrassment, or other dignitary harms), or social or economic harms (e.g., discrimination, stigmatization, loss of employment, loss of relationships; Prentice & Gordon, 2001).

The Common Rule (Protection of Human Subjects, 2005) requires researchers and the IRBs overseeing them to treat research participants with respect and dignity and to protect them from harm. Yet, the Common Rule provides little guidance to IRBs with respect to assessing and reducing threats of foreseeable physical violence that may affect research participants, researchers, or third parties. If much of the research evaluated by IRBs involves biomedical or therapeutic experiments that rely on intervention, these review boards may need additional information to appreciate the full range of concerns that may arise in the context of nonintervention studies conducted under high-risk circumstances. Several recommendations have been offered by the NRC (2003) to bolster the abilities of IRBs to adequately address the risks posed to vulnerable populations in nonintervention studies. First, investigators may need to justify the necessity of the nonintervention design of the research protocol in spite of the potential risks to the participants, the researchers, or third parties. Second, IRB members should have access to additional resources that provide training and education regarding nonintervention study methods (NRC, 2003; Seiber, 2001). This training should include a legal component.

Policymakers should consider whether modifications to federal research regulations would be helpful in encouraging greater consideration of risks of harm to third parties. Current regulations do not explicitly require IRBs to consider risk of harm to third parties, but the IRB may consider this risk if it chooses to do so. A more direct recognition and assessment of these risks should be incorporated into the review of nonintervention studies likely to involve a risk of harm to participants or third parties. Both researchers and IRBs should evaluate these risks prospectively to avoid harm and subsequent legal ramifications. Of course, some nonintervention studies will impose a much smaller risk to participants and others. Exempting these studies from rigorous review may be efficient and appropriate. These and other efforts may be necessary to ensure that the law encourages adequate consideration and protection of the unique risks posed to research participants and others during nonintervention studies conducted under high-risk circumstances.

Strengthening Privacy and Confidentiality Protections for Research Participants

Researchers engaged in nonintervention research have a strong interest in maintaining the confidentiality of the information they collect. Promises of nonintervention and other limitations such as confidentiality guarantees are frequently key to obtaining and maintaining the trust, participation, and consent of the research participants. Insufficient confidentiality protections may not only undermine the ongoing research study through violations of privacy and premature disclosure of data, but they may also endanger the ability of researchers to recruit participants for future studies on sensitive topics (Boruch & Cecil, 1979b; Wiggins & McKenna, 1996). However, if statutory confidentiality protections are too stringent, they could hinder subsequent efforts to engage in secondary research with previously collected data (Boruch & Cecil, 1979b), even if the data are not particularly sensitive. Breaches of confidentiality can also have serious negative consequences for research participants, including "social stigmatization, discrimination, loss of employment, emotional harm, civil or criminal liability, and, in some cases, physical injury" (NRC, 2003, p. 138). National reports have recognized the importance of establishing adequate measures to protect the privacy of research participants in studies involving illegal behaviors or sensitive topics (National Bioethics Advisory Commission, 2001; National Commission, 1979; NRC, 2003).

Researchers should use legal protections to maximize confidentiality whenever possible to reduce the harm to participants that may result from disclosure. Nevertheless, researchers engaged in nonintervention research who are confronted with risks of harm to research participants (e.g., suicide, abuse, violence) or risks of harm to third parties (e.g., violence, abuse) may be justified in releasing identifiable data or otherwise intervening to protect the safety of the participant or others. As a default position, researchers should avoid sharing information between participants and third parties unless one is in immediate danger and sharing the information is necessary to avert the risk of harm.

Researchers may build on the existing legal framework to protect the privacy of identifiable data in several ways. Efforts to protect confidentiality may include waiving written consent, obtaining a Certificate of Confidentiality (Public Health Services Act, 1988) to prevent data from being disclosed, or explaining the possibility that certain behaviors, such as child abuse, may be reported to authorities (NRC, 2003). Investigators have a legal obligation under the Common Rule (Protection of Human Subjects, 2005) to outline and explain applicable confidentiality procedures, "if any," to each research participant as a component of adequate informed consent (§ 46.116[a][5]). Researchers may also reduce the potential for confidentiality violations through study design, for example by limiting the amount of identifiable data collected and anonymizing data wherever possible (Margolin et al., 2005).

Certificates of Confidentiality (Public Health Services Act, 1988) provide the most substantial protection against compelled disclosure of identifiable data. However, the legal scope of protection offered by a certificate should be further explicated. Opinions from state legal authorities would help clarify the application of state reporting laws to research and the interaction between reporting laws and a certificate. Although prospective legal opinions will not always be followed in a subsequent judicial proceeding, such opinions would enhance the discussion and interpretation of these issues in advance of litigation and may even preclude litigation. Additional guidance from NIH would also be welcome. A discussion of the application of Certificates of Confidentiality could be added to the informed consent factors within the Common Rule (Protection of Human Subjects, 2005). Finally, the coverage of the certificate could be statutorily expanded to apply retroactively to data collected through research and later deemed sensitive or to apply to data collected regarding third parties.

Researchers should not attempt to avoid abuse and disease reporting requirements just to protect the privacy of their research data. Ethical responsibilities and legal duties compel researchers to report data to the appropriate authorities when such reporting can avert a risk of harm. Therefore, it is incumbent on investigators to inform potential research subjects as a part of the informed consent process of the possibility that researchers will disclose data pursuant to reporting requirements. The situation may be more complex when research data are sought for law enforcement or civil litigation purposes (Fischer, 1996). Such disclosures may undermine ongoing research studies, and researchers should use Certificates of Confidentiality to protect sensitive data from these entreaties when appropriate.

The creation of an evidentiary privilege between researchers and research participants could also provide additional confidentiality protection for some research data. Creating such a privilege, however, would not be easy and may not be necessary or desirable. Enhanced confidentiality protection for research data may be better served through the iterative processes established by federal Certificate of Confidentiality requirements (Public Health Services Act, 1988). Although obtaining a certificate is administratively more burdensome, the scope of confidentiality protection established under the certificate would certainly be broader and more predictable. The establishment of an evidentiary privilege could result in secondary legal consequences that may subject researchers to additional liability or responsibility. For instance, the recognition of a special relationship between researcher and research participant for purposes of the privilege could have ramifications on the applicable duties of care and duties to protect or warn that apply to researchers under tort law. Specifically, the existence of such a special relationship could increase the likelihood that researchers would face liability for failing to protect or warn third parties about foreseeable risks posed by research participants under their supervision. Because each state would have to establish the privilege separately, a varied legal structure could result, with different standards applicable across jurisdictions in multistate research studies. Scholars and researchers should continue to explore the possibilities and liabilities presented by a researcher–research participant privilege.

Legal recognition of stronger confidentiality protections will benefit research participants and give researchers additional discretion in how they may protect identifiable data when faced with a legal obligation to divulge information pursuant to judicial or other governmental processes. In evaluating the appropriate legal approach, it will be important to consider all of the possible ramifications of such enhanced protections and to establish rules that are consistent, procedurally fair, and adequately calibrated to balance competing societal goals.

Understanding the Growing Role of Litigation Related to Research

Over the past few years, litigation has increased against researchers and IRBs for adverse consequences that have occurred to research participants (*Gelsinger v. University of Pennsylvania*, 2000; *Grimes v. Kennedy Krieger Institute*, 2001). Several legal theories have been advanced in support of these claims, including allegations that the investigators, IRB members, institutions, and other related parties committed negligence by violating duties to protect research participants or duties to provide research participants with adequate informed consent. Although none of the publicly available decisions involve nonintervention research conducted under high-risk circumstances, several commentators have chronicled the developments of litigation in research more generally (Mello, Studdert, & Brennan, 2003). If case law were to recognize a "special relationship" between researcher and participant, it could increase the likelihood that negligence claims may be successfully brought against investigators or IRBs who violate duties created by that relationship. Although very few tort claims against IRBs and researchers have succeeded, researchers and IRB members should remain aware of the legal developments in this area.

Defining the Boundaries of Law in Nonintervention Research

Researchers, scientists, and clinical practitioners sometimes regard the law warily as an unwelcome presence that constrains scientific inquiry and imposes an oppressive bureaucracy of forms, review committees, and unnecessary oversight. Researchers engaged in studies involving controversial or innovative techniques may question how legal requirements developed for more conventional research may affect their studies. Thus, defining the boundaries of law serves an important purpose with regard to nonintervention research: It is helpful to know not only what the law demands but also when it yields to ethical or practical concerns.

Public Health Research and Public Health Practice

The boundaries of law may be explored through an examination of the distinction between public health research and public health practice. Public health practitioners and others have had difficulty defining the line between public health research and public health practice. Many nonintervention research studies have used the scientific techniques and conceptual approaches of public health. Population-based, nonintervention research uses some of the same tools and strategies that are used in public health practice—epidemiology, biostatistical analysis, interviews, and record reviews—yet the intent and purpose of the interaction differs. Public health research, like other research, focuses on the creation of generalizable knowledge, whereas public health practice seeks to improve the population's health, with the benefits primarily designed to accrue to that community (although not necessarily to specific individuals in the community; Amoroso & Middaugh, 2003; Fairchild, 2003; Fairchild & Bayer, 2004; Hodge, 2005; Hodge & Gostin, 2004).

Legal requirements vary depending on whether a public health initiative is characterized as practice or research. For instance, the HIPAA (1996) Privacy Rule provides exceptions for sharing identifiable information without consent for both public health practice and research, but these exceptions differ in scope and process (Hodge, 2005). PHI may be disclosed without consent for purposes of public health practice at the sole discretion of the public health agency. By contrast, a more thorough review process is required if the activity is characterized as research. As outlined, research protocols must meet specific, defined legal criteria such as IRB approval and informed consent. Similar activities classified as public health practice will not require any independent approval. Indeed, some types of public health efforts (e.g., disease reporting, epidemiological investigations) can be conducted without obtaining informed consent or a waiver of consent. Confidentiality protections available to public health research include Certificates of Confidentiality (Public Health Services Act, 1988), whereas data collected through public health practice will receive confidentiality protection through state privacy laws. State information privacy laws uniformly provide less confidentiality protection for identifiable data than a certificate.

The decision whether to characterize an activity as practice or research is typically made under law by the public health agency. Public health agencies may have guidelines that assist with this categorization or may make the determination on an ad hoc basis (Hodge & Gostin, 2004). When public health practice has been misclassified as research, public health practice initiatives will be restrained by the extra review and justification required of research. Alternatively, research that is mischaracterized as practice may not be subjected to a sufficiently rigorous review. Thus, it is important to have clear definitions and processes that make a distinction between research and practice.

Law and Ethics

The relationship between law and ethics provides another good example of the boundaries of law in the context of nonintervention research. The realms of law and ethics engage in a dynamic interplay. Although law and ethics occupy distinct spheres and roles in academic thought and professional practice, legal and ethical decision making are frequently ensnared in an inexorable embrace. In other words, the overlap between law and ethics is unavoidable and, in many cases, complementary.

Law and ethics intersect in multiple ways. First, law provides a system of rules that may incorporate or internalize ethical norms or values. In this respect, law acts as a reflection—or extension—of ethical norms (Diener & Crandall, 1978). In some cases, law reflects ethics because lawmakers explicitly enacted laws on the basis of their deeply ingrained ethical precepts or to address a specific ethical concern. Laws governing research with human participants have codified a set of procedures designed to protect human subjects in a way deemed ethical by our society.

Second, law allows for ethical norms and values to be applied within a legal framework that is, one hopes, consistent and transparent. This may occur within the context of the judicial system or through the application and enforcement of regulations. The human research subjects protections codified in the Common Rule (Protection of Human Subjects, 2005) provide a good example of how law may codify and enforce ethical considerations. The Common Rule places into an enforceable legal framework the ethical principles of autonomy, informed consent, justice, beneficence, and transparency. In addition to establishing that researchers and institutions conducting federally funded research assess the effect of these ethical concerns on human participants, the regulations establish IRBs, which act as explicit ethics committees subject to legal requirements.

Compliance with legal and ethical requirements, however, is often not analogous. If a research proposal has met the necessary legal requirements, it does not necessarily follow that all ethical concerns have been addressed (Berg et al., 2001). Even within the construct of the law, ethical frameworks provide a valuable tool to address situations that may place research participants, researchers, or others at risk of harm. Many laws remain vague when it comes to ethical issues. Often this is intentional. The law cannot be made to address all permutations of difficult and evolving dilemmas related to health care, life sciences, and related topics. For example, IRBs tend to focus on legalistic requirements for informed consent, whereas the ethical considerations require the informed consent process to be ongoing and interactive (Coleman, Menikoff, Goldner, & Dubler, 2005; Institute of Medicine, 2003). Decision makers and researchers in this field must consider not only whether they are guided or constrained by the law but also whether the ethical ramifications of the situation augur a preferred set of outcomes.

Third, laws may inform ethics. Ethical discussions, decisions, and analyses may be furthered and aided by the input of legal rules. As Fisher and Goodman noted in chapter 1, the application of a goodness-of-fit ethical model can greatly assist researchers in dealing with ethical dilemmas that arise during the conduct of nonintervention research. Law can provide guidance on these conundrums as well. However, legal guidance only goes so far to resolve ethical dilemmas. Law is not a substitute for ethical decision making. Rather, law and ethics together form a strong and complementary approach to protect high-risk human research subjects, researchers, and the general public. The combined approach is more than mutually reinforcing; it also provides researchers with guidance on how to assess and react to evolving situations that place them or their research participants at risk of harm or, even more important, allows for the mechanisms to prevent these harms from occurring in the first place through diligence and persistence.

CONCLUSION

Modern researchers in the United States have become adept at navigating the legal requirements necessary to conduct human subjects research. Yet legal challenges continue to manifest in the context of specific areas of research. As this chapter highlights, the interpretation and development of scholarship and analysis related to the application of the law to nonintervention research conducted under high-risk circumstances remains cursory and underexplored. However, the novel legal issues created by these studies deserve more concerted and careful evaluation. Indeed, these issues deserve no less attention than has previously been paid to traditional biomedical research. This discussion has identified several important legal challenges in this field. It is intended as a preliminary assessment of these complex and difficult issues, and it is hoped that it is the first of many examinations to outline and analyze the contours of unique legal situations that may arise during this type of research. The multifaceted legal framework described in this chapter presents a plethora of rules, obligations, and potential conflicts for researchers engaged in nonintervention research under high-risk circumstances. Successfully resolving these legal challenges will demand careful input from researchers, ethicists, lawyers, and research participants themselves. All those involved in this important research must continue to anticipate and explore these issues to achieve the dual goals of fostering useful research and protecting participants and others from harm.

REFERENCES

Amoroso, P. J., & Middaugh, J. P. (2003). Research vs. public health practice: When does a study require IRB review? *Preventive Medicine*, 36, 250–253.

Appelbaum, P. S., & Rosenbaum, E. (1989). Tarasoff and the researcher: Does the duty to protect apply in the research setting? *American Psychologist*, *44*, 885–894.

Barnes, M., & Krauss, S. (2001). The effect of HIPAA on human subjects research. *Health Law Reporter*, *10*, 1026–1036.

Bayer, R. (1991, May 23). Public health policy and the AIDS epidemic: An end to HIV exceptionalism? *New England Journal of Medicine*, *324*, 1500–1504.

Berg, J. W., Appelbaum, P. S., Lidz, C. W., & Parker, L. S. (2001). *Informed consent: Legal theory and clinical practice*. Oxford, England: Oxford University Press.

Boness, F. H., & Cordes, J. F. (1974). The researcher-subject relationship: The need for protection and a model statute. *Georgetown Law Journal, 62*, 243–272.

Boruch, R. F., & Cecil, J. S. (1979a). *Assuring the confidentiality of social research data*. Philadelphia: University of Pennsylvania Press.

Boruch, R. F., & Cecil, J. S. (1979b). On solutions to some privacy problems engendered by federal regulation and social custom. In M. L. Wax & J. Cassell (Eds.), *Federal regulations: Ethical issues and social research* (pp. 173–184). Boulder, CO: Westview Press.

Burris, S. (1994). Public health, "AIDS exceptionalism" and the law. *Marshall Law Review, 27*, 251–272.

Burris, S., Gable, L., Stone, L., & Lazzarini, Z. (2003). The role of state law in protecting human subjects of public health research and practice. *Journal of Law, Medicine & Ethics, 31*, 654–662.

Cal. Health & Safety Code § 11977 (2008).

Coleman, C. H., Menikoff, J. A., Goldner, J. A., & Dubler, N. N. (2005). *The ethics and regulation of research with human subjects*. Newark, NJ: LexisNexis.

Confidential Information Protection and Statistical Efficiency Act of 2002, Pub. L. No. 107-247, 116 Stat. 2962 (2002).

Currie, P. M. (2005). Balancing privacy protections with efficient research: Institutional review boards and the use of certificates of confidentiality. *IRB: Ethics & Human Research, 27*(5), 7–13.

Data Quality Act of 2001, Pub. L. No. 106-554 § 515, 114 Stat. 2763 (2001).

Diener, E., & Crandall, R. (1978). *Ethics in social and behavioral research*. Chicago: University of Chicago Press.

Fairchild, A. L. (2003). Dealing with Humpty Dumpty: Research, practice, and the ethics of public health surveillance. *Journal of Law, Medicine& Ethics, 31*, 615–623.

Fairchild, A. L., & Bayer, R. (2004, January 30). Ethics and the conduct of public health surveillance. *Science, 303*, 631–632.

Fischer, P. M. (1996). Science and subpoenas: When do the courts become instruments of manipulation? *Law and Contemporary Problems, 59*, 159–168.

Forsham v. Harris, 445 U.S. 169 (1980).

Fost, N., & Levine, R. J. (2007, November 14). The dysregulation of human subjects research. *JAMA, 298*, 2196–2198.

Freedom of Information Act of 1966, 5 U.S.C. 552 (1966).

Gelsinger v. University of Pennsylvania (Pa. C., No. 001885, complaint filed September 18, 2000). Retrieved July 1, 2008, from http://www.sskrplaw.com/links/healthcare2.html

Goldman, J., & Choy, A. (2001). Privacy and confidentiality in health research. In National Bioethics Advisory Commission, *Ethical and policy issues in research involving human participants: Vol. II. Commissioned papers and staff analysis* (pp. C1–C34). Bethesda, MD: U.S. Government Printing Office.

Gostin, L. O. (1995). Health information privacy. *Cornell Law Review, 80*, 451–528.

Gostin, L. O. (2000). Public health law: Power, duty, restraint. Berkeley: University of California Press.

Gostin, L. O., & Hodge, J. G., Jr. (1998). The "names debate": The case for national HIV reporting in the United States. *Albany Law Review, 61*, 679–743.

Gostin, L. O., & Hodge, J. G., Jr. (1999). Genetic privacy and the law: An end to genetics exceptionalism. *Jurimetrics, 40*, 21–58.

Gostin, L. O., Lazzarini, Z., Neslund, V. S., & Osterholm, M. T. (1996, June 26). The public health information infrastructure: A national review of the law on health information privacy. *JAMA, 275*, 1921–1927.

Grimes v. Kennedy Krieger Institute, Inc., 366 Md. 29 782A 2d 807 (2001).

Health Insurance Portability and Accountability Act of 1996, Pub. L. No. 104-191, 110 Stat. 1936 (1996).

Hodge, J. G., Jr. (2005). An enhanced approach to distinguishing public health practice and human subjects research. *Journal of Law, Medicine& Ethics, 33*,125–140.

Hodge, J. G., Jr. & Gostin, L. O. (2004). *Public health practice vs. research: A report for public health practitioners including case studies and guidance*. Atlanta, GA: Council of State and Territorial Epidemiologists.

Institute of Medicine. (2003). *Responsible research: A systems approach to protecting research participants*. Washington, DC: National Academies Press.

Jaffee v. Redmond, 518 U.S. 1, 116 S.Ct. 1923 (1996).

Kimmelman, J. (2005). Medical Research, Risk, and Bystanders. *IRB: Ethics and Human Research, 27*, vol. 4, 1–6.

Kulynych, J., & Korn, D. (2002). Use and disclosure of health information in genetic research: Weighing the impact of the new federal medical privacy rule. *American Journal of Law & Medicine, 28*, 309–324.

Margolin, G., Chien, D., Duman, S. E., Fauchier, A., Gordis, E. B., Oliver, P. H., et al. (2005). Ethical issues in couple and family research. *Journal of Family Psychology, 19*, 157–167.

Md. Stat. § 13-2002. (2007).

Mello, M. M., Studdert, D. M., & Brennan, T. A. (2003). The rise of litigation in human subjects research. *Annals of Internal Medicine, 139*, 40–45.

Myers, J. E. B. (1998). *Legal issues in child abuse and neglect practice*. Thousand Oaks, CA: Sage.

National Bioethics Advisory Commission. (2001). *Ethical and policy issues in research involving human participants*. Bethesda, MD: U.S. Government Printing Office.

National Commission for the Protection of Human Subjects of Biomedical and Behavioral Research. (1979). *Belmont Report: Ethical principles and guidelines for the protection of human subjects of research*. Washington, DC: U.S. Government Printing Office.

National Institutes of Health. (2003). *Protecting personal health information in research: Understanding the HIPAA Privacy Rule*. Washington, DC: U.S. Government Printing Office.

National Research Council. (2003). *Protecting participants and facilitating social and behavioral sciences research*. Washington, DC: National Academies Press.

Omnibus Consolidated and Emergency Supplemental Appropriations Act of 1999, Pub. L. No. 105-277 (1999).

O'Neill, R.M. (1996). A Researcher's Privilege: Does Any Hope Remain? *Law and Contemporary Problems, 59*, 35–49.

People v. Newman, 32 N.Y.2d 379 (1973).

Prentice, E., & Gordon, B. (2001). Institutional review board assessment of risks and benefits associated with research. In National Bioethics Advisory Commission, *Ethical and policy issues in research involving human participants: Vol. II. Commissioned papers and staff analysis* (pp. L1–L16). Bethesda, MD: U.S. Government Printing Office.

Privacy Act of 1974, 5 U.S.C. § 552a.

Protection of Human Subjects, 45 C.F.R. § 46 (2005).

Public Health Service Act § 301(d), 42 U.S.C. 241(d), as amended by Pub. L. No. 100-607 § 163 (1988).

Reiken, H. W. (1983). Solutions to ethical and legal problems in social research: An overview. In R. F. Boruch & J. S. Cecil (Eds.), *Solutions to ethical and legal problems in social research* (pp. 1–9). New York: Academic Press.

Schwartz, J. (2001). Oversight of human subject research: The role of the states. In National Bioethics Advisory Commission, *Ethical and policy issues in research involving human participants: Vol. II. Commissioned papers and staff analysis* (pp. M1–M20). Bethesda, MD: U.S. Government Printing Office.

Seiber, J. E. (2001). Privacy and confidentiality: As related to human research in social and behavioral science. In National Bioethics Advisory Commission, *Ethical and policy issues in research involving human participants: Vol. II. Commissioned papers and staff analysis* (pp. N1–N50). Bethesda, MD: U.S. Government Printing Office.

Singer, E. (2006). Access to research data: Reconciling risks and benefits. *Journal of Law & Policy*, 14, 85–114.Social research and privileged data. (1970). *Valparaiso University Law Review, 4*, 368–399.

Solove, D., & Rotenberg, M. (2003). *Health information privacy*. Aspen, CO: Aspen Publishing.

Southern Illinoisan v. Illinois Department of Public Health, 349 Ill. App.3d 431 (2004).

Tarasoff v. Regents of the University of California, 551 P.2d 334 (1976).

Uniting and Strengthening America by Providing Appropriate Tools Required to Intercept and Obstruct Terrorism Act of 2001, Pub. L. No. 107-56 (2001).

U.S. General Accountability Office. (2007). *Health information technology: Early efforts initiated but comprehensive privacy approach needed for national strategy*. Washington, DC: U.S. Government Printing Office.

United States v. Westinghouse Elec. & Mfg. Co., 339 U.S. 261 (1950).

Whalen v. Roe, 429 U.S. 589 (1977).

Wiggins, E. C., & McKenna, J. A. (1996). Researcher's reactions to compelled disclosure of scientific information. *Law and Contemporary Problems, 59*, 67–94.

Wolf, L. E., Zandecki, J., & Lo, B. (2004). The certificate of confidentiality application: A view from the NIH institutes. *IRB: Ethics & Human Research, 26*(1), 14–18.

II

CONDUCTING RESEARCH ETHICALLY

3

TELEPHONE SURVEYS OF TRAUMATIC EXPERIENCES AND OTHER SENSITIVE TOPICS

JENNIFER J. CERCONE, CARLA KMETT DANIELSON, KENNETH J. RUGGIERO, AND DEAN G. KILPATRICK

Public health, mental health, and substance abuse researchers often face situations in which they need accurate information from general population samples about sensitive topics that are stigmatizing and difficult to discuss. Such topics include history of illicit substance use, child maltreatment, interpersonal violence, mental disorders, delinquent or criminal behavior, and suicidal behavior. These kinds of experiences are often difficult for people to talk about, sometimes because of shame and stigma and sometimes because the experiences themselves are either illegal or socially sanctioned.

Researchers who want to gather data about these experiences face technical challenges about methodology (i.e., what are the methodologically sound ways to collect information about sensitive topics?) and research ethics (i.e., how can the information be collected in a way that reduces harm to research

This research was partially supported by Grant 93-IJ-CX-0023 from the U.S. Department of Justice, Office of Justice Programs, National Institute of Justice. Views expressed here do not necessarily represent those of the agencies supporting this research.

participants while obtaining data that are needed by society?). In addition to methodological and research participant protection issues, cost is also an issue for potential researchers. That is, if two research methods are equally sound methodologically and protect the rights of research participants in a similar fashion, then the method that is less costly offers some advantages.

The objective of this chapter is to describe one major alternative to in-person interviews for collecting data about sensitive topics—the telephone interview method. In the chapter, we cover the following topics: (a) an overview of telephone data collection methodology, including discussion of feasibility, reliability, and validity; (b) a discussion of the risks, safeguards, and benefits associated with telephone-based research; and (c) an illustration of some of these ethical issues by describing the methodology, selected findings, and safeguard procedures used in the National Survey of Adolescents (NSA), a telephone survey conducted with a large nationally representative sample of adolescents.

OVERVIEW OF TELEPHONE DATA COLLECTION METHODOLOGY

The use of the telephone as a means of collecting data has increased in recent years for a variety of reasons, ranging from its substantially lower cost than conducting in-person interviews to a growing appreciation that quality data can be collected using this method. As reviewed elsewhere (Galea et al., 2006), telephone-based research methods encompass two basic types of data collection procedures: (a) using the telephone to interview a preidentified list of individuals (i.e., list samples) and (b) using the random digit dial survey method to locate a representative sample of telephone households and respondents and then to interview respondents by telephone.

Galea et al. (2006) provided considerable procedural information about the mechanics of conducting both types of telephone studies, but we focus primarily on random digit dial telephone surveys. Briefly described, the random digit dial method involves first identifying telephone exchanges within the geographical area to be sampled. Next, telephone numbers are generated randomly within those exchanges to locate residential households that contain at least one household member within the sampling frame (i.e., adults, adult women, adolescents). If more than one eligible respondent in the sampling frame lives in the household, one is selected randomly for interview. A survey interviewer then describes the study to the respondent, obtains informed consent (almost always orally), and conducts the interview by telephone. As noted by Galea et al., most professional survey research firms use many quality control measures in their telephone interviews, including (a) careful interviewer selection, training, monitoring, and supervision; (b) constructing the actual interview measure in a computer-administered format in which questions are read verbatim and complex skip patterns can be used; (c) all interviewing is done at a control site so that interviewer behavior can be monitored on a real-time basis; and (d) respondent protection protocols are established so that interviewers who encounter distressed respondents can access assistance from trained mental health professionals.

Although open-ended questions can be included in telephone surveys, for the most part questions tend to be closed ended. Because of the difficulties that many people have in concentrating for extended periods over the telephone and their reluctance to tie up the telephone line for long periods of time, telephone interviews are generally of shorter duration than in-person interviews. This means that researchers using the telephone method must sometimes shorten or otherwise simplify some of the questions or measures that are typically used during in-person assessments. It also means that researchers must carefully construct the telephone survey instrument to ask questions in the precise fashion that they wish them to be asked. Generally, questions are pilot tested to make sure that their meaning is clear to respondents.

Two major advantages of random digit dial telephone surveys versus in-person surveys are reduced costs and enhanced ability to address language barriers to participation. These advantages are greatest when the sampling frame is geographically dispersed. For a national study, it has been estimated that a national household probability sample survey of 3,000 adult women would cost approximately three times as much as a comparable telephone survey (Boyle, personal communication, 2005). This is because of interviewer travel costs and the cost of making repeat visits to designated households when respondents are not home. Likewise, it is easy to switch to an interviewer who speaks another language in a centralized telephone interviewing facility, but it poses considerable logistical difficulties in an in-person household survey.

ARE TELEPHONE SURVEYS METHODOLOGICALLY SOUND?

One challenge in any research endeavor is to identify a methodology that is not only feasible and amenable to scientifically rigorous research designs but also reliable and valid for the study of the phenomenon of interest. Given the important role of epidemiological research, there are many advantages to conducting population-based surveys via telephone rather than by mail, via the Internet, or in person. First, mail questionnaires have low return rates and do not lend themselves to complex skip patterns that streamline the interview process. Second, recent technological advances notwithstanding, data from the 2000 U.S. census suggest that fewer households have Internet access (50%) than telephone access (95%), which calls into serious question the representativeness of findings from participants recruited via the Internet. Third, national in-person surveys are prohibitively expensive and exceed the budget of even the most generous extramural funding agency.

Thus, telephone survey methods are efficient for collecting information from large representative samples at relatively low cost.

Of course, the principles that apply to the design of methodologically sound surveys apply similarly to telephone-based interviews, as they do to in-person interviews and other methods of surveying participants. Fortunately, when telephone surveys are carefully designed, there is little risk of response bias or nondetection of critical variables of interest, as compared with in-person interview approaches (Dansky, Saladin, Brady, Kilpatrick, & Resnick, 1995; Midanik & Greenfield, 2003; Weeks, Kulka, Lessler, & Whitmore, 1983). These issues have been examined specifically in terms of sensitive topics such as detection of psychopathology and exposure to traumatic events using in-person versus telephone interview methods (e.g., Acierno, Resnick, Kilpatrick, & Stark-Riemer, 2003; Catlin & Murray, 1979; Lyneham & Rapee, 2005; Midanik & Greenfield, 2003; Pettigrew, Wilson, & Teasdale, 2003). For example, on the basis of objective police report data, no differences in rates of detection of victimization were observed, supporting both the reliability and the validity of the telephone method (Catlin & Murray, 1979). Another study (Paulsen, Crowe, Noyes, & Phohl, 1988) compared telephone and in-person assessment of *Diagnostic and Statistical Manual of Mental Disorders, Third Edition* (American Psychiatric Association, 1980) Axis I disorders, including anxiety disorders, affective disorders, alcoholism, and no mental health diagnosis using a structured diagnostic interview. Kappas ranging from .69 to .84 were obtained, even with a delay between in-person and telephone methods of 12 to 19 months (Paulsen et al., 1988).

POTENTIAL RISKS AND SAFEGUARDS IN TELEPHONE-BASED RESEARCH

Despite clear public health benefits associated with conducting well-designed survey research, the ethical implications of survey methodologies have long been the subject of debate. This debate is not specific to telephone-based methods because many of the major issues raised apply just as readily to in-person, Web-based, and other survey methods. Ethical concerns are particularly salient when sensitive topics are assessed, such as exposure to potentially traumatic events and the presence of significant mental health problems. The cost–benefit analysis plays a central role in ethical appraisals of psychological research (Bersoff & Bersoff, 1999). Although it is incumbent on investigators and the institutional review boards charged with overseeing their research to minimize adverse effects while maximizing benefits, it is important that decisions around these issues be based on empirical evidence rather than supposition or conjecture. This section explores the costs and benefits associated with the use of telephone surveys in the collection of sensitive self-report information and provides an illustration of an ethical approach to one such telephone survey through the presentation of the methodology and description of the consent process and participant protection protocol from the NSA, a national probability survey of 4,023 youths ages 12 to 17 years.

The principle of nonmalfeasance, or the imperative to do no harm, is central to the "Ethical Principles of Psychologists and Code of Conduct" (American Psychological Association [APA], 2002) and other health professionals (e.g., American Medical Association [AMA], 2004) and applies to conduct with research participants and clinical patients. It is therefore essential that investigators and institutional review boards anticipate, to the best of their ability, potential risks to participants and establish safeguards to reduce those risks. The potential risks and benefits of conducting research on sensitive topics have been broadly summarized elsewhere (e.g., Newman & Kaloupek, 2004). As noted, these issues generally apply to telephone-based as well as to in-person and Web-based administration of surveys. For the purposes of this chapter, we group the potential risks associated with telephone surveys of sensitive topics into three major categories: participants' (a) emotional distress associated with topics covered by the survey, (b) disclosure of risk of harm to self or others, and (c) privacy.

Emotional Distress Associated With Survey Topics

Potential Risks

One potential risk of telephone surveys of sensitive topics is that some participants may experience distress when asked questions pertaining to potentially traumatic events, mental health issues, substance abuse, and the like. In fact, empirical data consistently suggest that the risk of psychological harm from inquiries about sensitive topics is minimal and that participants often perceive benefits associated with having completed such surveys. Several studies have addressed this issue in the context of traumatic stress research and have found that asking people about their history of exposure to potentially traumatic events, such as physical or sexual assaults, produced no more than moderate distress among only a small proportion of participants and that even fewer participants reported still experiencing distress when contacted a few days after their participation in the study (e.g., Griffin, Resick, Waldrop, & Mechanic, 2003; Newman, Walker, & Gefland, 1999). In research conducted with New York City–area residents who were contacted via telephone between 1 and 6 months after the September 11, 2001, terrorist attacks (n = 5,774; Galea et al., 2002), only 1% (n = 58) overall described themselves as upset at the end of the interview, and only 0.3% (n = 19) of these indicated that they wanted assistance from a counselor after the research survey when asked by the interviewer. Thus, on the basis of the extant literature, it is reasonable to expect a very low occurrence of participant distress in telephone surveys on sensitive topics.

Safeguards

Although it is clear that only a small number of participants will experience emotional distress when asked sensitive questions in a telephone survey, investigators should nevertheless ensure that specific protocols are in place to assuage such distress when it does occur and provide referral options for such individuals. This is particularly important for telephone interviews in which, in contrast to in-person interviews, the investigators are further removed from the participants and have fewer options to intervene directly. The likelihood of distress can be reduced in a number of ways. For example, questions can be phrased as sensitively as possible, and prefatory statements can be given to orient and prepare participants for potentially sensitive questions. Moreover, interview questions and preambles can be tested for their effect in focus groups and pilot studies before being used with large numbers of participants. Proper training of interviewers is also essential and should stress the importance of acting professionally, ensuring that the participant is in a private setting and that it is a good time to do the interview, reading the questions as written (i.e., maintaining the structured format), and recognizing signs of participant distress (e.g., crying, undue hesitation). Real-time supervision and random monitoring of interviews can enhance interviewers' adherence to these guidelines.

When a participant does become distressed, it is important that interviewers respond in accordance with protocols intended to assuage distress. On recognizing distress, interviewers should ask participants whether they want to continue or whether they would rather suspend the interview; under no circumstances should interviewers pressure the participants to answer questions if they do not feel comfortable doing so. Of course, participants also always have the option of terminating participation simply by hanging up the phone. In fact, this may provide them with a greater sense of control than in-person interviews. Debriefing questions should also be used to assess distress and to provide participants with the option of talking with a licensed mental health professional about any issues that were raised by the interview. Licensed mental health professionals should be available for consultation when interviews are terminated by participant request or when participants indicate (e.g., via a question on the debriefing assessment) a wish to speak with a counselor. They should contact the participant, determine whether any further action is required, and provide treatment referrals as necessary.

Participant Disclosures of Risk of Harm to Self or Others

Potential Risks

A related risk concerns the possibility that participants may disclose a propensity for harm to self or others. Some telephone-based epidemiological research may focus directly on these issues, for example, to examine the population prevalence of and risk factors associated with suicidal and homicidal ideation and behavior. Such studies must have a thorough plan in place to respond to disclosures, particularly disclosures that suggest imminent risk of harm to self or other individuals. However, most telephone surveys on sensitive topics do not focus on the propensity for suicidal or homicidal ideation and behavior. Thus, for most studies, risk of disclosure is reduced by the exclusion of questions that directly assess this propensity, and many investigators intentionally refrain from including such questions for this reason. Nevertheless, although spontaneous disclosures are rare, they remain a possibility in any study in which mental health issues, criminal behavior, and other sensitive topics are assessed. For this reason, investigators must be prepared to respond appropriately to participants who are determined to be at risk of harm to self or others.

Safeguards

Although disclosures of propensity for harm to self or others are rare in telephone surveys, particularly when current homicidal and suicidal ideation are not assessed, it is nevertheless imperative that investigators be prepared to respond effectively to such disclosures in the unlikely event that they occur. This "obligation to screen and intervene" (Bersoff & Bersoff, 1999, p. 44) is predicated on the assumption that research participants are entitled to expect clinical services, or referral for clinical services, when they reveal a need to a health care professional, even in a research context.

The ethical response to such disclosures closely resembles the ethical response to distress of a more general nature, at least initially. That is, interviewers must be trained to recognize these disclosures for what they are and to put participants who make them in contact with a licensed mental health professional who can more thoroughly assess the situation and encourage and assist participants to identify and avail themselves of resources in their immediate environment. Often, no further action will be required. However, in the event that the danger to self or others appears imminent, investigators may need to be prepared to break confidentiality and involve the proper authorities.

Privacy Issues

Potential Risks

A third risk of participation in telephone surveys on sensitive topics is related to the possibility that participants will experience unwanted observation or interference as a result of their participation. It is possible, for example, that participants could be overheard by other members of the household or visitors to the household during the interviews. After the interviews themselves, the potential remains for sensitive information to be linked to participants unless appropriate care is taken to remove and secure all identifying information from databases containing interview responses.

Safeguards

Potential breaches of participant privacy during the interview itself are minimized by procedures such as informing participants that it is possible to call back at a more convenient time or prompting them to take steps to ensure their privacy (e.g., moving to a private room). In addition, questions may be modified so as to require only yes–no answers or other one-word responses, limiting the risk to participants should they be overheard. For example, instead of asking an open-ended question (e.g., "Can you please tell me about any stressful or traumatic events you have experienced in the past year?") it is preferable to ask behaviorally specific dichotomous-response-option questions (e.g., "During the past year, did anyone physically attack you with the intent to injure or kill you?"). This is sounder scientific practice in epidemiological research and also allows the respondent to answer a sensitive question with a simple yes-or-no response, the meaning of which cannot be understood by other individuals in the home who may overhear it. Potential breaches of participant privacy after the interview are minimized by procedures such as assigning participants ID numbers, storing identifying information separate from the data set, and restricting access to the master list.

POTENTIAL BENEFITS OF TELEPHONE-BASED EPIDEMIOLOGICAL RESEARCH

The principle of beneficence, or the imperative to do good, is also central to the ethics codes of psychologists and other health professionals (e.g., AMA, 2004; APA, 2002). As a result, the risks to participants are weighed against the benefits to participants and society. When risks are minor and measures are taken to address those risks, the cost–benefit ratio of telephone surveys of sensitive topics appears small.

Benefits to Participants

Not only is it rare for participants in nonintervention studies involving surveys of sensitive topics to report experiencing distress (as previously described), but some participants actually report benefiting from their involvement. For example, Newman et al. (1999) reported findings from a sample of 1,174 adult women in an HMO setting who completed paper-and-pencil questionnaires asking about physical and sexual assault experiences. A subset of these women ($n = 252$) were selected to participate in follow-up traumatic stress–focused interviews. When asked whether they gained something positive from their participation, most of the women were either neutral (61%)

or positive (23%) in their rating of the questionnaire portion of the research. However, the vast majority (86.1%) were positive about the interview portion of the research, and the remaining minority (13.9%) were neutral. None were negative. At 2-day follow-up, 85.8% of those interviewed said they had gotten something positive out of their participation in the study. Another study examined participant reactions to various trauma assessment procedures (Griffin et al., 2003). Almost 8 out of 10 participants (79%)—who included victims of domestic violence, rape, and physical assault—rated their participation in the clinical interviews as very or highly interesting, and only 5% said they would be unwilling to participate in a similar assessment study. These findings clearly demonstrate that a majority of participants in well-designed assessment studies of sensitive topics actually gain some benefit from their participation. Anecdotal evidence has also suggested that victims of crime, individuals with mental illness, and others dealing with issues of a sensitive nature appreciate the validation that comes from being told their experiences are important and that the information gathered from the survey will be used to learn how to help others in similar situations.

Benefits to Society

The benefits of telephone surveys on sensitive topics are even more apparent at a societal level. As noted previously, and covered in greater depth elsewhere (e.g., Galea et al., 2006), this methodology, when used to gather information from a national probability sample (as opposed to a convenience sample), provides researchers with opportunities to draw inferences from the data set to specific communities and to the U.S. population as a whole. This inferential ability is invaluable to the extent that it translates into the protection and promotion of the well-being of the population. For example, data from nationally representative samples can tell us about the prevalence and risk and protective factors associated with mental health, substance use, violence exposure, suicidality, and other issues of public health significance. These data, in turn, carry the potential to inform prevention and intervention efforts at the individual, community, and population levels. For this reason, the telephone survey method is used routinely by the Centers for Disease Control and Prevention, the federal agency charged with protecting the health of U.S. citizens.

Finally, as has been noted elsewhere (e.g., Kilpatrick, 2004), a truly comprehensive analysis of the ethics of research also considers the ramifications of not conducting research when more information is needed to guide the development of sound public policy and effective prevention and intervention strategies. Although others have rightly cautioned against conceiving health-related research as an absolute moral obligation without regard for competing demands on limited social resources (e.g., Callahan, 2003), it nevertheless remains the case that to adequately address the needs of individuals with traumatic experiences or other sensitive issues, further research is required.

NATIONAL SURVEY OF ADOLESCENTS: AN ILLUSTRATION OF ETHICAL TELEPHONE SURVEY RESEARCH

The NSA was a large epidemiological study sponsored by the National Institute of Justice to assess prevalence of, and risk and protective factors associated with, history of exposure to traumatic events, substance abuse, delinquency, posttraumatic stress disorder, depression, and suicidality among a national probability household sample of adolescents. The initial national probability sample was constructed through a multistage process. First, the United States was stratified geographically by census region, and a population-based subsample allocation was developed for each geographic stratum. Second, telephone banks within each geographic stratum were systematically selected using the comprehensive database of working telephone banks maintained by the survey research firm conducting the interviews. Third, random digit dial methodology was used to sample telephone households within the telephone banks selected in the second stage. Fourth, an adult respondent in each household selected was screened to determine whether the household was eligible for participation by asking whether there were any adolescents (between the ages of 12 and 17 years) who currently resided in the household or whether any other adolescent had lived in the household for at least 4 months within the previous year. After a household was deemed eligible, a parent or guardian was provided information about the purpose of the study, interviewed, and asked to provide permission to interview a randomly selected adolescent within the household.

All procedures, including sample selection and interviewing, were done by Schulman, Ronca, Bucavalas, Inc. (SRBI), a national survey research firm. Interviews were in a structured, computer-assisted format (using computer-assisted telephone interviewing technology) and involved behaviorally specific questions regarding the areas of study (e.g., victimization history). For example, sexual assault was assessed using a series of five questions specifically targeting different forms of unwanted sexual contact (e.g., "Has a man or boy put a sexual part of his body inside your private sexual parts, inside your rear end, or inside your mouth when you didn't want them to?"). On average, parent interviews were completed in 10 minutes and adolescent interviews, which occurred subsequent to the parent interview, were approximately 31 minutes in length.

In all, 5,367 households were deemed to be eligible. Of these households, 4,836 completed interviews (90.1% of eligible households). Furthermore, 4,236 parents gave permission for adolescent interviews (78.9% of eligible households; 87.6% of parents interviewed), and 4,023 adolescent interviews were ultimately completed (75% of eligible households; 83.2% of completed parent interviews; 95% of households with parental permission). With regard to the demographics of the study, 51.3% (*n* = 2,065) were male adolescents, 70.2% (*n* = 2,825) were White, non-Hispanic; 14.7% (*n* = 590) were Black, non-Hispanic; 7.8% (*n* = 314) were Hispanic; 3.5% (*n* = 139) were Native American; and 3.8% (*n* = 155) were reported to be of some other ethnic or racial background. Included in these numbers is an oversample of 862 adolescents from households in central cities in the United States as designated by the 1995 U.S. Bureau of the Census.

The primary results yielded by this study have been reported elsewhere (e.g., see Kilpatrick et al., 2000, 2003) and are beyond of the scope of this chapter. However, it is important to emphasize that study findings have clear and important public health implications. As an example, this study identified the U.S. population prevalence of adolescent sexual assault; physical assault; witnessed violence in the home, community, and school; and mental health disorders (i.e., posttraumatic stress disorder, major depressive episode, substance abuse and dependence, delinquent behavior, suicidality). Risk and protective factor findings for most of these outcomes have also had meaningful public health implications, as described elsewhere (e.g., Kilpatrick et al., 2000, 2003). After completion of the telephone interview, all 4,023 participants were asked whether they were willing to be contacted for a follow-up interview. In all, 98.8% (*n* = 3,973) gave permission to be recontacted, which indicates that the interview was not traumatic or stressful to the point to which the adolescent was not interested in further participation. In addition, no human subjects incidents were experienced during the NSA data collection.

Several safeguards were developed for this study to help protect the NSA adolescent participants, including having adequately trained interviewers, offering verification of the survey's authenticity to parents, ensuring privacy for the adolescents' responses, having an "adolescent in danger" protocol in place, and having resources in place for the few participants who may have reported distress following the interview. In the following sections, we discuss each safeguard in more detail.

Adequately Trained Interviewers

Interviewers were SRBI employees who received rigorous training in conducting structured interviews involving sensitive topics and had several years' experience doing so. In addition to the intensive training the interviewers had received from SRBI, the NSA investigators provided them with additional training before they began the NSA data collection. The training provided by the NSA investigators was specific to the interviews used in the project and focused on responding to various specific needs of adolescent respondents.

Offering Verification of the Survey's Authenticity

In this day and age of phone solicitation and crafty phone scams, it would stand to reason that some parents and guardians would question the authenticity of such a phone interview, which involved the assessment of personal information. Thus, the investigators provided several avenues for respondents to verify the survey's legitimacy. Specifically, respondents were offered a toll-free number to SRBI by the interviewers to verify the survey's authenticity. In addition, interviewers offered to send a letter to the parents or guardians before the interview, which included information on the general purpose and sponsorship of the study, the method by which their household had been selected, and the confidentiality of their responses. In the few cases in which additional information was requested, respondents were provided with the phone numbers of investigators of the study and the project officer at the funding institute (National Institute of Justice). There were only two calls to the investigators and only one call to the National Institute of Justice project officer out of approximately 10,000 parent–guardian and adolescent interviews conducted.

Ensuring Privacy for Adolescents' Responses

To increase the likelihood that adolescents could answer questions in an open and honest manner with a reasonable degree of privacy, two steps were taken. First, the interviewer specifically asked whether the adolescent was in a situation in which he or she could be assured of privacy and could answer in an open manner. If the adolescent indicated that he or she could not, the interviewer offered to call back at another time when privacy was more likely. Also, the interview questions were primarily asked in a close-ended format, so that the adolescent could respond to questions with a simple yes or no, a number (e.g., age, number of times an abusive incident occurred), or other one-word or phrase answers. Thus, anyone who may have been within earshot of the adolescent during the interview would have heard nothing but simple answers and would have been very unlikely to determine the topic of the questions. These steps appeared to result in a successful approach, as the number of interviews terminated before completion was very low and consistent with rates found with nonsensitive topics. Moreover, more than 99% of the adolescents agreed to answer the most sensitive questions (i.e., sexual assault history).

"Adolescent in Danger" Protocol

An "adolescent in danger" protocol was developed and in place for the purposes of the interview to appropriately detect and respond to participants who might be at acute risk for harm. A potential "adolescent in danger" was defined as an adolescent respondent who reported (a) being a victim of a sexual assault incident committed within the past year by an adult family member or caregiver living in the home that had not been reported to someone in authority such as the school, police, or child protection agency or (b) being seriously hurt in the context of a physical assault incident within the past year by a family member living in the home and for whom the incident had not been reported to someone in authority.

The computer-generated interview was programmed to automatically flag when a potential adolescent in danger was identified on the basis of these criteria. Once such an adolescent was identified, the interviewer informed the respondent that a professional connected with the study might need to recontact the participant in the future. The interviewer also immediately reported the case to one of the project coinvestigators (all doctoral-level, licensed mental health professionals), who were subsequently provided with identifying information regarding the teenager and the potential danger identified. A staff meeting was then conducted among the investigators to review each situation on a case-by-base basis to assess the potential harm resulting from the information provided and determine the need to recontact the adolescent for further clarifying information. In cases in which the adolescent was recontacted by the investigators, the adolescent was encouraged to talk with a protective adult in his or her immediate environment regarding the previous abusive incident. Furthermore, information was provided to each adolescent contacted via this protocol regarding referral to a qualified mental health or other responsible professional in the participant's community for further investigation and evaluation.

Among the very few NSA participants who needed to be recontacted, all youths had either already told a trusted adult about the prior unreported abusive experience or agreed to tell a trusted adult. In no instance was it necessary to break participant confidentiality to disclose the information collected in the interview to a parent or a third party (e.g., local Department of Social Services). Recently, Wave 1 data collection was completed for a new 10-year replication study of the NSA (i.e., the NSA 2005), in which the number of calls that had to be made in response to a similar adolescent in danger protocol was systematically evaluated. Overall, it was determined that only 29 out of the 3,614 adolescents who participated in the study (0.8%) needed to be recontacted by the investigators. In all of these follow-up cases, the adolescent indicated that he or she had told someone about the incident, agreed he or she would tell someone immediately, or no longer felt any danger or risk from the alleged perpetrator and no further steps beyond the phone call were necessary. As with the original NSA, in no case was it determined to be necessary to break confidentiality.

Resources for Participants Who Reported Distress

As anticipated, very few participants reported distress following the interview. However, for those who did report distress or were thought by the interviewer to be experiencing distress, the following steps were followed. First, the adolescent was asked whether he or she would like to talk with one of the project investigators, all of whom are licensed mental health professionals with significant experience in assisting victims of crime and other traumatic events. Second, adolescents who were perceived to be distressed were asked whether a member of the project team could contact them for follow-up to reassess distress levels and obtain additional information if necessary to ensure that any participants in need of mental health resources were provided assistance. Third, in such cases, a member (i.e., doctoral-level mental health professional) of the project team contacted the participant and assessed his or her current condition. In all incidents, when the project team member recontacted the adolescents, the respondent reported no significant distress during the follow-up phone call and no further action was necessary. If it had been determined that there was a need for clinical intervention with the adolescent, an appropriate mental health referral would have been arranged. This protocol was in place but never needed to be activated. Also, all adolescents who participated in the NSA were provided with the 1-800 telephone number of Child Help as a safeguard to assist with any potential current or future difficulties.

CONCLUSION

The telephone survey is a feasible method for collecting information about sensitive topics from population-based samples. It is much cheaper, permits greater quality control, and provides a more anonymous context than in-person interviews. Although more expensive than an Internet survey, a telephone survey provides greater coverage of the total population because at present, many more households have telephones than Internet access. That is not to say that telephone surveys are the perfect research methodology. The small percentage of the U.S. population who do not live in households with telephones are excluded from such surveys. However, telephone surveys represent a good compromise of cost, coverage, and anonymity. Most important, on the basis of the cost–benefit exploration presented here, there is strong evidence that this type of research can be conducted safely, as long as proper precautions are taken, and that the information gained from such studies can be invaluable in informing the development and target population of prevention and intervention programs. Finally, institutional review boards and other regulatory bodies should heavily weigh the available data on telephone-based research on sensitive topics when reviewing human subjects protocols.

REFERENCES

Acierno, R., Resnick, H. S., Kilpatrick, D. G., & Stark-Riemer, W. (2003). Assessing elder victimization: Demonstration of a methodology. *Social Psychiatry and Psychiatric Epidemiology, 38*, 644–653.

American Medical Association Council on Ethical & Judicial Affairs. (2004). *Code of medical ethics: Current opinions with annotations* (2004–2005 ed.). New York: American Medical Association Press.

American Psychiatric Association. (1980). *Diagnostic and statistical manual of mental disorders* (3rd ed.). Washington, DC: Author.

American Psychological Association. (2002). Ethical principles of psychologists and code of conduct. *American Psychologist, 57*, 1060–1073.

Bersoff, D. M., & Bersoff, D. N. (1999) Ethical perspectives in clinical research. In P. C. Kendall, J. N. Butcher, & G. N. Holmbeck (Eds.), *Handbook of research methods in clinical psychology* (2nd ed., pp. 31–53). New York: Wiley.

Callahan, D. (2003). *What price better health? Hazards of the research imperative.* Berkeley: University of California Press.

Catlin, G., & Murray, S. (1979). *Report on Canadian victimization survey methodological pretests.* Ottawa, Ontario, Canada: Statistics Canada, Special Survey Group.

Dansky, B. S., Saladin, M. E., Brady, K. T., Kilpatrick, D. G., & Resnick, H. S. (1995). Prevalence of victimization and posttraumatic stress disorder among women with substance use disorders: Comparison of telephone and in-person assessment samples. *International Journal of the Addictions, 30*, 1079–1099.

Galea, S., Ahern, J., Resnick, H. S., Kilpatrick, D. G., Bucuvalas, M., Gold, J., et al. (2002, March 28). Psychological sequelae of the September 11 terrorist attacks in New York City. *New England Journal of Medicine, 346*, 982–987.

Galea, S., Bucuvalas, M., Resnick, H. S., Boyle, J., Vlahov, D., & Kilpatrick, D. G. (2006). Telephone-based research methods in disaster research. In F. H. Norris, S. Galea, M. Friedman, & P. Watson (Eds.), *Methods for disaster mental health research* (pp. 111–128). New York: Guilford Press.

Galea, S., Nandi, A., Stuber, J., Gold, J., Acierno, R., Best, C. L., et al. (2005). Participant reactions to survey research in the general population after terrorist attacks. *Journal of Traumatic Stress, 18*, 461–465.

Griffin, M. G., Resick, P. A., Waldrop, A. E., & Mechanic, M. (2003). Participation in trauma research: Is there evidence of harm? *Journal of Traumatic Stress, 16*, 221–227.

Kilpatrick, D. G. (2004). The ethics of disaster research: A special section. *Journal of Traumatic Stress, 17*, 361–362.

Kilpatrick, D. G., Acierno, R. E., Resnick, H. S., Saunders, B. E., & Best, C. L. (2000). Risk factors for adolescent substance abuse and dependence: Data from a national sample. *Journal of Consulting and Clinical Psychology, 68*, 19–30.

Kilpatrick, D. G., Ruggiero, K. J., Acierno, R. E., Saunders, B. E., Resnick, H. S., & Best, C. L. (2003). Violence and risk of PTSD, major depression, substance abuse/dependence and comorbidity: Results from the National Survey of Adolescents. *Journal of Consulting and Clinical Psychology, 71*, 692–700.

Lyneham, H. J., & Rapee, R. M. (2005). Agreement between telephone and in-person delivery of a structured interview for anxiety disorders in children. *Journal of the American Academy of Child & Adolescent Psychiatry, 44*, 274–282.

Midanik, L. T., & Greenfield, T. K. (2003). Telephone versus in-person interviews for alcohol use: Results of the 2000 National Alcohol Survey. *Drug and Alcohol Dependence, 72*, 209–214.

Newman, E., & Kaloupek, D. G. (2004). The risks and benefits of participating in trauma-focused research studies. *Journal of Traumatic Stress, 17*, 383–394.

Newman, E., Walker, E. A., & Gefland, A. (1999). Assessing the ethical costs and benefits of trauma-focused research. *General Hospital Psychiatry, 21*, 1–10.

Paulsen, A. S., Crowe, R. R., Noyes, R., & Phohl, B. (1988). Reliability of the telephone interview in diagnosing anxiety disorders. *Archives of General Psychiatry, 45*, 62–63.

Pettigrew, L. E. L., Wilson, J. T. L., & Teasdale, G. M. (2003). Reliability of ratings on the Glasgow Outcome Scales from in-person and telephone structured interviews. *Journal of Head Trauma Rehabilitation, 18*, 252–258.

U. S. Bureau of the Census. (2001). Home computers and internet use in the United States: August 2000. *Current Population Reports, P23-207*, 1–12.

Weeks, M. F., Kulka, R. A., Lessler, J. T., & Whitmore, R. W. (1983). Personal versus telephone surveys for collecting household health data at the local level. *American Journal of Public Health, 12*, 1389–1394.

4

LONGITUDINAL RESEARCH IN SCHOOL BULLYING: ADOLESCENTS WHO BULLY AND WHO ARE BULLIED

LANG MA, ERIN PHELPS, JACQUELINE V. LERNER, AND RICHARD M. LERNER

Bullying in adolescence is a ubiquitous and complex instance of interpersonal violence with multiple developmental implications, ones that are best brought to light through longitudinal research. Youth involvement in bullying, especially as it occurs naturalistically in key contexts of adolescence, most particularly in school, is also methodologically challenging to assess, particularly when the course of bullying is studied longitudinally over several years. At the same time, such naturalistic or descriptive research presents significant ethical challenges to the longitudinal researcher (e.g., Fisher, 2002, 2003; Fisher, Higgins-D'Alessandro, Rau, Kuther, & Belanger, 1996; O'Sullivan & Fisher, 1997).

Longitudinal research pertinent to school bullying among adolescents raises important ethical issues. As we examine in this chapter, because bully-

We are grateful to Celia B. Fisher for her helpful suggestions regarding this chapter. The research reported in this chapter was supported in part by a grant from the National 4-H Council.

ing involves the repeated exposure to negative actions against which bullied youths cannot adequately defend themselves, longitudinal researchers must balance the scientific goals of their research with their responsibility to protect participants from immediate and future harm (i.e., from repeated bullying). At the same time, this protection has to occur within the context of honoring participants' confidentiality.

In other words, in tracking their longitudinal sample, researchers know who specifically may be involved in bullying (as a bully or a victim) at any one time, and as noted, perhaps more important, researchers may be able to predict who may be likely to be involved in such violence in the future and how such involvement may diminish significant attainments in adolescence, such as academic achievement and life skills. As a consequence, the need to observe the naturalistic developmental course of school bullying to generate a sound empirical foundation for description, explanation, and ultimately optimization of research must be weighed against the need to protect young participants from harm and also to honor pledges of confidentiality given to them when they agree to be involved in the research (e.g., Fisher, 1994; Fisher, Higgins-D'Alessandro, et al., 1996; Fisher, Hoagwood, & Jensen, 1996; Fisher et al., 2002; O'Sullivan & Fisher, 1997).

The purpose of this chapter is to discuss the ethical tension between maintaining the empirical foundations of one's research—specifically, maintaining a rigorous, state-of-the-art longitudinal study of adolescent development, one that includes an assessment of the course of bullying within the school context—and adequately addressing the ethical challenges of such research, chiefly protecting young people from harm and respecting their confidentiality (e.g., Fisher, Higgins-D'Alessandro, et al., 1996; Fisher, Hoagwood, et al., 1996; O'Sullivan & Fisher, 1997). To underscore the significance of this dilemma, we first review what is known about school bullying in adolescence and discuss why obtaining sound empirical information about the longitudinal course of such behavior is important for both basic and applied scientific interests. The problems of school bullying, for the bully and the victim, are far from insignificant or transitory. Such problems have implications for academic performance and social and emotional functioning within and across time. As such, if developmental scientists are to have a firm empirical basis for interventions to either diminish or prevent bullying or to promote positive outcomes among youths involved in bullying, it is crucial that the sort of longitudinal work we describe in this chapter be done. Accordingly, we use the 4-H Study of Positive Youth Development (PYD; Gestsdottir & Lerner, 2007; Jelicic, Bobek, Phelps, Lerner, & Lerner, 2007; Lerner et al., 2005; Phelps et al., 2007; Theokas & Lerner, 2006) as a sample case of the nature and potential effect of such research. Finally, we discuss the ethical challenges of longitudinal research on school bullying and make recommendations for future research.

SCHOOL BULLYING: DEFINITION, PREVALENCE, AND IMPLICATIONS

School bullying (peer victimization, peer harassment) is usually defined as a subset of aggressive behaviors among schoolchildren and adolescents. A young person is being bullied when he or she is repeatedly exposed to negative actions on the part of one or more other youths, such as physical assaults, cruel teasing, being called bad names, and rumor spreading; the youth who is bullied is unable to effectively defend himself or herself (Smith et al., 1999). Young people who are involved in bullying play different roles and have different bullying statuses: Some are bullies who pick on peers; some are victims who are picked on by peers; and some are bullies in certain situations and victims in other situations (bully–victims). Some youths are bystanders who are not directly involved in bullying (O'Connell, Pepler, & Craig, 1999; Smith et al., 1999).

Bullying is prevalent among schoolchildren and adolescents in different nations and cultures, making it an issue of significant universal concern for adolescent health and well-being (Nansel et al., 2001; Smith et al., 1999). For example, in a survey of approximately 130,000 primary and junior high school students in Norway, about 15% of the students were involved in bullying with some regularity. Approximately 9% were victims, 7% were bullies, and 1.6% were bully–victims (Olweus, 1999). In the first study of bullying in a national representative sample of U.S. youths (15,686 students in Grades 6–10), which used similar measures of bullying, a total of 29.9% reported involvement in bullying, with 13.0% as bullies, 10.6% as victims, and 6.3% as bully–victims (Nansel et al., 2001).

Being involved in bullying is associated with various social, emotional, and academic challenges (Nansel et al., 2001; Smith & Brain, 2000; Smith et al., 1999) and hence underscores the implications of bullying for healthy behavioral and mental functions. Being bullied predicts higher anxiety, greater depression, low self-esteem, peer rejection, suicidal behaviors, and aggression (Hodges, Boivin, Vitaro, & Bukowski, 1999; Hodges & Perry, 1999; Rigby, 2001). Recent research has suggested that bullying others and being bullied are positively related to substance use and fighting (Nansel, Overpeck, Haynie, Ruan, & Scheidt, 2003). Adolescents who bully are as likely to carry weapons and engage in violence in the streets as either perpetrators or victims (Andershed, Kerr, & Stattin, 2001). Early experience as a bully in school is a significant predictor of juvenile delinquency, later affiliation with gangs, and criminality in adulthood (Hazler, 1994; Holmes & Brandenburg-Ayres, 1998).

Given the prevalence of bullying and the developmental implications suggested by existing research, studies of its individual and contextual bases and of its effect on youth development within and across time have importance both for understanding this large group of young people and for devising policies and programs pertinent to prevention of bullying and to promotion of positive developmental outcomes among youths. Nevertheless, we have emphasized that the potential effect of such longitudinal research must be balanced with steps to address the important ethical challenges intrinsic to such scholarship. This dilemma is made all the more complicated when the researcher recognizes that bullying has potentially profound negative implications for healthy development. Thus, there is great need to collect data that elucidate the bases of bullying across life.

IMPORTANCE OF LONGITUDINAL RESEARCH ABOUT BULLYING

In this section, we take academic competence as an example to discuss the importance of longitudinal bullying research from a developmental systems theoretical perspective. Research has indicated that being involved in bullying has implications for academic development. Being a bully is associated with lower GPA and self-perceived academic achievement (Nansel et al., 2001; Yang, Chung, & Kim, 2003), and being bullied correlates with lower GPA and lower self-perceived academic competence (Neary & Joseph, 1994; Yang et al., 2003). However, although there are differences in academic competence between youths who engage in bullying versus those who do not, these differences cannot simply be attributed to different bullying statuses. There are three reasons for this. First, most studies about bullying and academic competence have used cross-sectional data (e.g., Nansel et al., 2001), and as such, the research findings cannot be used to establish antecedent–consequent relationships between bullying status and academic competence. Juvonen, Nishina, and Graham (2000) reported one of the few studies that used longitudinal data, and their study showed that changes in perceived victimization, along with self-worth and loneliness, across a 1-year period predicted subsequent GPA and absenteeism. Second, because of the cross-sectional nature of the research, it is not possible to control for prior years' academic competence when examining the relationships between bullying and academic competence. Third, these studies also did not control for demographic characteristics that can predict youth academic competence (e.g., Yang et al., 2003). These demographic characteristics include the youth's sex (Morrison, Rimm-Kauffman, & Pianta, 2003), race or ethnicity (Liaw & Brooks-Gunn, 1994), and indicators of family socioeconomic status, such as maternal education and household income (Jimerson, Egeland, & Teo, 1999; Morrison et al., 2003). Researchers should investigate whether being involved in bullying accounts for lower academic competence above and beyond such demographic factors and prior years' academic competence.

Little research has explored why bullying others is associated with poorer academic competence. Nevertheless, studies have suggested that adolescents who bully tend to be engaged in other problem behaviors, including substance abuse and serious violent behaviors (Andershed et al., 2001; Nansel et al., 2003), and they are more likely to participate in juvenile delinquency and gang activities (Hazler, 1994; Holmes & Brandenburg-Ayres, 1998). Therefore, bullies may spend less time and energy on schoolwork and hence have lower levels of academic competence.

Academic competence predicts youths' continuing schooling (or, conversely, lack of academic competence predicts dropping out of school), career opportunities, potential income, and family stability (Goldschmidt & Wang, 1999; Hauser, 1997; Rumberger & Larson, 1998; Swanson & Schneider, 1999). Given the pervasiveness of school bullying and its negative implications for academic competence, as suggested by extant research, it is essential to study the development of adolescents' academic competence in the context of bullying.

To understand why some adolescents who are involved in bullying can do well academically, and hence suggest entry points for interventions to enhance academic competence of adolescents who bully and who are bullied, it may be useful to adopt a developmental systems theoretical perspective. Such a theoretical perspective underscores that plasticity—that is, the potential for systematic change—is an inherent characteristic of individuals. Plasticity arises as a result of the coactions between the contexts and the individual. The potential for plasticity suggests the utility of exploring the attributes of individuals and settings that together may promote positive developmental outcomes (Lerner, 2002, 2004). Attributes of individuals and contexts that are linked to positive developmental outcomes have been termed *developmental assets* (Benson, Scales, Hamilton, & Sesma, 2006). We conducted research about bullying to identify potential developmental assets that may promote academic competence of youths who bully and who are bullied (Ma, Phelps, Lerner, & Lerner, 2007).

Our work in the 4-H study of PYD (Ma et al., 2007) aligns with other studies that have identified some variables that may promote positive academic competence among youths, particularly those who are at risk of low academic competence because of they are of a racial or ethnic minority or come from a low-income or remarried family (e.g., Boyce Rodgers & Rose, 2001; Englund, Luckner, Whaley, & Egeland, 2004; Kim & Rohner, 2002; Morrison et al., 2003; Rosenfeld, Richman, & Bowen, 2000; Sirin & Rogers-Sirin, 2004; Waxman, Huang, & Padrón, 1997).

However, few studies have tested whether and to what extent these developmental assets for academic competence can work in the context of bullying. Research about bullying usually adopts a deficit model, focusing on problems and negative developmental outcomes, such as lower academic competence, that are associated with bullying. Researchers rarely examine what factors in the contexts and in youths themselves can promote positive academic outcomes for those who bully and who are bullied. This omission may explain why there is a lack of empirical work examining what could possibly enhance academic competence for adolescents who bully and who are bullied.

A developmental systems theoretical perspective frames the 4-H study of PYD (Gestsdottir & Lerner, 2007; Jelicic et al., 2007; Lerner et al., 2005; Phelps et al., 2007; Theokas & Lerner, 2006). This national longitudinal study of the individual and ecological bases of PYD in adolescence has explored whether ecological variables, such as parent support, teacher support, and peer support, and individual variables, such as educational expectations and school engagement, promote academic competence among adolescents who are involved in bullying as bullies and victims. To facilitate discussion of the dilemma between, on one hand, the methodological requirements and substantive significance of longitudinal research about youth bullying and, on the other hand, the ethical challenges of such investigations (e.g., Fisher, Higgins-D'Alessandro, et al., 1996; Fisher, Hoagwood, et al., 1996; O'Sullivan & Fisher, 1997), it is useful to describe the 4-H study of PYD and note some of our recent findings regarding bullying (Ma et al., 2007).

AN OVERVIEW OF THE 4-H STUDY OF POSITIVE YOUTH DEVELOPMENT

Our bullying research is conducted as a part of the 4-H study of PYD, a national, longitudinal study of PYD that began in 2002 by studying across 13 states about 1,700 fifth graders and about 1,200 parents. At this writing, it includes about 4,000 students and 2,000 parents from 25 states. The 4-H study is designed to test a theoretical model about the role of developmental assets in promoting PYD, as conceptualized by the "five Cs" of competence, confidence, connection, character, and caring and by the "sixth C" of contribution (Lerner, 2004), and in the reduction of problem and risk behaviors. More details of the methodology of the 4-H study have been presented in prior reports (Gestsdottir & Lerner, 2007; Jelicic et al., 2007; Lerner et al., 2005; Theokas & Lerner, 2006).

In brief, the 4-H study used a form of longitudinal sequential design (Baltes, Reese, & Nesselroade, 1988). Data from fifth graders were gathered in Wave 1 of the study during the 2002 through 2003 school year, and these fifth graders were the initial cohort in this design and the only cohort in Wave 1. To maintain at least initial levels of power for within-time analyses and to assess the effects of retesting, subsequent waves of the study involved the addition of a "retest control" cohort of youths of the current grade level of the initial cohort; these additional cohorts were then followed longitudinally. For instance, in Wave 2 of the study, in which the current grade level of the initial cohort was Grade 6, a retest control group of sixth graders, new to the study, was added; these youths became members of the second longitudinal cohort. Similarly, subsequent waves of the study introduced a new cohort that is then followed longitudinally.

Data were collected by contacting schools or, in a few cases, structured, out-of-school program settings. Measurement involved collection of student and family demographic data and, in turn, information about bullying status. We used the two global questions from the Olweus Bullying Questionnaire (Olweus, 1996) to appraise adolescents' experiences of bullying peers and being bullied by peers in the past couple of months. We then created bullying status dummy variables to indicate an adolescent's bullying status as to one of the four categories: bully, victim, bully–victim, and bystander. Because the bully–victim group was too small, and thereby statistically problematic, this group was excluded from analysis. We also assessed ecological and individual variables that may promote academic competence, including parent support, teacher support, peer support, educational expectations, and school engagement. Finally, we assessed academic competence as indexed by self-reported grades and self-perceived academic competence (the details of these measures are described elsewhere; Lerner et al., 2005; Ma et al., 2007).

Study results suggested that involvement in bullying as a bully negatively predicted academic competence above and beyond the influences of sex, maternal education, and academic competence in the prior year. This finding held when self-reported grades and self-perceived academic competence were used as the outcome variables, respectively (Ma et al., 2007), and is consistent with results from previous investigations (e.g., Nansel et al., 2001; Neary & Joseph, 1994). In addition, our research extends previous research by using longitudinal data and by revealing that the negative effect of bullying on academic competence is retained even when the influences of demographic background and baseline academic competence are taken into account.

Another key finding from our research is that both educational expectations and school engagement were found to serve as developmental assets in the context of bullying. These two variables acted to enhance academic competence concurrently for adolescents who were involved in bullying as bullies and victims in an interactive manner (Ma et al., 2007). From a developmental systems theoretical perspective, every youth has the potential to develop positively, given adequate developmental assets in his or her life (Lerner, 2002, 2004). When ecological variables and individual variables were entered into a regression model, being a bully versus being a victim was no longer a significant predictor of academic competence; what really counted in predicting academic competence was educational expectations and school engagement (Ma et al., 2007). The results suggest that given sufficient positive individual assets, victims and bullies can achieve academic competence in spite of their negative experiences of being involved in bullying.

Thus, the 4-H study provides some useful information for school bullying interventions by identifying some individual variables—educational expectations and school engagement—as developmental assets that enhance academic competence for adolescents involved in bullying. Future longitudinal research with a more complex model that includes both developmental assets, such as educational expectations and school engagement, and risk factors, such as depression and absenteeism, would help clarify how developmental assets may offset the influences of the risk factors in predicting academic competence for adolescents who bully and who are bullied.

The 4-H study expands understanding of the relationships between bullying and academic competence by using longitudinal data to examine the effects of bullying on academic competence with the influences of demographic background and baseline academic competence controlled. Overall, the results to date indicate that involvement in bullying impairs academic competence, above and beyond the influences of adolescent sex, maternal education, and prior year academic competence. This finding suggests the need for broadly based bullying interventions, including alleviation, prevention, and promotion, given the pervasiveness of bullying. In particular, this finding highlights the importance of addressing the issue of academic competence in bullying interventions, which is still more or less rarely a target of such work.

ADDRESSING ETHICAL ISSUES IN THE LONGITUDINAL STUDY OF ADOLESCENT INVOLVEMENT IN BULLYING

The 4-H study has provided, and will continue to provide, important information about the immediate and longer term implications of being involved in school bullying, as either a victim or a bully, on significant psychosocial behaviors, such as academic competence. In fact, because it is longitudinal, the data set can alert researchers, and policymakers and practitioners, to the likely effects across their lives of adolescents' involvement in bullying. Such knowledge is indisputably important for both basic science and applied concerns. Yet, such knowledge of the within- and across-time covariates of involvement in bullying means that developmental scientists are necessarily placed in an ethically challenging situation.

The 4-H study constitutes a "naturalistic" assessment of the role of individual and ecological variables in the course of school bullying. The study is naturalistic in the sense that we appraise and describe patterns of covariation between school bullying and other school-based behaviors "as we find them" among our participants, and there is no educational or intervention component, although—as we envision the implications of our research—we believe there is import for subsequent application to educational policies and programs. Moreover, because the 4-H study is longitudinal, the identities of the adolescents, and thus their responses, are known to the senior members of the research team. Therefore, we have an ongoing relationship with the adolescents as well as personal knowledge about whether a particular adolescent is a bully or a victim. Given our definition of being bullied—which, as noted earlier in this chapter, involves the repeated exposure to negative actions on the part of one or more other youths, actions that the bullied youth is unable to effectively defend himself or herself against—youths who are bullied are in a situation they cannot by themselves escape. Accordingly, ethical issues are raised because researchers need to balance the scientific goals and quality of the research with the responsibility to protect participants from harm. Complicating this issue further is the fact that we also need to respect and protect our participants' rights to confidentiality. For instance, as researchers conducting longitudinal research, can we study the natural course of bullying phenomena, which we know have immediate and longer term negative consequences, for both bullies and victims, and not intervene? If we do not intervene, are we sending an implicit message that we do not care about bullying or that we do not think that reports of it are important enough to elicit our action? Given such questions, we may ask whether we can conduct methodologically appropriate, indeed cutting-edge, research and at the same time fulfill our ethical responsibilities to protect the welfare of our participants—to act to avoid further harmful actions toward victims, to prevent bullies from continued enactment of their aggressive behaviors, and to avoid the diminution of the school climate that occurs when bullying goes unchecked—while maintaining the confidentiality promised to youth participants and to their parents when agreement to be involved in the research was solicited.

We, the authors, believe that the answer to this question is yes. Our view is based on the results of important and, in fact, ingenious research conducted by Fisher and her colleagues. Fisher, Higgins-D'Alessandro, et al. (1996) noted that research pertinent to developmental risks among youths raises ethical concerns when an investigator learns that participants are in jeopardy. They assessed the views of 7th, 9th, and 11th graders in regard to three options researchers might enact in such circumstances: (a) taking no action and maintaining confidentiality, (b) reporting the problem to a concerned parent or adult, or (c) facilitating adolescent self-referrals. Youths judged these options in regard to several instances of potential youth risk, that is, delinquency, substance abuse, child maltreatment, and life-threatening behaviors (e.g., suicide). They reported that maintaining confidentiality was viewed favorably in regard to risks that were seen by youths as not severe or under the circumstances in which reporting risks to adults would increase risks for the young person. However, confidentiality was viewed unfavorably, and reporting risks to adults was judged as favorable when the risk situation involved either suicide or child maltreatment; this latter category within the Fisher, Higgins-D'Alessandro, et al. study is the closest to the situation involving youth bullying, in which the victim of bullying is certainly being maltreated.

Fisher, Higgins-D'Alessandro, et al. (1996) interpreted their findings to suggest that even when participant confidentiality is assured, which is the case with traditional informed consent procedures, middle school–age adolescents—that is, youths of the age level of most of the 4-H study participants—may anticipate being helped when they reveal to researchers that they are a victim of violent behavior. Given such expectations, it may be that longitudinal researchers should act to inform school personnel and/or parents of the fact that youths are involved in bullying, especially when the adolescent reports that he or she is a victim. Indeed, and as we have suggested, Fisher, Higgins-D'Alessandro, et al. (1996) noted that

> an investigator's failure to help a teenager who has disclosed such problems may unintentionally send messages that the problem is unimportant, that no services are available, or that knowledgeable adults can not be depended on to help children in need. (p. 2096)

Other research by Fisher and her colleagues has provided evidence that parents as well as adolescents expect researchers to ignore promises of confidentiality and to act to protect youths experiencing violence from further harm. O'Sullivan and Fisher (1997) studied the ratings of 14 risks and of four reporting policies provided by a group of mothers and their adolescent children. The four reporting policies were taking no action, providing a referral to the teenager, telling a parent, or informing a school counselor. Parents were most likely to consent to studies with policies that indicated that they would be informed. In turn, parents were least likely to consent if no actions were planned by the investigator. Adolescents regarded student referrals as favorable with respect to all instances of risk and preferred this option over confidentiality policies in regard to research pertinent to sexually transmitted diseases and, pertinent to the 4-H study focus on bullying, to harassment.

Again, then, and for both youths and parents, the work of Fisher and her colleagues provides data that put into doubt the ethical stance that it is appropriate to take no action when an investigator discovers that a teenager has been involved in violent (e.g., harassing) behaviors, such as bullying (O'Sullivan & Fisher, 1997). From this research, we can conclude that the correct course for researchers conducting longitudinal research involving problematic behaviors such as bullying—both in regard to protecting participants from current or future harm and with respect to acting in manners desired by adolescent participants and their parents—is to refer youths for help (be they bullies or victims) and also to inform parents and school personnel that study participants are involved in these problematic behaviors.

Such conduct will enable the longitudinal researcher to identify the characteristics that are associated with identification as a bully or as a victim of bullying and, at the same time, to take actions that will maximize the probability that the social interactions involved in bullying phenomena will be ethically addressed. We agree, then with the observation of Fisher, Higgins-D'Alessandro, et al. (1996) that

> maintaining a balance between scientific responsibility and participant welfare will continue to be a difficult ethical challenge for scientists en-

gaged in expanding our knowledge of the developmental strengths and vulnerabilities of urban youth. Incorporating participant perspectives into our ethical decision making has the potential to contribute to both the continued development of our science and the individuals whose participation make the science possible. (p. 2097)

Recognizing that both youths and parents want researchers to take action when behaviors associated with bullying occur gives developmental scientists conducting longitudinal research the prerogative, and in fact the mandate, to act to stop such behaviors from diminishing the present and future quality of life of the young people participating in their research.

Such actions will not reduce the opportunity for these researchers to identify whether particular variables indeed predict involvement in bullying within their sample and will at the same time enable these scholars to use their privileged position—as observers of the developmental life course of adolescents—to act to remove young people from circumstances in which they face being bullied. Indeed, the creative researcher, acting in this ethically sensitive manner, can then work to assess the sequelae of such actions on the subsequent development of bullies and their victims.

For example, if the investigator is using the self-referral method across the waves of the longitudinal study, the survey that is being used can include items asking whether the student did seek counseling independently or as a result of the survey. These data could then be used as a covariate, predictor, or dependent variable, depending on hypotheses about how such counseling and referrals influence the trajectory of bullying. A similar approach can be taken for those whose bullying reports call for disclosure to parents or counselors. Thus, effectively addressing the ethical challenges of youth bullying can actually enhance the quality of the longitudinal investigation, adding important information about how referrals or disclosures can ameliorate problems of bullying and, as such, help move naturalistic and descriptive studies closer to the point of informing interventions aimed at optimization.

Given, then, the potential synergies between conducting ethically appropriate research on youth bullying and conducting scientifically valid and useful research on this topic, it is crucial for longitudinal investigators to develop and deploy action strategies for institutional ethical procedures. In the concluding section of this chapter, we discuss some of the options available to longitudinal researchers.

MEETING THE CHALLENGES OF LONGITUDINAL RESEARCH ABOUT BULLYING

We have noted that there are relatively few longitudinal studies of bullying among youths. Neither the 4-H study, nor any other longitudinal investigation of this topic of which we are aware, has effectively instituted solutions to the ethical challenges involved in this research. Of course, it would be ideal to institute ethical procedures before conducting longitudinal research on youth bullying. However, the strategies suggested in this section can be put into place before study implementation or for already launched longitudinal studies.

Fisher and her colleagues have suggested referral and informed consent strategies that can be adopted for longitudinal research involving children (Fisher, 1994, 2002, 2003; Fisher, Higgins-D'Alessandro, et al., 1996). For instance, investigators might explore with school administrators what types of counseling options for bullying problems currently exist at the school, suggest that such options be put in place, or work with the school to identify resources in the community that can counsel youths involved in bullying. Because developmental scientists are not ordinarily trained to conduct such counseling themselves, identifying appropriate resources for students is critical. After identifying referral options, at each wave of assessment students can be provided with a list of in-school and out-of-school referrals for bullying problems. This action would communicate to students that the investigators believe the problem of bullying is an important one and that there is help for those in need. At the same time, such action protects student confidentiality. Alternatively, at each assessment period, questionnaires distributed to students can include a place for them to check a box that indicates that they would like to see the school counselor about this problem. Because the investigator can identify each student from the subject identification number on the questionnaire, the form can also indicate that the investigator will let the counselor know about the student's desire to meet with him or her.

Another procedure that may be introduced to address the ethical challenges of bullying research, one that may be especially important given the physical risk of being bullied and the legal risk of serious harm caused by a bully, involves the investigators identifying indicators in the data that would warrant a disclosure to school authorities, physicians, or parents. These criteria should be empirically based, and all members of the research team should be trained in identifying when the criteria are met and in enacting the procedures for disclosure. As Fisher (2003) discovered, there are important cultural differences in students' preferences for referrals to parents, school counselors, and practitioners outside of school. Not only must all members of the research team become sensitive to these cultural variables, but meetings with student representatives and parents will also be useful in providing researchers with information pertinent to such sensitivity. Students will help researchers identify their preferred referral and disclosure procedures.

Whatever decisions are made about the referral and disclosure policy for a study need to be communicated to parents and youths in the parent permission and youth assent forms. O'Sullivan and Fisher (1997) found that a majority of parents would give permission for their child to participate in a study on adolescent risk if the permission form noted that even in the absence of informing them, their children would be referred for counseling if a problem was identified. Fisher (2002) noted as well that many parents report they would be satisfied with referral procedures as long as their child gets needed help. Finally, because there are potential legal, employment, and other consequences that might arise when researchers are studying youth bullying, it is advisable that all of these recommended actions for addressing ethical challenges be coupled with the researchers obtaining a U.S. Department of Health and Human Services Certificate of Confidentiality (see chap. 2, this volume). This certificate protects the investigator from being forced by subpoena to provide confidential information to law enforcement, but does not limit the investigator from disclosing information that she or he believes is vital to the welfare of a participant or a third party. Fisher (2002, 2003; Fisher, Hoagwood, et al., 1996) has provided further details about this certificate.

CONCLUSION

Investigators conducting longitudinal research on youth bullying may take a range of appropriate steps to institute ethical actions, either before they launch such studies or even after the research has commenced. As we have discussed, implementation of such ethical procedures does not come at the cost of good science. In fact, science may be enhanced by such actions. Indeed, Fisher's perspective (e.g., 2003; O'Sullivan & Fisher, 1997) rings as true in the study of youth bullying as it does in other areas of research pertinent to the development of adolescents. That is, the standards of good science and good ethics can and should exist in a win–win situation, one in which researchers improve both the quality of their empirical work and the quality of the contributions to the well-being of youths and the health of society.

REFERENCES

Andershed, H., Kerr, M., & Stattin, H. (2001). Bullying in school and violence on the streets: Are the same people involved? *Journal of Scandinavian Studies in Criminology & Crime Prevention, 2*(1), 31–49.

Baltes, P. B., Reese, H. W., & Nesselroade, J. R. (1988). *Life-span developmental psychology: Introduction to research methods.* Hillsdale, NJ: Erlbaum.

Benson, P. L., Scales, P. C., Hamilton, S. F., & Semsa, A., Jr. (2006). Positive youth development: Theory, research, and applications. In W. Damon & R. M. Lerner (Eds.-in-chief) & R. M. Lerner (Ed.), *Handbook of child psychology: Vol. 1. Theoretical models of human development* (6th ed., pp. 894–941). Hoboken, NJ: Wiley.

Boyce Rodgers, K., & Rose, H. A. (2001). Personal, family, and school factors related to adolescent academic performance: A comparison by family structure. *Marriage & Family Review, 33*(4), 47–61.

Englund, M. M., Luckner, A. E., Whaley, G. J. L., & Egeland, B. (2004). Children's achievement in early elementary school: Longitudinal effects of parental involvement, expectations, and quality of assistance. *Journal of Educational Psychology, 96*, 723–730.

Fisher, C. B. (1994). Reporting and referring research participants: Ethical challenges for investigators studying children and youth. *Ethics & Behavior, 4*, 87 – 95.

Fisher, C. B. (2002). Participation consultation: Ethical insights into parental permission and confidentiality procedures for policy-relevant research with youth. In R. M. Lerner, D. Wertlieb, & F. Jacobs (Eds.), *Handbook of applied developmental science—Promoting positive child, adolescent, and family development through research, policies, and programs: Vol. 4. Adding value to youth and family development: The engaged university and professional and academic outreach* (pp. 371–396). Thousand Oaks, CA: Sage.

Fisher, C. B. (2003). Adolescent and parent perspectives on ethical issues in youth drug use and suicide survey research. *Ethics & Behavior, 13*, 302–331.

Fisher, C. B., Higgins-D'Alessandro, A., Rau, J. B., Kuther, T. L., & Belanger, S. (1996). Referring and reporting research participants at risk: Views from urban adolescents. *Child Development, 67*, 2086–2100.

Fisher, C. B., Hoagwood, K., Boyce, C., Duster, T., Frank, D. A., Grisso, T., et al. (2002). Research ethics for mental health science involving ethnic minority children and youths. *American Psychologist, 57*, 1024–1040.

Fisher, C. B., Hoagwood, K., & Jensen, P. (1996). Casebook on ethical issues in research with children and adolescents with mental disorders. In K. Hoagwood, P. Jensen, & C. B. Fisher (Eds.), *Ethical issues in research with children and adolescents with mental disorders* (pp. 135–238). Hillsdale, NJ: Erlbaum.

Gestsdottir, S., & Lerner, R. M. (2007). Intentional self-regulation and positive youth development in early adolescence: Findings from the 4-H Study of Positive Youth Development. *Developmental Psychology, 43*, 508–521.

Goldschmidt, P., & Wang, J. (1999). When can schools affect dropout behavior? A longitudinal multilevel analysis. *American Educational Research Journal, 36*, 715–738.

Hauser, R. M. (1997). Indicators of high school completion and dropout. In R. M. Hauser, B. V. Brown, & W. R. Prosser (Eds.), *Indicators of children's well-being* (pp. 152–184). New York: Russell Sage Foundation.

Hazler, R. J. (1994). Bullying breeds violence: You can stop it. *Learning, 22*, 38–41.

Hodges, E. V. E., Boivin, M., Vitaro, F., & Bukowski, W. M. (1999). The power of friendship: Protection against an escalating cycle of peer victimization. *Developmental Psychology, 35*, 94–101.

Hodges, E. V. E., & Perry, D. G. (1999). Personal and interpersonal antecedents and consequences of victimization by peers. *Journal of Personality and Social Psychology, 76*, 677–685.

Holmes, S. R., & Brandenburg-Ayres, S. J. (1998). Bullying behavior in school: A predictor of later gang involvement. *Journal of Gang Research, 5*(2), 1–6.

Jelicic, H., Bobek, D., Phelps, E. D., Lerner, R. M., & Lerner, J. V. (2007). Using positive youth development to predict contribution and risk behaviors in early adolescence: Findings from the first two waves of the 4-H Study of Positive Youth Development. *International Journal of Behavioral Development, 31*, 263–273.

Jimerson, S., Egeland, B., & Teo, A. (1999). A longitudinal study of achievement trajectories: Factors associated with change. *Journal of Educational Psychology, 91*, 116–126.

Juvonen, J., Nishina, A., & Graham, S. (2000). Peer harassment, psychological adjustment, and school functioning in early adolescence. *Journal of Educational Psychology, 92*, 349–359.

Kim, K., & Rohner, R. P. (2002). Parental warmth, control, and involvement in schooling: Predicting academic achievement among Korean American adolescents. *Journal of Cross-Cultural Psychology, 33*, 127–140.

Lerner, R. M. (2002). *Concepts and theories of human development* (3rd ed.). Mahwah, NJ: Erlbaum.

Lerner, R. M. (2004). *Liberty: Thriving and civic engagement among America's youth.* Thousand Oaks, CA: Sage.

Lerner, R. M., Lerner, J. V., Almerigi, J. B., Theokas, C., Phelps, E., Gestsdottir, S., et al. (2005). Positive youth development, participation in community youth development programs, and community contributions of fifth-grade adolescents: Findings from the first wave of the 4-H Study of Positive Youth Development. *Journal of Early Adolescence, 25*, 17–71.

Liaw, F., & Brooks-Gunn, J. (1994). Cumulative familial risks and low birth weight children's cognitive and behavioral development. *Journal of Clinical Child Psychology, 23*, 360–372.

Ma, L., Phelps, E., Lerner, J. V., & Lerner, R. M. (2007). *Pathways to academic competence for adolescents who bully and who are bullied: Findings from the 4-H Study of Positive Youth Development.* Unpublished manuscript, Institute for Applied Research in Youth Development, Tufts University, Medford, MA.

Morrison, E. F., Rimm-Kauffman, S., & Pianta, R. C. (2003). A longitudinal study of mother-child interactions at school entry and social and academic outcomes in middle school. *Journal of School Psychology, 41*, 185–200.

Nansel, T. R., Overpeck, M. D., Haynie, D. L., Ruan, W. J., & Scheidt, P. C. (2003). Relationships between bullying and violence among US youth. *Archives of Pediatrics & Adolescent Medicine, 157*, 348–353.

Nansel, T. R., Overpeck, M., Pilla, R. S., Ruan, W. J., Simons-Morton, B., & Scheidt, P. (2001, April 25). Bullying behaviors among US youth: Prevalence and association with psychosocial adjustment. *JAMA, 285*, 2094–2100.

Neary, A., & Joseph, S. (1994). Peer victimization and its relationship to self-concept and depression among schoolgirls. *Personality and Individual Differences, 16*, 183–186.

O'Connell, P., Pepler, D., & Craig, W. (1999). Peer involvement in bullying: Insights and challenges for intervention. *Journal of Adolescence, 22,* 437–452.

Olweus, D. (1996). *The Revised Olweus Bully/Victim Questionnaire* [Mimeo]. Bergen, Norway: Research Center for Health Promotion (HEMIL Center), University of Bergen.

Olweus, D. (1999). Norway. In P. K. Smith, Y. Morita, J. Junger-Tas, D. Olweus, R. F. Catalano, & P. Slee (Eds.), *The nature of school bullying: A cross-national perspective* (pp. 28–48). London: Routledge.

O'Sullivan, C., & Fisher, C. B. (1997). The effect of confidentiality and reporting procedures on parent-child agreement to participate in adolescent risk research. *Applied Developmental Science, 1,* 187–199.

Phelps, E., Balsano, A., Fay, K., Peltz, J., Zimmerman, S., Lerner, R. M., & Lerner, J. V. (2007). Nuances in early adolescent development trajectories of positive and of problematic/risk behaviors: Findings from the 4-H Study of Positive Youth Development. *Child and Adolescent Clinics of North America, 16,* 473–496.

Rigby, K. (2001). Health consequences of bullying and its prevention in schools. In J. Juvonen & S. Graham (Eds.), *Peer harassment in school: The plight of the vulnerable and victimized* (pp. 310–331). New York: Guilford Press.

Rosenfeld, L. B., Richman, J. M., & Bowen, G. L. (2000). Social support networks and school outcomes: The centrality of the teacher. *Child & Adolescent Social Work Journal, 17,* 205–226.

Rumberger, R. W., & Larson, K. A. (1998). Student mobility and the increased risk of high school drop out. *American Journal of Education, 107,* 1–35.

Sirin, S. R., & Rogers-Sirin, L. (2004). Exploring school engagement of middle-class African American adolescents. *Youth & Society, 35,* 323–340.

Smith, P. K., & Brain, P. (2000). Bullying in schools: Lessons from two decades of research. *Aggressive Behavior, 26,* 1–9.

Smith, P. K., Morita, Y., Junger-Tas, J., Olweus, D., Catalano, R. F., & Slee, P. (1999). *The nature of school bullying: A cross-national perspective.* London: Routledge.

Swanson, C. B., & Schneider, B. (1999). Students on the move: Residential and educational mobility in America's schools. *Sociology of Education, 72,* 54–67.

Theokas, C., & Lerner, R. M. (2006). Observed ecological assets in families, schools, and neighborhoods: Conceptualization, measurement and relations with positive and negative developmental outcomes. *Applied Developmental Science, 10,* 61–74.

Waxman, H. C., Huang, S. L., & Padrón, Y. N. (1997). Motivation and learning environment differences between resilient and nonresilient Latino middle school students. *Hispanic Journal of Behavioral Sciences, 19,* 137–155.

Yang, K., Chung, H., & Kim, U. (2003). The effects of school violence on the psychological adjustment of Korean adolescents: A comparative analysis of bullies, victims, and bystanders. In K. Yang & K. Hwang (Eds.), *Progress in Asian social psychology: Conceptual and empirical contributions. Contributions in psychology* (pp. 263–275). Westport, CT: Praeger.

5

SUICIDE IN A NATURAL HISTORY STUDY: LESSONS AND INSIGHTS LEARNED FROM A FOLLOW-UP OF VIETNAM VETERANS AT RISK FOR SUICIDE

RUMI KATO PRICE, LI-SHIUN CHEN, NATHAN K. RISK, ASHLEY HUGHES HADEN, GREGORY A. WIDNER, DAVID M. LEDGERWOOD, AND COLLINS E. LEWIS

Contemporary studies of suicide and suicidal behavior span genetics, biology, psychiatry, psychology, epidemiology, social sciences, and social work, among others (Maris, 1993). They have produced a wealth of information with regard to psychiatric, personality, family history, and environmental risk factors (Vaillant & Blumenthal, 1990), as well as potential genetic and other biologic mechanisms that underlay vulnerability to such behaviors (van Heeringen, 2003). Yet predicting who will commit suicide and when it will occur remains difficult for clinicians and family members (O'Connor &

Preparation of this article was supported in part by the Independent Scientist Award (K02DA00221) and research grants (R01DA09281, R01MH060961) to Rumi Kato Price, Joe Young Sr. Funds from the State of Michigan, and National Institute on Drug Abuse Grant R21021839-01A1 to David M. Ledgerwood.

Sheehy, 2000, p. 127; Pokorny, 1983), making targeted, cost-effective suicide prevention a major challenge (Mann et al., 2005). Furthermore, unless a study uses a sample at high risk of depression, suicide is rarely observed in epidemiologic studies. When suicide occurs, chances are that investigators may not even be aware of the incident unless longitudinal tracking of the causes of death is part of the study aims.

Our longitudinal study of a cohort of Vietnam veterans observed a suicide after a standard psychiatric epidemiology assessment; this provided us with a unique scientific opportunity and a moral obligation to learn from this incident. In this chapter, we introduce background information on suicide risk of Vietnam veterans and how one suicide changed the course of this longitudinal study. We then describe how we used epidemiologic tools to enhance prediction of suicidality, which in turn was used to design a new study focused on suicidality in middle-aged men. We explain how we attempted to balance the need to pursue scientific inquiries with the ethical need to protect the participants by providing clinical care urgently needed by some study members. We close with recommendations about how large-scale epidemiologic studies can fill gaps in knowledge in suicide research and ethical guidelines that will benefit both researchers and study subjects.

At the time of this writing, the United States has been engaged in the Operation Iraqi Freedom/Operation Enduring Freedom (OIF/OEF) conflicts for more than 5 years. Anecdotal accounts of OIF/OEF veterans committing suicide began appearing by early 2004 ("Iraq Military Suicides at 21," 2004). The military has been keenly aware of the impact of a potential increase in suicide and suicidality rates among OIF/OEF service members and veterans. The annual rates of suicide among OIF-deployed Army service members were between 10.5 and 24.0 per 100,000 for the period of 2003 to 2007, yielding an average rate of 18.5 per 100,000. The average rate is considerably higher than a comparable civilian population and approximately 50% higher than the Army as a whole (Office of the Surgeon Multi-National Force–Iraq, Office of the Command Surgeon, & Office of the Surgeon General United States Army Medical Command, 2008). We hope our experience with Vietnam veterans at risk for suicide will help guide researchers and clinicians when examining the mental health and suicidality of the new generation of Iraq and Afghanistan veterans in years to come.

SUICIDE AND SUICIDALITY IN VIETNAM VETERANS

Throughout this chapter, *suicide* is defined as "an act of voluntarily and intentionally taking one's own life" (Murphy, 1992, p. 10); we use it interchangeably with "committed suicide." *Suicide attempt* is a physical act to accomplish suicide (Soubrier, 1993). *Suicidal behavior* or nonfatal *suicidality*, however, is less clearly defined. Therefore, this term is defined empirically in terms of specific behaviors such as suicide attempt, suicide plan, and suicide ideation.

Suicide and Suicidality in Middle-Aged U.S. Men

Suicide rates vary by age, ethnicity, and gender. Rates are higher in elderly people, Caucasians, and men. When our last follow-up study started in 2001, suicide rates in the United States were 23.16 per 100,000 men and 6.90 per 100,000 women in the 40 to 60 age group (Centers for Disease Control & Prevention, 2008), and rates have been relatively stable over the past 3 decades (Riggs, McGraw, & Keefover, 1996). The suicide rate among youth men ages 15 to 24 was 16.54 per 100,000, and the rate among elderly men age 70 years or older was 35.18 per 100,000 (Centers for Disease Control & Prevention, 2008). Thus, the suicide rate for middle-aged men is actually higher than the rate for men in younger age groups, although not as high as the elderly group in which suicide rates have been highest (Waern, Rubinowitz, & Wilhelmson, 2003). Perhaps reflective of the reluctance of men in the middle-aged group to seek help, there is a critical gap in our knowledge about the epidemiology and prevention of suicide in middle-aged men (Moller-Leimkuhler, 2003).

Are Vietnam Veterans at Increased Risk of Suicide?

Approximately 9.2 million individuals served in the U.S. military during the Vietnam era (August 1964 to April 1975); of them, 3.4 million were deployed to Vietnam. Three decades later, Vietnam veterans make up about 22% of U.S. men in the 40 to 60 age group.[1] Estimates of completed suicide among Vietnam-era veterans, however, vary by report (Pollock, Rhodes, Boyle, Decoufle, & McGee, 1990). Evidence for an excess risk of suicide among Vietnam veterans is equivocal (Bullman & Kang, 1995), depending on many factors including deployment to Vietnam (Watanabe & Kang, 1995), military branch (Crane, Barnard, Horsley, & Adena, 1997), rank, age group, years since discharge (Centers for Disease Control, 1987), and draft eligibility (Hearst, Newman, & Hulley, 1986). It is difficult to assess the excess risk of suicide among Vietnam veterans accurately in part because of a "healthy worker effect" (Crane et al., 1997). Veteran cohorts tend, in general, to be healthier than their civilian counterparts because of the selection process for military service, as well as a requirement to maintain a specified level of physical fitness during service. Indeed, mortality studies of veterans show that their overall mortality rate is significantly lower than the rates among civilian groups. This appears to hold true across different time periods, genders (Thomas, Kang, & Dalager, 1991), and nationalities (Crane et al., 1997).

[1]Calculated using data from Census 2000.

We based our research on risk of suicide and suicidality in Vietnam-era veterans on two large national surveys. The National Mortality Follow-back Survey contains information about deceased individuals (Centers for Disease Control & Prevention, 1998), and the National Longitudinal Alcohol Epidemiologic Survey (Grant, Peterson, Dawson, & Chou, 1994) includes measures of suicidal ideation and suicide attempts from in-person interviews (Grant & Hasin, 1999). Among deceased men in the 40 to 60 age group, male Vietnam-era veterans were found to have a significantly increased risk of completed suicide relative to other men of the same age group (5.6% vs. 2.9% respectively; odds ratio [OR] = 1.96, 95% confidence interval [CI] = 1.23–3.12). Among living members surveyed by the National Longitudinal Alcohol Epidemiologic Survey, there was a nonsignificant increased risk for attempted suicide compared with other men of the same age group (2.7% vs. 1.8% respectively; OR = 1.51, 95% CI = 0.95–2.39). The significant odds ratio for completed suicide, however, should be interpreted cautiously, because the overall mortality of Vietnam veterans was lower than that of other men because of the healthy worker effect. From the National Mortality Follow-back Survey and vital statistics sources, we estimated that the proportion of completed suicides among male Vietnam-era veterans ages 40 to 60 in 1993 was 22.64 per 100,000, compared with 20.43 per 100,000 in other men of the same age group. Although the veteran population did have a slightly higher suicide death rate ratio of 1.11, it was not significantly different (95% CI = 0.64–1.58). Thus, results of completed suicide using the National Mortality Follow-back Survey data represented a higher proportion of deaths attributable to suicide among Vietnam-era veterans compared with other men of the same age group, but not the rate of completed suicide per se (Price et al., 2006).

Although conclusive evidence has not been found for increased risk for suicide and suicidality in Vietnam-era veterans, risks appear to be elevated among select subgroups, such as Vietnam veterans with combat exposure (Farberow, Kang, & Bullman, 1990) or physical injury (Bullman & Kang, 1996). Psychiatric disorders in general (Fontana & Rosenheck, 1995; Thompson, Katz, Kane, & Sayers, 2000), and more specifically posttraumatic stress disorder (PTSD; Drescher, Rosen, Burling, & Foy, 2003; Kramer, Lindy, Green, Grace, & Leonard, 1994), depression (Farberow et al., 1990), and alcoholism (Fu et al., 2002; Windle, 2004), are associated with suicide and nonfatal suicidality among veteran populations. Comorbidity of PTSD, depression, and other psychiatric difficulties also appears to be associated with greater exposure to traumatic events (Beckman et al., 1998; Engdahl, Dikel, Eberly, & Blank, 1998).

We began the third wave of surveys of a cohort of Vietnam veterans without much attention to the potential of encountering suicide and nonfatal suicidality, largely because of the 2-decade hiatus in contacting the cohort. The cohort was selected to oversample those who were exposed to heroin and other opiates while stationed in Vietnam. On the basis of data collected within 12 months after these men returned from Vietnam, 78% reported that they had been under enemy fire at least once. In retrospect, combat-induced PTSD, in combination with a history of heavy illicit drug use, should have been good indicators for increased risk of suicidality in these men.

HOW ONE SUICIDE CHANGED THE COURSE OF THE STUDY

The Washington University Vietnam Era Study (VES) cohort of 1,227 men originated from surveys in 1972 and 1974 that were initiated by the White House Special Action Office for Drug Abuse Prevention and contracted to Washington University (Robins, 1974). A total of 943 veterans were included in the database in 1971. About half of the sample was randomly drawn from a list of Army servicemen (pay grades E1–E9) who had positive urine tests for opiates, amphetamines, or barbiturates at the time of their departure from Vietnam in September 1971. This sampling frame represented the drug-positive population, which was estimated at 10.5% of the 13,760 Army enlisted returnees in September 1971. The other half, the "general" sample of the 1972 survey, was randomly drawn from the total population of Army enlisted returnees leaving Vietnam in September 1971. To ensure that the categories of drug-positive and drug-negative veterans were mutually exclusive, drug-positive members who appeared in the general sample (n = 39; Robins, 1974) were reassigned to the drug-positive sample. In the 1974 survey, nonveteran controls (n = 284) were recruited from Selective Service registrations and individually matched to those in the general sample with respect to draft eligibility, draft board location, age, and education completed by the time of the veteran's entry into service (Robins & Helzer, 1975).

For the third wave of interviews conducted from 1996 through 1997 (VES-III), more than 93% of the surviving members (n = 1,024) were located. The VES-III fieldwork was discontinued after 841 members had been interviewed (82.1% interview rate), exceeding our recruitment goal (see Table 5.1 for sampling information). Response rates for the two follow-ups reflected attrition, deaths, failure to locate, and interview refusals (Price, Risk, & Spitznagel, 2001).

Suicide Incident

In August 1996, the principal investigator of VES-III received notification from a veteran's wife that he committed suicide approximately 3 weeks after finishing the follow-up interview. At the time of the interview, the respondent did not report a prior history of suicide attempt or any suicidal ideation. An adverse event report was filed with the Washington University Institutional Review Board (IRB) and the IRB of the St. Louis Veterans Af-

TABLE 5.1
Washington University Vietnam-Era Study Samples

Sample category	DEROS-positive veterans[a]	DEROS-negative veterans[b]	Nonveteran controls[c]	Total
Target sample size	512	431	284[c]	1,227
Interviewed in (*n* [%])				
1972[d]	484 (94.5)	414 (96.1)	Not included	898 (73.2)
1974[d, e]	309 (60.4)	262 (60.8)	284 (100)	855 (69.7)
1996–1997[d]	323 (63.1)	320 (74.3)	198 (69.7)	841 (68.5)
Demographic characteristics of those interviewed in 1996–1997 ($n = 839$)[f]				
Mean age (*SD*)	46.5 (2.0)	48.0 (4.1)	46.9 (1.6)	47.3 (3.0)
Race (%)				
White	62.2	82.5	88.8	76.2
Black	28.5	9.4	6.1	16.0
Hispanic	5.3	5.3	4.6	5.1

Note. From "Remission From Drug Abuse Over a 25-Year Period: Patterns of Remission and Treatment Use," by R. K. Price, N. K. Risk, and E. L. Spitznagel, 2001, *American Journal of Public Health, 91,* p. 1108. Copyright 2001 by the American Public Health Association. Adapted with permission from the American Public Health Association.

[a]DEROS-positive veterans were those whose urine tested positive for opiates, amphetamines, or barbiturates at the Date Eligible for Return from Overseas (DEROS) program. This sample consisted of those who were drawn randomly from the DEROS-positive veteran pool of 1,400 Army-enlisted men who departed from Vietnam in September 1971 and includes 39 who were also included in the general sample.

[b]Selected randomly from the total 13,760 Army-enlisted men who departed at the same time, excluding those who also were selected in the DEROS-positive sample.

[c]Selected from the Selective Service records of men who had never been in service and matched individually to the general sample surveyed in 1974. Because a series of replacements was allowed, the target sample could not be clearly defined.

[d]Percentages in parentheses are based on the target sample total for each sampling category.

[e]By design, career soldiers who had been in the military for longer than 3 years and those living in sparsely populated states were dropped.

[f]The demographic characteristics are based on respondents interviewed in 1996–1997 for each sampling category excluding 2 respondents for whom data were mostly missing (DEROS-positive veterans, $n = 323$; D-negative veterans, $n = 319$; and nonveterans, $n = 197$).

fairs (VA) Medical Center, which had provided oversight for collaboration in the consortium of VA investigators. The investigators attended a hearing at the St. Louis VA Medical Center and submitted a report to the funding agency (the National Institute on Drug Abuse). Fieldwork was stopped until the Washington University IRB determined that the potential iatrogenic effect of the interview (Fisher, 2004) was "possible but not probable."

Implementing Suicide Prevention

The local IRB requested an amendment to the written consent form to include an "imminent harm" clause. It was intended to allow the interviewer to break the pledge of complete confidentiality and consult with a mental health professional to decide the course of action if the respondent indicated that he posed harm to himself or others. The IRB also requested that the study team devise a mechanism that would be likely to prevent another suicide. In response, the investigators implemented a suicide prevention protocol based on the methods used by the local Life Crisis Services. Consultation was obtained from Washington University psychiatrists, psychologists, social workers, and mental health professionals with expertise in treating Vietnam veterans from the Readjustment Counseling Service (the official name for Vet Centers).

The field interviewers had been hired by a subcontract data collection firm, and changes had to be implemented at the end of the annual contract. The field interviewers did not possess clinical qualifications; thus, any changes had to be simple. A "Closing Statement" protocol was created to allow interviewers to assess risk of suicide and to refer the study subject for immediate intervention at a local Vet Center or a local suicide hotline within minutes. In the preexisting assessment, the interviewer had to rely on three questions about suicidality: (a) whether the respondent indicated that he had ever "frequently thought of committing suicide," (b) when those thoughts first started, and (c) when they last occurred. In the Closing Statement, the interviewer was instructed to provide contact information for a local suicide hotline, local Vet Center, and VES hotline if the respondent was considered suicidal. The interviewer initiated consultation if the respondent refused this offer or when several other indicators of suicidality were present (such as emotional instability, previous suicide attempts, excessive alcohol and/or drug use, severe depression, etc.). The suicide hotline personnel (trained clinician) used additional forms to evaluate the intensity of current suicidal thoughts and specific suicidal plans.

Following Up At-Risk Cohort Members

The investigators needed to monitor the implementation of the Closing Statement. By the time the Closing Statement was implemented, about two thirds of the data collection had been completed. For those interviews that had already been completed, we compiled information manually on those who met the criteria for the suicide prevention follow-up. For those interviews yet to be completed, interviewers were instructed to provide the follow-up information as soon as the interview was ended and the first-stage editing was in process. The Closing Statement provided a mechanism to identify those who met the criteria for suicide prevention follow-up. However, it did not resolve questions regarding how long the research team was ethically obliged to follow up with increased-risk study participants, nor how to do such a follow-up. The investigators and study team members began compiling clinical vignettes, based on a risk management perspective (Clark & Fawcett, 1992). The vignettes essentially consisted of a brief summary of risk factor items and the interviewer's subjective observation of suicidality risk. The resulting internal documents yielded the first glimpse of the levels of suicidal risk among this cohort. By the middle of 1997, 39 out of 783 interviewed cases (5.0%) reported active suicidal ideation and were identified as "currently suicidal cases." The proportions of active suicidal cases were correlated with the sampling status set in 1972 and 1974: 7.1% among drug-positive veterans, 4.9% among drug-negative veterans, and 2.0% among comparison nonveterans. Three of the 39 cases were identified as high risk at the time of contact, meaning that an attempt would be likely in the near future (usually within a few months), and thus, staff made immediate referrals.

The investigators also obtained valuable qualitative information about factors associated with suicidality and barriers to psychiatric care. For example, 1 respondent was deemed to be at medium risk on the basis of his well-thought-out suicide plan with intention to use carbon monoxide, previous suicide attempts, recent loss of a daughter, active daily marijuana and alcohol use, and lack of psychiatric care. He had previously refused mental health care, but despite his stated lack of interest, the investigators referred him to a local Vet Center. Another respondent was also categorized as medium risk on the basis of his severe alcohol use, depression, lack of psychiatric care, financial problems, and PTSD. He showed interest in referrals to a VA psychiatrist and substance abuse program, a community mental health center, and Alcoholics Anonymous. The clinical vignettes revealed a significant lack of psychiatric and substance abuse care. Among the 39 veterans at risk of suicide, only 27.8% were receiving some form of psychiatric care.

HOW ONE SUICIDE GAVE A BIRTH TO A NEW STUDY

By the end of 1996, 10.5% (n = 129) of the entire cohort was lost through death: 17.4% of those who were drug positive, 7.4% of those who were drug negative, and 2.8% of the nonveterans (Price, Risk, Murray, et al., 2001). Urine drug status at time of departure from Vietnam was an excellent discriminator for mortality and morbidity in part because this one-shot test indicated the inability of narcotics-using servicemen to abstain from use for only a matter of several days. Nine death certificates confirmed suicide between 1971 and 1996, and all of these were among the veterans (Table 5.2, far right column). All but 1 of the suicides was Caucasian, and all but 1 had enlisted voluntarily. The standard mortality ratios for the most common causes of death among drug-negative veterans fell within the ranges expected for a general population of middle-aged men. Suicide was higher among drug-negative veterans than among drug-positive veterans (2.0 vs. 1.5, respectively). The lifetime nonfatal suicidality rate was 8.6% among nonveterans interviewed in 1996–1997. In comparison, 15.7% of the 641 interviewed veterans reported suicidality (weighted prevalence including frequent thoughts of suicide, plans of suicide, or suicide attempts) sometime in their lives. In our veteran sample, African American veterans were more likely than Cauca-

TABLE 5.2
Nonfatal Suicidality and Completed Suicide by Demographic Characteristics Among Veteran Sample Members

Demographic characteristic	Interviewed in 1996–1997 (*N* = 641)					
	No lifetime nonfatal suicidality (*n* = 517)		Nonfatal suicidality reported[a] (*n* = 124)		Completed suicide 1971–1996 (*n* = 9)	
	n	%	*n*	%	*n*	%
Race						
Caucasian	392	86.3	87	13.8	8	
African American	98	78.4	26	21.7	—	
Other	27	70.1	11	29.9	1	
Enlistment[b]						
Draftee	218	93.1	23	6.9	1	
Volunteered	288	76.3	97	23.7	8	
Drug urinalysis status in1971[c]						
Drug negative	271	85.0	48	15.1	5	
Drug positive	246	76.4	76	23.6	4	

Note. No completed suicide was found among nonveterans. Lifetime nonfatal suicidality among nonveterans was 8.6%. Percentages are weighted to adjust for oversampling of drug-positive veterans. From "Post-Traumatic Stress Disorder, Drug Dependence and Suicidality Among Male Vietnam Veterans With a History of Heavy Drug Use," by R. K. Price, N. K. Risk, A. Haden, C. Lewis, and E. Spitznagel, 2004, *Drug and Alcohol Dependence, 76*(Suppl.1), p. S36. Copyright 2004 by Elsevier. Reprinted with permission.
[a]Includes frequent thoughts of committing suicide, planning suicide, or suicide attempt; lifetime assessment.
[b]Excluding missing cases.
[c]Sampling status based on urinalysis testing at the time of departure from Vietnam.

sian veterans to report suicidality (21.7% vs. 13.8%, respectively). Those who had enlisted voluntarily were more likely than draftees to report suicidality (23.7% vs. 6.9%, respectively), as were those with a drug-positive urinalysis status in 1971 as compared with drug-negative veterans (23.6% vs. 15.1%, respectively; Table 5.2; see also Price, Risk, Haden, Lewis, & Spitznagel, 2004).[2]

Two Factors Uniquely Contributed to the VES Veterans' Increased Risk of Suicidality

Was one suicide over 1 year a random occurrence? On the basis of the estimates mentioned earlier, we would have to have interviewed 4,300 to 4,400 veterans to observe one completed suicide on average within 1 year of the observational period. We observed one with one sixth of this number in the field. Two factors appeared to have particularly contributed to increased

[2]The percentages among veterans were weighted to adjust for oversampling of the drug-positive veterans.

risk of suicidality among veterans in this cohort: high levels of opiate use and combat trauma exposure during their duty in Vietnam. Indeed, further analyses of several outcomes, including suicidality, illicit drug use, health problems and social functioning, by heroin use in Vietnam showed that of 19 indicators, odds ratios were significantly higher for all but two (unemployed 2 or more years or divorced one or more times in the past 10 years before the 1996–1997 survey) among those who reported heroin use while they were stationed in Vietnam, compared with matched nonveterans in the general sample of this cohort (see Table 5.3). Although one might expect that those veterans who used heroin in Vietnam would be at higher risk of using illicit drugs later in life, the odds ratio, in fact, was highest (OR = 9.6, 95% CI = 2.3–40.5) for suicide attempt among all indicators. The odds ratios for veterans who did not report any heroin use in Vietnam were higher for suicide attempt and plan than those for nonveterans, although they were nonsignificant (OR = 3.7, 95% CI = 0.7–17.6, and OR = 3.0, 95% CI = 1.0–9.3, for attempt and plan, respectively).[3] On the basis of these results, it appears that factors other than opiate use also affected increased suicide risk.

PTSD may be such an additional contributing factor. Several years after the 1996 suicide incident, we were able to assess how PTSD and drug abuse contributed to risk of suicidality over the adult life course of our cohort members. We used longitudinal data (although retrospectively assessed) constructed from VES-III to examine the relationships among PTSD, drug dependence, and suicidality over time. A suicidality measure was constructed from questions on attempt, plan, and frequent thoughts of committing suicide, in conjunction with lifetime, recency, and onset information. Psychiatric diagnoses based on the *Diagnostic and Statistical Manual of Mental Disorders* (4th ed., or *DSM–IV*; American Psychiatric Association, 1994) were derived from the information on recency and onset for each symptom of PTSD, major depression, and adult antisocial personality. Retrospective information was available for yearly *DSM–IV* diagnoses of alcohol dependence and dependence on illicit drugs. Using the time-dependent Cox regression analysis applied to 25 years of information over all veterans interviewed, we examined the effects of PTSD and drug dependence, controlling for alcohol dependence, major depression, adult antisocial personality, and demographic characteristics. As expected, the hazard ratio for major depression was the largest at 3.21, but the hazard ratio for drug dependence was the next largest at 2.06. The hazard ratio for PTSD was nonsignificant when an interaction term of PTSD × Time Since 1972 was simultaneously entered, but the inter-

---

[3]The percentages are unweighted in Table 5.3 because heroin use in Vietnam was very colinear with drug-positive status. Here, the purpose was to examine the long-term outcomes if the veterans did use heroin in Vietnam. No attempt is made to generalize the results to the entire sample of the 1971 returnees. No weights exist for nonveterans because they were matched to the general-sample veterans. Odds ratios were not adjusted for sampling status (drug-positive status) because the extreme collinearity caused unstable estimates.

TABLE 5.3
Increased Risk Associated With Heroin Use During Deployment in Vietnam: Comparisons With Nonveterans (n = 839)

	Veterans				
	In-Vietnam heroin users (n = 394)		In-Vietnam heroin nonusers (n = 248)		Nonveterans[a]
Outcome and time frame	%	OR[b]	%	OR[b]	(n = 197; %)
Nonfatal suicidality					
Attempt since 1972	9.9	9.6**	3.2	3.7	1.0
Plan since 1972	12.4	6.8***	5.7	3.0	2.0
Frequent thoughts since 1972	18.8	3.6***	8.5	1.6	5.6
Illicit drug use					
Opiates					
Past 10 years	13.2	6.5***	2.0	1.2	2.0
Past 3 months	4.6	4.8*	0.8	0.9	1.0
Cocaine					
Past 10 years	29.4	4.7***	5.7	1.0	6.6
Past 3 months	10.2	6.9**	2.0	2.5	1.0
Marijuana					
Past 10 years	51.5	6.3***	17.7	1.5	13.7
Past 3 months	27.7	6.2***	9.3	1.9	5.6
Health problems (past year)					
Hepatitis[c]	5.8	4.2*	0.4	0.3	1.5
Diabetes	8.6	2.0	6.5	1.5	4.6
Arthritis	21.3	1.7*	14.1	1.1	13.2
High blood pressure	23.4	1.9**	24.2	1.7*	13.7
Employment					
Fired 1+ times					
First 10 years	7.9	4.4*	2.8	2.2	1.5
Past 10 years	7.9	3.7*	4.4	2.1	2.0
Unemployed 2+ years out of 10 years					
First 10 years	13.5	7.9***	5.2	4.8*	1.5
Past 10 years	7.6	2.4	2.8	1.4	2.5
Marriage (divorced 1+ times)					
First 10 years	30.5	1.7**	26.2	1.3	20.3
Past 10 years	23.6	1.5	16.9	1.0	17.8

Note. [a]Includes veterans and nonveterans followed up and interviewed in 1996–1997. Out of nonveterans who were interviewed in 1996–1997, 12 (6.1%) used heroin during the time period in which their matched veterans were in deployment.
[b]Odds ratios (OR) were adjusted for age and race and are based on nonveteran OR being 1.0.
[c]Includes both viral hepatitis and hepatitis resulting from alcohol use.
*$p < .05$. **$p < .01$. ***$p < .001$.

action term itself was significant (hazard ratio = 1.31, p = .049). Further inspection of the yearly interaction effects indicated that the effect of PTSD on suicidality became significant around 1974. Additional analyses indicated that the potentially causal role of drug dependence on PTSD and suicidality was limited to young adulthood. For later adulthood periods starting in respondents' early 30s (or early 1980s), however, we observed stronger effects of suicidality and PTSD on continuation of drug dependence. This suggests drugs were used to self-medicate symptoms of suicidality and PTSD (Price et al., 2004).

In part on the basis of these findings, a new ongoing "suicide" study (VES-IV) used subsamples of the VES veterans cohort interviewed in 1996–1997 and focused on protective factors mitigating suicide risks as they entered the second half-century of their lives. In this study, we attempt to integrate qualitative measures with traditional epidemiological quantitative measures to best examine interactions between risk and protective factors.

Prospectively Predicting Suicidality

Improving prediction of suicidality was one of the scientific aims of the new study. In proposing the sampling design for the new suicide study, we developed a model that aimed to predict who would be at risk of suicidal ideation several years after the last assessment. Logistic models for suicidal ideation in the past 4 years were created using measures created for the VES-III survey. The models included 21 predictors measuring depression, substance abuse, health problems, PTSD, antisocial personality disorder, and family history, assessed for the period since 1972 or lifetime. The resulting additive scale ranged from 0 to 25 and appeared to be a good discriminating scale of suicidal ideation up to 1996, even though values of some odds ratios were unimpressive (see Table 5.4).[4] The resulting scale and the report of past suicidal ideation were used to identify the higher risk subsample veterans. Those respondents with a score greater than or equal to 17 were considered higher risk. Those veterans with prior suicidal ideation whose score was below 17 (n = 56) were also included in the sample as higher risk cases. In the resulting higher risk subsample, 63 (56.3%) out of 112 veterans had a prior suicidal ideation. A contrasting lower risk subsample was defined as those with a score less than or equal to 4. The lower risk subsample included twice as many veterans as did the higher risk subsample to maximize statistical power. Of the 250 veterans who fell into this lower risk subsample, 246 (98.4%) had no prior suicide ideation. Because the new study would be more labor intensive than the VES-III, the middle group was dropped from further follow-up.

By October 2005, we had completed 350 interviews. The sampling scheme of the higher risk groups versus the lower risk groups generally differentiated suicidal ideation since their VES-III interviews in 1996 and 1997 (see Table 5.5). Since their VES-III interviews, 17 (7.8%) of lower risk re-

[4]An exponentially based model, which is a more logical option mathematically, provided a multiplicative scale with too wide a spread to be considered stable.

TABLE 5.4
Logistic Model Predicting Suicidal Ideation Among Veterans in the Past 4 Years ($n = 641$)

Measures obtained from Vietnam Era Study—III	Odds ratio	p
Depressive symptoms[a]		
Depressed mood	1.88	.173
Lack of interest	1.75	.290
Diminished or increased appetite	0.96	.922
Insomnia or hypersomnia	1.08	.870
Moving slowly or restlessness	0.91	.831
Fatigue or lack of energy	1.12	.797
Feelings of worthlessness or guilt	4.67	<.001
Difficulty in concentrating or confusion	1.25	.615
Thoughts of suicide	Q	—
Substance use		
Drug use[b]	0.90	.825
Alcohol dependence[c]	0.86	.704
Health problems[d]		
Two or more health problems	2.12	.052
Current health is poor	1.77	.221
Current health is worse than last year	1.51	.317
Posttraumatic stress disorder[e]	3.05	.003
Antisocial personality (ASP) syndrome		
Four or more adult ASP symptoms	1.24	.605
Four or more childhood ASP symptoms	1.25	.547
Family history		
Family member depressed	0.96	.919
Family member with alcohol problems	0.84	.639
Family member hospitalized for mental or drug problems	1.46	.353
Family member committed suicide	0.68	.450

Note. Based on the veteran sample only ($n = 641$). Q = the outcome and predictor variables were "quasi-separated" (values of a part of two vectors were identical). Thus, the predictor was excluded from the results because the odds ratio was not estimable. All measures covered the period between 1972 and VES-III interviews in 1996 and 1997, except childhood ASP symptoms. p = the significance level of the beta estimate; *DSM–IV* = *Diagnostic and Statistical Manual of Mental Disorders* (4th ed.; American Psychiatric Association, 1994).
[a]Symptoms included in the diagnostic criteria for lifetime *DSM–IV* major depression.
[b]Use five times or more of illicit drugs (sedative, stimulants, marijuana, opiates, cocaine, PCP, inhalants, or hallucinogens).
[c]*DSM–IV* lifetime dependence criteria.
[d]Self-reported major diagnosed medical illnesses since 1972.
[e]*DSM–IV* lifetime criteria.

spondents and 64 (48.5%) of higher risk respondents reported suicidal ideation. Suicidal ideation in the past month was reported by 15.9% of the higher risk group compared with 0.5% of the lower risk group. The scale has a better specificity than sensitivity, consistent with other reports of high-risk sample follow-up (Beautrais, 2004). Although 17 respondents from the lower risk group had expressed suicidal ideation since their VES-III interviews, the number of those who had attempted suicide since the time of the interview or of those who actively expressed suicidality at the time of their VES-IV (fourth wave) interview was minimal. In brief, the empirically based predic-

TABLE 5.5
Suicidal Ideation and Attempt Outcomes Since Last Interview in 1996–1997 Among Veterans Interviewed in the Fourth Wave of the Vietnam Era Study ($n = 350$)

	Lower risk % (n = 218)		Higher risk % (n = 132)	
Data compiled to date	%	n	%	n
Suicidal ideation since 1996–1997	7.8	17	48.5	64
Suicide attempts since 1996–1997	0.9	2	18.2	24
Active suicidal ideation (past month)	0.5	1	15.9	21

tive scale that we developed was very helpful for allocating clinical resources and providing assistance to those who most needed such help.

BALANCING SCIENCE AND CLINICAL CARE

To address ethical obligations to the study participants, we introduced a number of strategies in the new suicide study. If the study had been conducted in a clinical setting, clinical resources would be readily available. In such controlled environments, psychiatrists and other qualified mental health professionals can implement appropriate assessment and communication techniques (Hendren, 1990). However, because our new study was being conducted in the community for epidemiologic study aims, other assessment and intervention methods were required. The research investigators had to be versed in both epidemiologic assessment and clinical care. One factor that accounted for the successful execution of the study was the on-call availability of psychiatrists for the project. Because only one third of the study sample were considered at a higher risk of suicidality, it was neither necessary nor cost-efficient to staff field interviewers solely on the basis of clinical qualifications. The study's fieldwork instead needed a good mix of seasoned clinical interviewers who could accurately detect level of suicidality among higher risk respondents and lay interviewers who could complete standardized interviews in a cost-efficient fashion with those not requiring a clinical follow-up. Through a series of training sessions, we released some professional interviewers who participated in the earlier VES-III data collection because it was difficult to train them for the clinical aspects of the new study. Instead, we hired master's-level clinicians with training from a local life crisis center.

Identifying Veterans at Imminent Risk of Suicide

The greatest ethical challenge we faced was gauging our ability to identify veterans who were so close to making a suicide attempt that the costs of potential harm would outweigh the benefit of collecting scientific data (Fisher, Pearson, Kim, & Reynolds, 2002). Having experienced one completed suicide, one more encounter with a suicide death in a suicide study would be enough to halt the investigation. From an ethical perspective, preventing potential harm to human subjects must come before the research. Nonetheless, the critical problem was the unpredictable nature of the timing of suicide and suicide attempt. Using a community sample, one estimate of suicide attempt incidence rate is 99.1 per 100,000 per year (or 0.10%; Kuo, Gallo, & Tien, 2001). Although this estimate cannot be directly applied to our study, we estimated that at most, there were only going to be a few participants who would require immediate hospitalization during the time the research team would be in contact with them.

Many attempts at identifying veterans at imminent risk of suicide were made while we were developing the interview protocol. A complicated algorithm was developed to systematically assess the risk levels while carrying out an in-person interview. However, a laptop and computer-assisted interview would have been needed to manage an automated algorithm computation while asking questions. Pilot testing with local veterans who had clinical symptoms of PTSD led us to decide not to use a laptop because the sound of computer keys clicking was simply inappropriate when a veteran began to show emotional distress while discussing his suicidal episode. Interviewers conducting a complicated assessment in the field by themselves was judged infeasible because we wanted to minimize false negatives (see Hallfors et al., 2006, for a similar experience). In the end, we decided that that the interviewer needed to know only two things: One was whether he or she should call 911 to arrange for an ambulance to send the respondent to the hospital (imminent risk) because the danger to the respondent and the study's legal liability were considered to outweigh consideration for the respondent's preferences. The other was whether the interview should proceed, even if an immediate hospitalization is unwarranted. For example, if the interviewer observed a sign of extreme agitation, anger, or a nonimminent but high level of suicidality or heard that a loaded gun was available close by, the interviewer was instructed to use the best clinical judgment or call the central fieldwork office. The imminent risk assessment was reduced to seven questions related to the timing of the suicide plan, details of the plan, and intervention possibility (Figure 5.1). A decision was made to abort the interview if the interviewer checked the imminent risk or high-risk box. A flow chart was provided to accompany the assessment (Figure 5.2). We discovered that once trained on imminent risk assessment, most interviewers did not have to follow the flow chart step by step to figure out what to do. Out of 350 interviews completed to this date, only 1 case required us to follow the step-by-step assessment of this form.

ST-SUP1. SUICIDE RISK ASSESSMENT - IMMEDIATE STOP

ID#

1. TIMING OF SUICIDE PLAN IF ST7a=04 (PLAN TO ATTEMPT < 24 HOURS), R IS AT IMMINENT RISK. **CHECK BOX HERE. →**	**IMMINENT**
2A. TIMING OF SUICIDE PLAN IF ST7a = 03, (ATTEMPT > 24 HOURS & WITHIN A WEEK) **CHECK BOX HERE. →**	
2B. DETAILS OF PLAN GO TO ST5 TO ST7. CHECK BOXES BELOW	

IF ST8a = 01-08. **Method/how well thought out**	**IF ST8b1 OR ST8b2 OR ST8b3 OR ST8b4 =01.** **Has means or method now; or used in past**	**IF ST9a = 01-03.** **Location known or planned**	**IF ST10=00.** **Intervention not possible** **If 2 or more boxes checked. →**

2C. IF BOXES ARE CHECKED FOR BOTH 2A AND 2B, R IS AT HIGH RISK.	**HIGH**
3. ARE THERE OTHER INDICATIONS OF HIGH RISK SUCH AS FLORID EXPRESSION OF ANGER WITH ACUTE DEPRESSION, HOMICIDAL IDEATION, REPEATED REFERENCE TO SUICIDE WITH NO TIME FRAMEWORK? **CHECK BOX HERE. →**	HIGH RISK

INTERVIEWER: IF A BOX FOR IMMINENT RISK OR HIGH RISK IS CHECKED, STOP THE INTERVIEW AND GO TO SECTION RT.

Figure 5.1. Suicide Risk Assessment Form to determine whether the interview must be aborted to move to an intervention.

Building Clinical Flexibility Into the Structured Instrument

Most veterans answered questions about suicide openly (although initially reluctantly) in the VES-III survey. Nonetheless, because of the fluid and uncertain timing of these disclosures, we decided to construct an instrument for the current study that has built-in flexibility to deviate from the standard progression and ask pertinent questions when needed to obtain indication of suicidality. For example, because suicidality questions are so sensitive, they should not be asked right at the start of the interview. However, if the respondent reports past or present suicidal ideation in a beginning life chart section (where we obtain year-to-year landmark events to help the respondent reconstruct time sequences of past events), the interviewer can

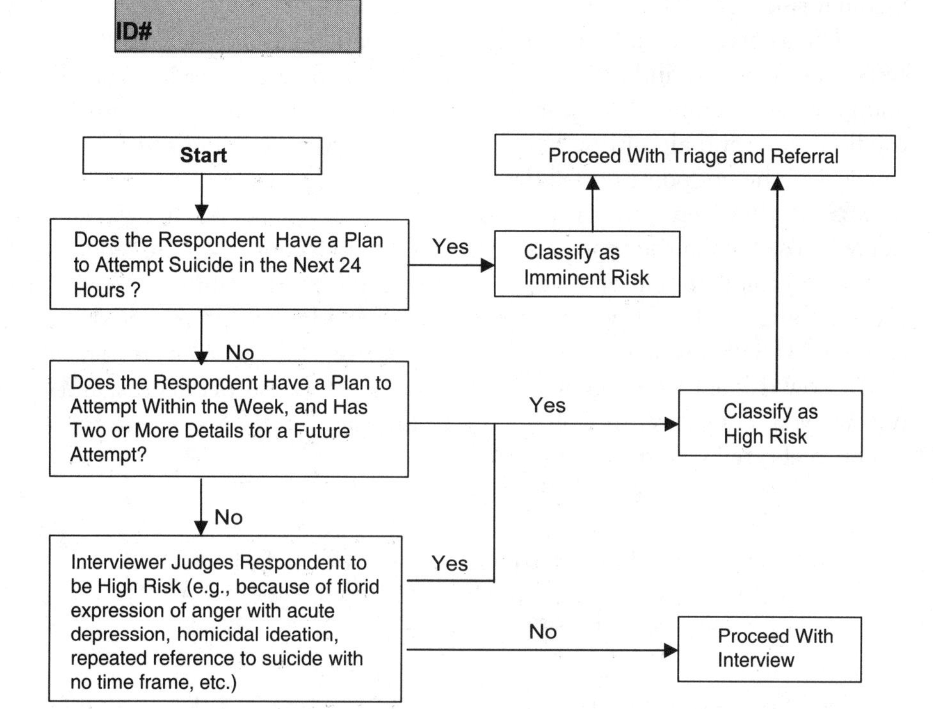
SR-SUP2. RISK ASSESSMENT FORM - FLOW CHART
FOR MEDIUM OR LOWER RISK
ID#
Start
Proceed With Triage and Referral
Does the Respondent Have a Plan to Attempt Suicide in the Next 24 Hours ?
Yes
Classify as Imminent Risk
No
Does the Respondent Have a Plan to Attempt Within the Week, and Has Two or More Details for a Future Attempt?
Yes
Classify as High Risk
No
Interviewer Judges Respondent to be High Risk (e.g., because of florid expression of anger with acute depression, homicidal ideation, repeated reference to suicide with no time frame, etc.)
Yes
No
Proceed With Interview

Figure 5.2. The flow chart to direct interviewers in using the Suicide Risk Assessment Form.

skip to the suicidality assessment section to obtain the maximum amount of information and proceed to assess the respondent for imminent or high risk using the using the suicide risk assessment form (Figure 5.1). If the respondent is judged not to be at imminent or high risk, the interviewer would then resume structured assessments.

Determining the Appropriate Intervention–Prevention Path

Data from the clinical follow-up of cohort members interviewed in the earlier VES-III indicated on one hand that a number of higher risk sample members would have a level of suicidal ideation. On the other hand, more than half were expected to be psychiatrically healthy, albeit with some expected changes in status. To determine each respondent's risk level, another risk assessment form was devised for respondents with levels of suicide risk lower than imminent or high. A flow chart was provided to direct hand-scoring of each respondent's risk score, which was modeled on our suicidality prediction scale used to develop the sampling scheme. This postinterview risk assessment was developed primarily for the interviewer to call back and recommend or offer other assistance to those who meet the criteria of the medium risk.

The intervention and referral flow chart were used to guide an intricate system of decisions and actions. The completion of the interview was the endpoint for veterans who fell into the low- or no-risk categories defined in the flow chart and algorithm. For those who fell into medium or higher risk categories, the endpoint varied depending on the individual condition. As in VES-III, they went into the pool for clinical follow-up. The case was considered closed when the triage was completed or risk concerns were reduced. Out of 350 completed interviews, 61 were logged onto the clinical follow-up list. Of them, 1 (1.6%) was considered at high risk of a future suicide attempt, 42 (68.9%) were considered at medium risk, 13 (21.3%) were considered at low risk but were followed up because of interviewer concerns, and 4 (6.6%) were considered miscellaneous follow-ups. To date, one interview has been aborted (see the next section).

NEED TO DEVELOP GUIDELINES FOR EPIDEMIOLOGIC RESEARCH INVOLVING HUMAN SUBJECTS AT INCREASED RISK OF SUICIDE

Suicide is undoubtedly a sensitive topic, and studies of suicide and suicidality touch on many ethical and legal aspects of research (Maris, Berman, & Silverman, 2000). The existing literature on ethical and legal responsibilities in relation to potential suicide attempts, however, tends to focus on clinical practice. The American Psychiatric Association's guidelines for assessment and treatment of suicidal patients (Steering Committee on Practice Guidelines, 2003) outline the conduct of a thorough psychiatric evaluation for suicidal behavior by psychiatrists. Simon (2004) has put forth hospital admission and discharge suicide risk assessments for use in evaluating psychiatric patients' risk of self-harm. Although the information is useful, such guidelines are not easy to implement in an epidemiologic study setting. In closing, we reflect on the epidemiologic research practice that we implemented to help guide the development of future research guidelines for non-intervention epidemiologic studies.

Institutional Barriers: What Happens When a Study Is Defined as a Suicide Study?

The VES-IV suicide study is considerably different from the earlier VES-III because we wanted to assess situation-specific protective factors that might mitigate contemporaneous suicide risk. Nonetheless, the aims of this study remain essentially those of an observational study. Although in-depth questions were asked about suicidal episodes, they are not much different from "why questions" typical of journalistic inquiries. Moreover, we reinterviewed respondents who had already participated several years earlier. Once the study was defined as a suicide study, however, perceptions of the study changed in many ways. For example, our IRB recommended that we abort one case on the basis of the respondent's agitated state at the contact phase, even though he had previously been interviewed in VES-III several years go. In another case, a national network media outlet approached the study to interview some of our respondents for a report of long-term mental heath consequences of the Vietnam War. Although the jurisdiction of the VA IRB was limited because respondents were ascertained from their respective communities, it denied our request for the media interviews, overriding our local IRB's approval.

Perhaps the most damaging institutional barrier was the definition of a serious adverse event (SAE). Federal regulations for the protection of human subjects (Protection of Human Subjects, 2005) require researchers to immediately report SAEs to the local institutional IRB. Although the term *unanticipated problems* used in Protection of Human Subjects (2005) is not explicitly defined, it commonly refers to death, life-threatening conditions, or unanticipated events. However, our local IRB SAE reporting criteria are more expansive and include "hospitalization unless preplanned." One of the study's clinical protocols, however, was to send the respondent to the hospital if he was deemed to be at imminent or high risk, thus qualifying as an unplanned hospitalization meeting a SAE criterion, even though the intent was to protect the respondent. The main reason for this irony lies in the fact that the paradigmatic model of SAE used by our IRB is a drug clinical trial, which is ill suited for a natural history study with a clinical intervention component. For a social and behavioral nonintervention study of a high-risk sample, adverse events, including even death, occur as part of a natural event. Definitions of adverse events require a more flexible approach, including different criteria for social and behavioral sciences.

How Can Epidemiologic Studies Increase the Knowledge on Suicide and Suicidality?

Although suicide and suicide attempts are rare, they should be considered naturally occurring events, like any other health problem. Suicide and suicidality should not be treated any differently than other serious mental health problems. For both ethical and scientific reasons, large-scale epidemiologic studies conducted with funding from the federal government should implement sound protocols that assess suicidality and provide systematic follow-up of suicidal respondents. For example, the National Survey of Drug Use and Health conducted annually by the Substance Abuse and Mental Health Services Administration (e.g., Substance Abuse and Mental Health Services Administration, 2003) includes approximately 70,000 individuals ages 12 and older. According to our conservative estimates using the National Longitudinal Alcohol Epidemiologic Survey in the U.S. general population, suicide attempt and suicidal ideation rates for the past year before the interview (1992) were 0.32% and 1.38%, respectively.[5] Thus, during the National Survey of Drug Use and Health fieldwork, more than 150 respondents would attempt suicide over 1 year, and more than 950 would express their suicidality to interviewers. If clear guidelines and a mandate for follow-up assessments of those individuals were in place, the resulting data would provide rich sources of information that are not biased by sampling specifics. Such efforts, however, must also be combined with a careful clinical follow-up protocol to protect both the respondents and the projects.

CONCLUSION

Using a longitudinal study of a cohort of Vietnam veterans with a history of high levels of opiate use and combat experience while stationed in Vietnam, we documented how one completed suicide gave study investigators an opportunity to learn about the suicide risk in this population and factors that contributed to the increased risk of suicide and to develop systematic assessments of suicidality and protective factors that mitigate suicidal risk in face of life adversity. Nonintervention studies of suicide and suicidality lack clear human subjects protection models such as those adopted in clinical trials. The need exists to develop research guidelines for epidemiologic research to help fill the gaps in the knowledge of suicide research. Furthermore, ethical guidelines need to be developed to help assist those study subjects at increased risk of suicide, whether the study involves investigation of suicide and suicidality. The National Institute of Mental Health provides comprehensive guidelines for intervention research of suicidality, including intervention designs, monitoring, risk management, and informed consent (Pearson, Stanley, King, & Fisher, 2001). Similar scientific, ethical, and legal guidelines should be developed for nonintervention studies in which suicide and nonfatal suicidality may be observed with reasonably predictable probabilities.

REFERENCES

American Psychiatric Association. (1994). *Diagnostic and statistical manual of mental disorders* (4th ed.). Washington, DC: Author.

[5]Unpublished data. The estimates are somewhat conservative because the skip patterns of the National Longitudinal Alcohol Epidemiologic Survey questionnaire eliminates those who have attempted suicide or had suicidality in the past year but did not endorse the standard depression "gateway" question of feeling blue or depressed for a 2-week interval. Timing is based on the entire depressive episode.

Beckman, J., Moore, S., Feldman, M., Hertzberg, M., Kirby, A., & Fairbank, J. (1998). Health status, somatization, and severity of posttraumatic stress disorder in Vietnam combat veterans with posttraumatic stress disorder. *American Journal of Psychiatry, 155*, 1565–1569.

Beautrais, A. L. (2004). Further suicidal behavior among medically serious suicide attempters. *Suicide and Life-Threatening Behavior, 34*, 1–11.

Bullman, T., & Kang, H. (1995). A study of suicide among Vietnam veterans. *Federal Practitioner, 12*, 9–13.

Bullman, T., & Kang, H. (1996). The risk of suicide among wounded Vietnam veterans. *American Journal of Public Health, 86*, 662–667.

Centers for Disease Control. (1987, February 13). Postservice mortality among Vietnam veterans. *JAMA, 257*, 790–795.

Centers for Disease Control & Prevention. (1998). *National Mortality Followback Survey—Provisional data 1993*. Hyattsville, MD: National Center for Health Statistics.

Centers for Disease Control & Prevention. (2008). *WISQARS injury mortality report*. Office of Statistics and Programming, National Center for Injury Prevention and Control. Retrieved September, 25, 2008, from http://webapp.cdc.gov/sasweb/ncipc/mortrate10_sy.html

Clark, D., & Fawcett, J. (1992). Review of empirical risk factors for evaluation of the suicidal patient. In B. Bongar (Ed.), *Suicide: Guidelines for assessment, management and treatment* (pp. 16–48). New York: Oxford University Press.

Crane, P., Barnard, D., Horsley, K., & Adena, M. (1997). *Mortality of Vietnam veterans: The Veteran cohort study. A report of the 1996 retrospective cohort study of Australian Vietnam veterans*. Canberra, Australian Capital Territory, Australia: Department of Veterans' Affairs.

Drescher, K., Rosen, C., Burling, T., & Foy, D. (2003). Causes of death among male veterans who received residential treatment for PTSD. *Journal of Traumatic Stress, 16*, 535–543.

Engdahl, B., Dikel, T., Eberly, R., & Blank, A. J. (1998). Comorbidity and course of psychiatric disorders in a community sample of former prisoners of war. *American Journal of Psychiatry, 155*, 1740–1745.

Farberow, N., Kang, H., & Bullman, T. (1990). Combat experience and postservice psychosocial status as predictors of suicide in Vietnam veterans. *Journal of Nervous and Mental Disease, 178*, 32–37.

Fisher, C. (2004). Ethics in drug abuse and related HIV risk research. *Applied Developmental Science, 8*, 91–103.

Fisher, C., Pearson, J., Kim, S., & Reynolds, C. (2002). Ethical issues including suicidal individuals in clinical research. *IRB: Ethics & Human Research, 24*(5), 1–6.

Fontana, A., & Rosenheck, R. (1995). Attempted suicide among Vietnam veterans: A model of etiology in a community sample. *American Journal of Psychiatry, 152*, 102–109.

Fu, Q., Heath, A., Bucholz, K., Nelson, E., Glowinski, A., Goldberg, J., et al. (2002). A twin study of genetic and environmental influences on suicidality in men. *Psychological Medicine, 32,* 11–24.

Grant, B., & Hasin, D. (1999). Suicidal ideation among the United States drinking population: Results from the National Longitudinal Alcohol Epidemiologic Survey. *Journal of Studies of Alcohol, 60,* 422–429.

Grant, B., Peterson, A., Dawson, D., & Chou, P. (1994). *Source and accuracy statement for the National Longitudinal Alcohol Epidemiologic Survey.* Rockville, MD: National Institute on Alcohol Abuse & Alcoholism.

Hallfors, D., Brodish, P., Khatapoush, S., Sanchez, V., Cho, H., & Steckler, A. (2006). Feasibility of screening adolescents for suicide risk in "real-world" high school settings. *American Journal of Public Health, 96,* 282–287.

Hearst, N., Newman, T., & Hulley, S. (1986, March 6). Delayed effects of the military draft on mortality: A randomized natural experiment. *New England Journal of Medicine, 314,* 620–624.

Hendren, R. (1990). Assessment and interviewing strategies for suicidal patients over the life cycle. In S. K. D. Blumenthal (Ed.), *Suicide over the life cycle* (pp. 235–252). Washington, DC: American Psychiatric Press.

Kramer, T. L., Lindy, J. D., Green, B. L., Grace, M. C., & Leonard, A. C. (1994). The comorbidity of post-traumatic stress disorder and suicidality in Vietnam veterans. *Suicide and Life-Threatening Behavior, 24,* 58–67.

Kuo, W., Gallo, J., & Tien, A. (2001). Incidence of suicide ideation and attempts in adults: The 13-year follow-up of a community sample in Baltimore, Maryland. *Psychological Medicine, 31,* 1181–1191.

Mann, J. J., Apter, A., Bertolote, J., Beautrais, A., Currier, D., Haas, A., et al. (2005, October 26). Suicide prevention strategies. A systematic review. *JAMA, 294,* 2064–2074.

Maris, R. (1993). The evolution of suicidology. In A. Leenaars (Ed.), *Suicidology: Essays in honor of Edwin Schneidman* (pp. 3–21). Northvale, NJ: Jason Aronson.

Maris, R., Berman, A., & Silverman, M (2000). Ethical, religious, and philosophical issues in suicide. In R. Maris, A. Berman, & M. Silverman (Eds.), *Comprehensive textbook of suicidology* (pp. 456–479). New York: Guilford Press.

Moller-Leimkuhler, A. (2003). The gender gap in suicide and premature death or: Why are men so vulnerable? *European Archives of Psychiatry and Clinical Neuroscience, 253,* 1–8.

Murphy, G. (1992). *Suicide in alcoholism.* New York: Oxford University Press.

O'Conner, R., & Sheehy, N. (2000). *Understanding suicidal behavior.* Leicester, England: BPS Books.

Office of the Surgeon Multi-National Force–Iraq, Office of the Command Surgeon, and Office of the Surgeon General United States Army Medical Command. (2008). *Mental Health Advisory Team (MHAT) V: Operation Iraqi Freedom 06-08: Iraq, Operation Enduring Freedom 8: Afghanistan.* Retrieved September 25, 2008, from http://www.armymedicine.army.mil/reports/mhat/mhat_v/mhat-v.cfm

Pearson, J., Stanley, B., King, C., & Fisher, C. (2001). *Issues to consider in intervention research with persons at high risk for suicidality*. Bethesda, MD: National Institute of Mental Health. Retrieved July 7, 2008, from http://www.nimh.nih.gov/health/topics/suicide-prevention/issues-to-consider-in-intervention-research-with-persons-at-high-risk-for-suicidality.shtml

Pokorny, A. (1983). Prediction of suicide in psychiatric patients: Report of a prospective study. *Archives of General Psychiatry, 40*, 249–257.

Pollock, D., Rhodes, P., Boyle, C., Decoufle, P., & McGee, D. (1990). Estimating the number of suicides among Vietnam veterans. *American Journal of Psychiatry, 147*, 772–776.

Price, R. K., Ledgerwood, D., Risk, N. K., Virgo, K., Spitznagel, E., & Lewis, C. (2006). *Risk of completed and attempted suicide in middle-aged Vietnam-Era veterans: Results from two national samples*. Unpublished manuscript.

Price, R. K., Risk, N. K., Haden, A., Lewis, C., & Spitznagel, E. (2004). Post-traumatic stress disorder, drug dependence and suicidal ideation among male Vietnam veterans with a history of heavy drug use. *Drug and Alcohol Dependence, 76*(Suppl. 1), S31–S43.

Price, R. K., Risk, N. K., Murray, K., Virgo, K., Spitznagel, E., & Robins, L. (2001). Twenty-five year mortality of U.S. servicemen deployed in Vietnam: Predictive utility of early drug use. *Drug and Alcohol Dependence, 64*, 318.

Price, R. K., Risk, N. K., & Spitznagel, E. L. (2001). Remission from illicit drug use over a 25-year period. Patterns of remission and treatment use. *American Journal of Public Health, 91*, 1107–1113.

Protection of Human Subjects, 45 C.F.R. § 46 (2005).

Riggs, J., McGraw, R., & Keefover, R. (1996). Suicide in the United States, 1951-1988: Constant age-period-cohort rates in 40- to 44-year-old men. *Comprehensive Psychiatry, 37*, 222–225.

Robins, L. (1974). *The Vietnam drug user returns* (SAO Monograph, Series A, No. 2). Washington, DC: U.S. Government Printing Office.

Robins, L., & Helzer, J. (1975). Drug use among Vietnam veterans—Three years later. *Medical World News Psychiatry, 16*, 44–49.

Simon, R. (2004). *Assessing and managing suicide risk guidelines for clinically based risk management*. Washington, DC: American Psychiatric Publishing.

Soubrier, J.-P. (1993). Definitions of suicide. In A. Leenaars (Ed.), *Suicidology: Essays in honor of Edwin Schneidman* (pp. 35–41). Northvale, NJ: Jason Aronson.

Steering Committee on Practice Guidelines. (2003). Practice guidelines for the assessment and treatment of patients with suicidal behaviors. *American Journal of Psychiatry 160*(11, Suppl.), 1–60.

Substance Abuse & Mental Health Services Administration. (2003). *Results from the 2002 National Survey on Drug Use and Health: National findings* (DHHS Pub. No. SMA 03-3836). Rockville, MD: Substance Abuse & Mental Health Services Administration, Office of Applied Studies.

The Struggle for Iraq: Iraq Military Suicides at 21. (2004, January 15). *The New York Times*. Retrieved September 25, 2008, from http://query.nytimes.com/gst/fullpage.html?sec=health&res=990DE7DF1130F936A25752C0A9629C8B63

Thomas, T., Kang, H., & Dalager, N. (1991). Mortality among women Vietnam veterans, 1973–1987. *American Journal of Epidemiology, 134*, 973–980.

Thompson, R., Katz, H., Kane, V., & Sayers, S. (2000). Cause of death in veterans receiving general medical and mental health care. *Journal of Nervous and Mental Disease, 190*, 789–792.

Vaillant, G., & Blumenthal, S. (1990). Introduction—Suicide over the life cycle: Risk factors and life-span development. In S. Blumenthal & D. Kupfer (Eds.), *Suicide over the life cycle* (pp. 1–14). Washington, DC: American Psychiatric Press.

van Heeringen, K. (2003). The neurobiology of suicide and suicidality. *Canadian Journal of Psychiatry, 48*, 292–300.

Waern, M., Rubinowitz, E., & Wilhelmson, K. (2003). Predictors of suicide in the old elderly. *Gerontology, 49*, 328–334.

Watanabe, K., & Kang, H. (1995). Military service in Vietnam and the risk of death from trauma and selected cancers. *Annals of Epidemiology, 5*, 407–412.

Windle, M. (2004). Characteristics of alcoholics who attempted suicide: Co-occurring disorders and personality differences with a sample of male Vietnam era veterans. *Journal of Studies on Alcohol, 55*, 571–577.

6

USING PUBLIC DATA: ILLUSTRATIONS FROM DOMESTIC VIOLENCE RESEARCH

CATHERINE CERULLI AND CHRISTOPHER D. THOMAS

Researchers may be overwhelmed by the complex web of federal and state statutes that mandate human subjects protection in data collection, storage, and reporting. Research protocols must be in compliance with the law, and those working with vulnerable populations may have subjects who are protected by additional statutory mandates, such as children, prisoners, and those who are mentally ill. In addition, studies that explore violence and other high-risk behaviors may have complex protocols regarding their methodology's legality. This chapter provides examples of domestic violence studies for which the law and science intersect to illustrate how to use statutes to access data and how research can inform policy. We demonstrate how laws can assist researchers in accessing data and describe how researchers and attorneys can collaborate to conduct sound empirical research to inform public policy.

WHY RESEARCHERS NEED TO UNDERSTAND LAW AND LAWYERS NEED TO UNDERSTAND RESEARCH

Case Scenario

A Hispanic man physically and sexually abused his wife for years. He was the father of the victim's four children, who often witnessed the vio-

> lence. The victim did not speak or read English. On one particular occasion, her husband assaulted her in front of their four children, pulling down a china cabinet on top of her, causing serious physical injury. Her medical records indicated brain damage as a result of prior head trauma. The police charged the defendant with Assault Third, a misdemeanor (N.Y.P.L. § 120). The prosecutor wanted to amend the information before the court to include the charge Endangering the Welfare of a Child (N.Y.P.L. § 260.10). In 1996, New York State case law and statutes did not prohibit a parent from assaulting another parent in the presence of children, nor from stabbing a parent, despite years of reports in the medical, psychological, and social scientific literature reporting that witnessing violence harms children. Four years later, on different facts, the highest court in New York, the Court of Appeals, issued a ruling stating that under certain circumstances, abusing one's partner in front of the children can be construed as endangerment (*People v. Johnson*, 2000). As of January 2008, the legislature has not codified that case by statute.

In this case, the prosecutor attempted to amend the charges before the court and used medical, psychological, psychiatric, and social scientific research articles in drafting the Memorandum of Law. Yet, as an attorney she did not have the training necessary to interpret the research, for example, she did not fully understand such terms as *random sample* and *statistically significant*. Barnard and Greenspan (2003) argued in the *Journal of Legal Education* that law students need more skills in conducting empirical research. Equally as important, health researchers—especially those conducting research on high-risk populations—should become well acquainted with relevant legal precepts that may affect the conduct of their research. Researchers conduct studies within sociolegal environments that regulate their conduct, their subjects' informed consents, and even the very variables they are studying. For example, one cannot study homicide and access to weapons without considering both the effects and the intersection of state and federal gun control laws. Moreover, even though research is frequently conducted for the purpose of informing or changing social policy, researchers and lawyers generally know little about one another's disciplines. This chapter illustrates how researchers can use the law to gain access to untapped sources of data on sensitive topics with high-risk populations, focusing particularly on domestic violence.

THE INTERSECTION OF RESEARCH AND LAW IN INVESTIGATING DOMESTIC VIOLENCE: THE ARREST EXPERIMENT

When researchers began studying domestic violence in the late 1970s, little was known about the causes of domestic violence, nor its frequency and severity. As a result, many myths were promulgated that were unsupported by empirical research: "The children didn't see the abuse, so it won't hurt them," "A victim is in more danger if they leave," and "Men receive lenient sentences when they kill their partners." For more than 2 decades, social scientists have been examining these issues to provide more informed answers. However, it is often difficult to translate new evidence-based information into policy; at other times, merely one single empirical study is used as the basis for passing law, long before the generalizability of the findings is known (Sherman & Berk, 1984).

For example, to assess whether arrest reduced recidivism, Sherman et al. (1984) conducted the first study to assess how different police responses to domestic violence (mediation, separation, and arrest) affected perpetrators' recidivism rates. The findings from their first study showed that perpetrators who were arrested did not recidivate at the same rate as those who were not (Sherman & Berk, 1984). This study made headlines (Fessenden, 1989; Goodman, 1983). Legislators, anxious to do something to protect their constituents, passed laws either mandating arrest or suggesting arrest as the preferred response. However, a few years later duplication studies showed mixed reviews. A second study found that arrest after a call for service to a home was only effective against married and/or employed perpetrators (Maxwell, Garner, & Fagan, 2001; Sherman, 1992). In fact, for unemployed perpetrators, there was an increase in recidivism. Years later, with multiple replications, results yielded a more complex picture in which rates of recidivism were found to be significantly influenced by the perpetrator's stake in conformity (Sherman, 1992). A more recent study that combined data from six studies has now reported that arrest is successful as a deterrent to future violence only under certain circumstances (Maxwell et al., 2001). However, in 1994, New York State was the last state in the country to pass some form of either mandatory or permissive arrest for domestic violence cases. This history of mandatory arrest illustrates how legal advocates and policymakers need to better understand empirical research, and researchers need to better appreciate the many ways in which science is used (and misused) to inform law.

Despite the progress that has been made toward understanding the effects of mandatory arrest, there are still many unanswered questions surrounding domestic violence, and more research is needed to explore both the causes and the consequences of intimate partner violence. Federal and state governments are currently sponsoring considerable research under the Violence Against Women Act of 2000, reenacted in December 2005. These federally funded projects sometimes require the study data to be archived, depending on the budget available. Many researchers choose the Inter-university Consortium for Political and Social Research (ICPSR) to archive their data. This data archive permits other researchers to explore the datasets, run different analyses, and perhaps answer different questions. The federal statutes are not simply important for what happens to collected data, but for study methodology and access to data. The ICPSR currently houses many data sets available for researchers' use on myriad issues including homicide, crime, and violence.

Federal Statutes

Archived Data

In a study exploring gender differences in sentencing (Cerulli, 2004), all secondary data were either publicly archived or available through simple institutional review board (IRB) approval processes. This study assessed how the courts adjudicated a sample of Ohio homicide cases from charging to sentencing stages to ascertain whether there was a difference between intimate homicides and otherwise comparable homicides committed in nonintimate relationships. The study was grounded in Black's (1976) *The Behavior of Law*, exploring the amount of law applied (arrest, prosecution, indictment, and sentencing) and the victim–offender relationship. Although Black's discussion focused on statutes and databases for the homicide study, the research methodology is generalizable to research projects studying many social problems, including suicide and child abuse.

The Federal Bureau of Investigation (FBI) maintains an archive called the Supplementary Homicide Reports (SHRs). We drew the homicide sample from the 1996 Ohio SHRs. Although there are some difficulties in using the SHRs (discussed in Cerulli, 2004), the benefits of such analyses far outweighed the disadvantages (Traugott, 1990) for this particular study because the SHRs provide rich detail regarding victim–offender relationships for homicide cases.

The FBI began collecting the SHRs in 1961 (Riedel, 1990). In cases of homicide, law enforcement officials complete the report, in conjunction with the Uniform Crime Reports (see Riedel, 1990, and Biderman & Lynch, 1991, for detailed discussions of the Uniform Crime Reports, including their history and evaluation reports). The SHRs include the circumstances (location, motive, method), victim and offender sociodemographic information, and the relationship between the parties (Maxfield, 1989). Since 1961, the FBI has revised the form several times to expand the circumstances of the murders and the victim–offender relationship categories (Maxfield, 1989). The SHRs are available on the Internet via the National Archive of Criminal Justice Data, sponsored by the Bureau of Justice Statistics, United States Department of Justice, and operated by the ICPSR (http://www.icpsr.umich.edu/).

Using the Federal Freedom of Information Statute to Access Data

Although researchers may choose to access archived data, they can also seek to collect data via federal public access statutes under the federal Freedom of Information Act (FOIA; 1966). This federal statute dictates that a federal employee must respond to a researcher's request within 20 working days. However, the agency may request an extension of time to respond to the inquiry. The extension must set forth the reason for the agency's needing more time to answer whether it has and can provide the documents. Each federal agency promulgates its own guidelines for answering such inquiries. The FOIA places the burden of the response on the government to either provide the information or demonstrate that the records requested are exempt under one of nine exempt categories (national security, personnel rules, federally mandated statutory exceptions, trade secrets, agency memoranda and policy discussions, personal privacy, ongoing law enforcement investigations, banks, and oil and gas wells) or three exclusions for law enforcement agencies (undercover operations, FBI informants, and counterintelligence or terrorism exceptions; Wright & Carr, 2001, p. 14:5). Each agency has a designated employee who acts as the FOIA liaison, and the federal agencies' Web sites identify these individuals. There is a special section of the statute that addresses costs associated with using the FOIA. The act specifically states that the disclosing agency may charge duplication fees for requests from educational entities for research (Wright & Carr, 2001, p. 14:4). The person filing the request may also file a companion fee waiver (Wright & Carr, 2001, p. 14:4).

State Statutes

Using State Freedom of Information Statute to Access Data

In addition to using archived publicly available FBI SHRs, the intimate homicide study also relied on the Ohio Availability of Public Records for Inspection and Copying (O.R.C. § 149.43), a state statute permitting access to court, legal, and medical information, in particular.[1] This statute provides access to documentation in the courts, police departments, and prosecutors' offices, including court docket sheets. Some of this information is also available via the Internet.

Using State-Archived Data

Just as many federally funded projects archive their data on the ICPSR Web site, state agencies now use the Internet to provide access to their publicly available data. This public access reduces the burden on employees to search for, duplicate, and process information subject to state freedom of information requests.

[1]"(A)(1) 'Public record' means any record that is kept by any public office, including, but not limited to, state, county, city, village, township, and school district units, except that public record does not mean any of the following: [omissions noted]. (B) All public records shall be promptly prepared and made available for inspection to any person at all reasonable times during regular business hours. Upon request, a person responsible for public records shall make copies available at cost, within a reasonable period of time. In order to facilitate broader access to public records, governmental units shall maintain public records in a manner that they can be made available for inspection in accordance with this division."

In Ohio, many of the courts maintain Web sites that house electronically scanned records of court proceedings. For the intimate homicide study, the electronically stored docket sheets provided a great deal of information for coding and entry into a database. The court record provides the amount of bail, a variable of potential interest indicating whether female or male intimate homicide offenders are assigned higher bail figures. The court record also notes whether there was a waiver of indictment, indicating whether a defendant chose not to be indicted and took a plea bargain. The document also records whether and when there is a plea and to what charges. For the intimate homicide study, these are critical time periods captured in the analysis. The court record also indicates whether the court accepted the plea and whether there was a request for a presentence report. In some states, this presentence report may be available for review. The court record provides the term of the sentence and a release date, if known.

In the intimate homicide study, one defendant's attorney motioned the court for a judicial release. If the researcher had only reviewed the term of the sentence, important information would have been missed. Although the defendant was sentenced harshly, 5 to 25 indeterminate years, in fact, within 1 year someone appealed for judicial release on the defendant's behalf. The availability of this information via the Internet greatly expedited much of the fieldwork of the Ohio intimate homicide study. There were fewer demands placed on agencies for copying and mailing documents, and the researcher had reduced travel and lodging expenses.

Using State Health Laws

In addition to reliance on the Availability of Public Records for Inspection and Copying (O.R.C. § 149.43) statute, the intimate homicide study also relied on a statute governing the release of coroner's records (O.R.C. §§ 313.09 and 313.10). This statute provides for the availability of records from the coroner's office that are public record and available pursuant to a written request. The Health Insurance Portability and Accountability Act of 1996 (HIPAA), discussed in chapter 2, has significantly limited access to medical information. However, the particular state statute governing the coroner's reports provides access to decedents' records because HIPAA governs only live patients. The primary investigator provided the university's IRB with a copy of the statute to assist the board in making its decision. An informed, empowered IRB board is more likely to rule in favor of the research protocol if they understand the statutorily provided access to the data. Additionally, some states' health statutes provide exceptions, allowing disclosures for research purposes.

The primary investigator of the intimate homicide study provided each county coroner a copy of the statute, an SPSS grid with the victims' names identified by a cross-check of the SHR, and secondary newspaper analysis. The grid contained blank cells when victims' names were unknown. The coroners actually completed the grids using their own database searches. Although the statute requires public access to the coroner's records, each county responded to the requests differently. Although some provided full reports, others provided one-page summary documents. Some counties automatically run toxicology reports on the victims' blood, but other counties do not. The reports were unique to the circumstances of each county.

Statutory Limitations

When researchers write the methodology section of a grant, they must consider the time frame within which the sample will be drawn. If the cases of interest are still pending, access may be denied. Similar to the FOIA, some states have limitations and exemptions to their public information statutes. In Ohio, the sample was drawn from 1996 homicides to ensure the cases were closed and not under either investigation or prosecution. Likewise, certain agencies such as the courts do not have the staff and resources to duplicate large case files for public dissemination. In these instances, New York State law delineates when and how one can access public records by "inspection" (Wright & Carr, 2001, p. 15:10; N.Y. Judiciary Law § 225-b). In New York State, the Uniform Justice Court Act (§ 2019-a) provides how and when the court clerk must provide public access to court records: "The records and dockets of the court except as otherwise provided by law shall be at reasonable times open for inspection to the public" (Wright & Carr, 2001, p. 15:10).

Although the intimate homicide study was a retrospective document review, it is also possible to conduct a study in courthouse settings for both recruiting subjects and collecting data via court-based files (Cerulli & Tomkins, 2000). In some states, one can recruit at courthouses because they are public buildings. Even if the court is closed to the public, there may be a statutory way to access the data. For instance, in New York State Family Court, a statute exists that permits the Chief Judge of Family Court to open court records under certain circumstances (N.Y. C.L.S. Family Court Act § 166, 1998).

Statutes as Variables

In addition to using statutes to gain access to data, researchers may want to consider whether the various statutes themselves could be important variables in the study. In the intimate homicide study described earlier, the homicide statute was used to capture the seriousness of the offense at the four main stages of discretion: arrest, indictment, conviction, and sentence. The discretionary decision makers (police, prosecutors, judges, and juries) apply the homicide statutes horizontally across the stages and the seriousness of the charge may be different across space and time.

The Bureau of Justice diagram in Figure 6.1 demonstrates the many stages of discretion in adjudicating a homicide case. When police respond to

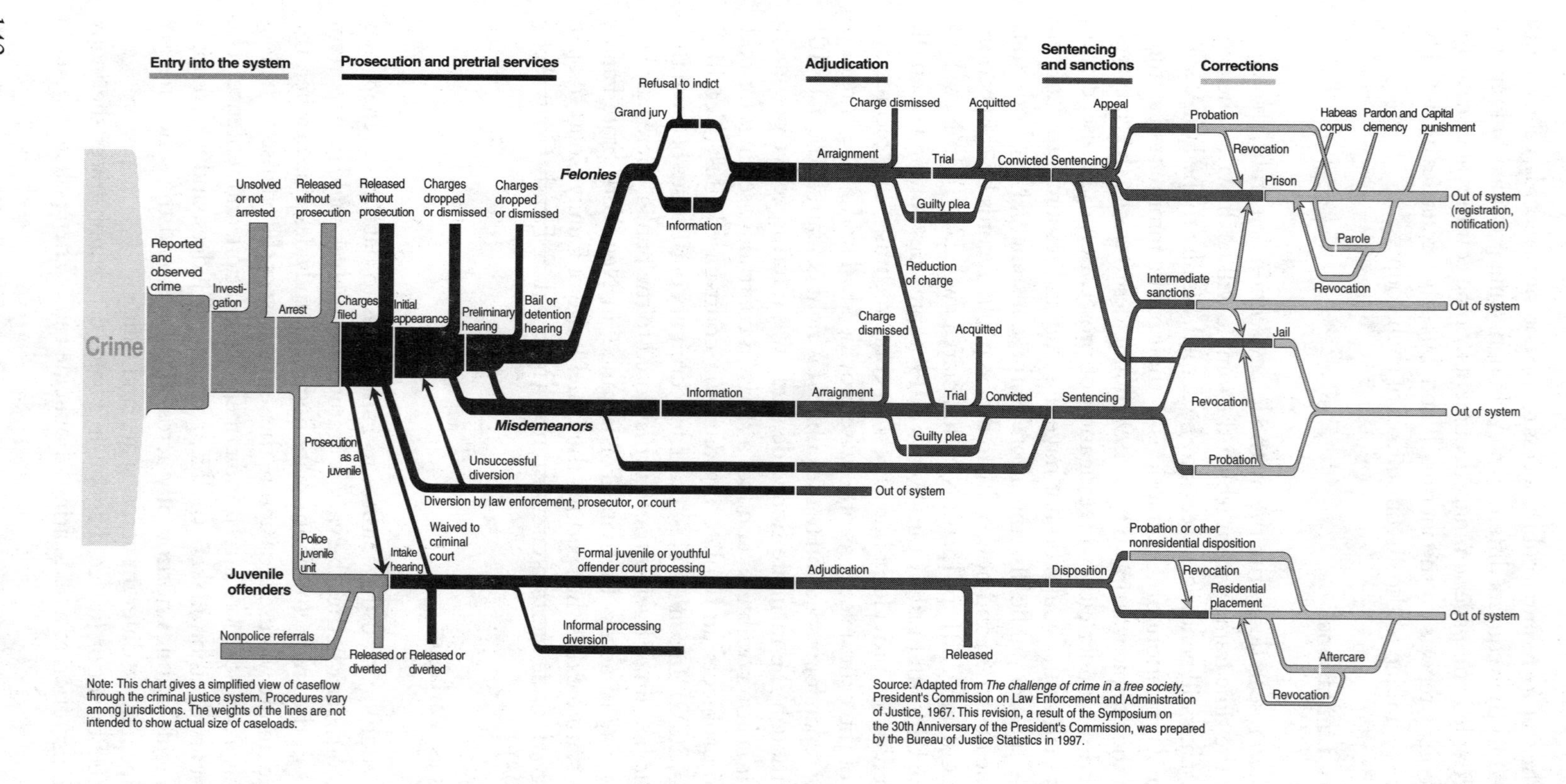

Figure 6.1. What is the sequence of events in the criminal justice system? From "The Criminal Justice System Flowchart," by the U.S. Department of Justice Office of Justice Programs Bureau of Justice Statistics. Retreived October 22, 2008, from http://www.ojp.usdoj.gov/bjs/flowchart.htm

a crime scene, they can charge from the most serious crime, aggravated murder (O.R.C. § 2903.01), with a possible sentence of death, to a homicide misdemeanor (O.R.C. § 2903.05), with a possible 6-month sentence or probation. The prosecutor may choose to either increase or decrease the seriousness of the homicide charge. In addition, the investigation results may warrant other charges, such as the Firearm Enhancement Statute. This statute enhances a defendant's commitment to prison. In the intimate homicide study, these homicide statutes were variables entered into the model and considered as "acts of discretion." Also, the Firearm Enhancement Statute was a dichotomous variable that influenced case outcome for plea bargaining. It was possible that a particular defendant did not get an original sentence reduced but had the Firearm Enhancement charge taken in satisfaction of the homicide plea, essentially making that charge disappear.

How to Access the Statutes

When one considers using statutes for research purposes, the law can be complex and confusing, particularly for nonattorney researchers. The law is constantly changing, and sometimes in practice the real-world application of the law is significantly different than it appears in print. Indeed, a court could overrule a recently enacted statute tomorrow.

Many law schools maintain Web tutorials on locating statutes by topic. A pending statute could have an impact on a researcher's research plans. For example, in the intimate homicide study, a major legislative reform to the sentencing statute was passed in the middle of the data collection year. In July 1996, the midpoint of the data collection year, Ohio's legislature passed a sentencing reform bill that incorporated determinate sentencing, life without parole, and mandatory minimums, and all but eliminated parole. The new sentencing structure applied to any offender who committed an offense on or after July 1, 1996. This legislative change had to be taken into account in the data collection, analysis, and writing phases. Had the statute not been noted, the results would have implied judges were sentencing more severely, when in fact there was a statutory change mandating judicial behavior.

Although this issue is beyond the scope of this chapter, one must also consider possible conflicts of law between federal and state statutes. For example, although federal funding sources may accept IRB approval for the release of study funds, the methodology may not meet state requirements, especially in the areas of informed consent, mandatory child abuse reporting, accessing court-based data, and state statutory sealing provisions. Although state law could perhaps be used to unseal records, any such release would be dependent on the particular facts of the case. It would be imprudent to secure federal funding and gain IRB permission only to have to abort a project subsequently because of state laws that block access to data or subjects. An example might be a Violence Against Women research grant to study recidivism wherein a researcher will access state criminal records. Although the federal review committee may approve such a project, the state criminal code may seal criminal records under certain circumstances, making the project undoable without court approval. Along these lines, researchers should not rely on practitioners to know the relevant state statutes governing access to internal agency records. A letter on that agency's counsel's letterhead can prevent future disasters.

Finally, researchers should not assume that statutory state mandates requiring certain documentation will actually result in certain paperwork. For instance, in New York there is a mandatory arrest statute for domestic violence (N.Y. Crim. Proc. Law § 140). Much of the domestic violence research currently underway in New York relies on forms generated from domestic violence police calls, the Domestic Incident Report (N.Y. Crim. Proc. Law § 140.10[5]). Police officers must complete a Domestic Incident Report when they are "investigating a report of a crime or offense between members of the same family or household as such terms are defined."[2] Members of the same family are defined as

> (a) persons related by consanguinity or affinity; (b) persons legally married to one another; (c) persons formerly married to one another; and (d) persons who have a child in common, regardless whether such persons have been married or have lived together at any such time. (N.Y. Crim. Proc. Law § 530.11(1)

In two studies conducted in conjunction with police departments, chart reviews revealed that police complete Domestic Incident Reports in only 50% to 60% of cases (Cerulli, Edwardsen, Hall, Conner, & Chan, 2006; Cerulli, Marinucci, & Reixach, 2002; Cerulli, Marinucci, Reixach, Tomkins, & Vella, 2001). Researchers using these mandatory forms may be receiving data on only half the calls for service to homes in some communities. Officers cite many reasons for not completing these forms, including but not limited to the offender not being at the scene, the victim requesting nonpunitive relief, and being out of the actual paper form. It is imperative that researchers conducting any research based on police response and documentation understand the difference between calls for service and arrests. It is readily conceivable, for example, that domestic violence calls for service may be increasing, whereas arrests are declining. Similarly, in studying the effects of mandatory arrest, it is important to consider the extent to which the researchers have access to interviewing victims who make calls to the police, yet whose perpetrators are not arrested. This illustrates that what is statutorily mandated is not necessarily enacted in practice.

In one homicide case review, a victim who killed her batterer had the police at her home more than 30 times during her relationship with her

[2]N.Y. Criminal Procedure Law Section 140.10 (5) dictates when a Domestic Incident Report must be completed.

batterer before the homicide. However, only one arrest was noted in the police reports. Additionally, there were no mandatory reports on file with either the police department or the courts. This ethnographic study has resulted in training materials for officers that may have an impact on police practice in the future.

Findings Affecting Policy

In a Family Court study of Protection Order Petitions (POP; Cerulli & Tomkins, 2000), researchers compared the criminal histories noted in court files with information publicly available via the New York State Department of Correctional Services Inmate Information Web site (http://www.docs.state.ny.us). Research staff entered subjects' name, date of birth, and race to search for matches. They then verified those individuals with a match on sociodemographic variables by cross-checking the information on ethnic origin and county of commitment. After 206 searches, they located 13 cases (6%) in which the subject had served time in a state prison. In 8 of those cases, the judge issuing the protection order was unaware of the subjects' incarceration because there was no notation on the POP. In all POPs, either the paperwork was unclear or there was no indication that the subjects were on parole. Five POPs were also unclear regarding whether the subjects had a felony conviction or were known to the Department of Probation.

The project staff learned that despite issuing POPs, the family court judges were not able to access the subjects' official criminal histories and often relied on either the victims' information or subjects' self-reports. As a result of the research project, judges now have access to criminal histories from the New York State Department of Criminal Justice Services. This study was conducted with limited financial resources, used public data, and had an impact on policy.

CONCLUSION

Are statutes barriers to researchers, or can researchers work with legal practitioners to promulgate better research? The worlds of law and research have historically built many bridges on issues. Examples include competency decisions, patent law, trademark applications, personal injury law, and medical malpractice. Many of these partnerships are profit generating for the attorneys engaging in the work. However, in the important arena of research on suicide, violence, and substance abuse with vulnerable populations such as children, victims, and defendants, we have barely laid the foundations for building that bridge, with researchers and lawyers still viewing each other with suspicion.

Despite the statutes providing access to the public data, and IRBs approving such studies, researchers still have a responsibility to use the data with care. Although secondary data are often deidentified, low base-rate phenomena such as suicide and homicide make "reidentification" a possibility. As demonstrated with the Ohio homicide study, it is possible to couple the SHRs with newspaper articles and learn the identities of the victims and perpetrators. Furthermore, when reporting such findings, case descriptions can violate privacy rights. The memory of our deceased subjects' voices must drive our decisions about how and what to publish. Our ethical obligations remain the same despite the public nature of the data. Also, as researchers we may want to consider the extent to which our use of publicly available data can have an impact on policy.

It is time to reconsider how research can affect the law. In cases involving child custody decisions, perhaps empirical evidence on the effects of violence on children can be considered. In cases involving mentally ill offenders, studies on the beneficial effects of assertive community treatment can be considered. Rather than rely simply on studies that report on the effects of mandatory arrest, we can track victims and offenders longitudinally to see how the entire adjudication process affects them as individuals and their relationships with each other and their children. It may be time to use science to study the law rather than simply direct it. Additionally, it may be time for scientists to consider the law as a variable worthy of measurement.

REFERENCES

Barnard, J., & Greenspan, M. (2003). Incremental Bar admission: Lessons from the medical profession. *Journal of Legal Education, 53*, 340–367.

Black, D. (1976). *The behavior of law.* San Diego, CA: Academic Press.

Cerulli, C. (2004). *Does intimacy provide leniency from the law? A study of Ohio criminal homicide cases involving different victim–offender relationships.* Unpublished doctoral dissertation, State University of New York at Albany.

Cerulli, C., Edwardsen, E., Hall, D., Conner, K. R., & Chan, K. L. (2006). *Exploring the use of medical and legal documentation in evidence-based prosecution.* Manuscript submitted for publication.

Cerulli, C., & Tomkins, S. (Eds.). (2000). *Monroe County Family Court domestic violence intensive intervention court evaluation, March 1999–March 2000.* Buffalo: Family Violence Clinic, State University of New York at Buffalo School of Law.

Cerulli, C., Marinucci, K., & Reixach, K. (2002). *Rochester Safe Start technical assistance report Phase II.* Buffalo: Family Violence Clinic, State University of New York at Buffalo School of Law.

Cerulli, C., Marinucci, K., Reixach, K., Tomkins, S., & Vella, E. (2001). *Rochester Safe Start technical assistance Phase I: Rochester Police Department file review.* Buffalo: Family Violence Clinic, State University of New York at Buffalo School of Law.

Chan, K., Tiwari, A., Leung, W. C., Ho, H. & Cerulli, C. (2007). Common correlates of suicidal ideation and physical assault among male and female university students in Hong Kong. *Victims and Violence, 22(3), 290–301.*

Fessenden, F. (1989, January 5). Home violence arrests increasing. *Newsday*, p. 27.

Freedom of Information Act of 1966, 5 U.S.C. 552 (1966).

Goodman, E. (1983, April 19). Using "muscle" against wife beaters. *Washington Post*, p. A21.

Health Insurance Portability and Accountability Act of 1996, Pub. L. 104-1936 (1996).

Maxfield, M. G. (1989). *Circumstances in supplementary homicide reports: Variety and validity. Criminology, 27*, 671–695.

Maxwell, C. D., Garner, J. H., & Fagan, J. A. (2001). *The effects of arrest on intimate partner violence: New evidence from Spouse Assault Replication Program*. Washington, DC: National Institute of Justice, U.S. Department of Justice.

N.Y. C.L.S. Family Ct. Act § 166 (1998).

N.Y. Crim. Proc. Law § 140.

N.Y. Jud. Law § 225-b.

N.Y. Penal Law § 120.

N.Y. Penal Law § 260.10.

Ohio Rev. Code § 149.43.

Ohio Rev. Code § 313.09.

Ohio Rev. Code § 313.10.

Ohio Rev. Code § 2903.01.

Ohio Rev. Code § 2903.05.

People v. Johnson, 95 NY2d 368 (2000).

Riedel, M. (1990). Nationwide homicide data sets: An evaluation of the Uniform Crime Reports and the National Center for Health Statistics data. In D. MacKenzie, P. J. Baunach, & R. R. Roberg (Eds.), *Measuring crime: Large-scale, long-range efforts*. Albany: State University of New York Press.

Sherman, L. (1992). The variable effects of arrest on criminal careers: The Milwaukee domestic violence experiment. *Criminology, 83*, 137–145.

Sherman, L., & Berk, R. (1984). Police response to domestic violence incidents. *American Sociology Revue, 49*, 261–271.

Uniform Justice Court Act § 2019-a. 18 U.S.C. Sec. 922(g)(1).

Violence Against Women Act of 2000, Pub. L. No. 106-386, 114 Stat. 1491 (2000).

Wright, J. B., & Carr, B. G. (Eds.). (2001). *Legal handbook for New York state journalists*. Albany: New York State Bar Association.

III

RESPONDING TO THREATS OF VIOLENCE

7

ETHICAL DILEMMAS IN CONDUCTING FIELD RESEARCH WITH INJECTION DRUG USERS

DAVID R. BUCHANAN

Psychologists and other social scientists are committed to investigating health and social problems to learn how their toll on society can be reduced. Problems such as suicide, homicide, HIV/AIDS, domestic violence, and child abuse are major causes of morbidity and mortality and present poignant humanitarian concerns as well. The two principal ethical obligations in conducting health research are (a) to protect human subjects and (b) to generate new knowledge. Ethical dilemmas arise because these moral duties can conflict. As researchers seek to gain knowledge, their research sometimes threatens the health and welfare of the participants.

In conducting investigations into the etiology of health problems with high-risk populations, for example, researchers may face fundamental ethical dilemmas about how to proceed if or when they learn about threats of harm to the participants themselves in the case of suicide or to third parties in cases of threatened violence or about exposure to life-threatening diseases. To what extent are researchers responsible for preventing violence, infection, or the breakdown of individual participants? Under what circumstances should researchers be considered morally obligated to sacrifice sound research methods and override promises to protect the confidentiality of the participants to try to prevent harm to uninvolved third parties or to intervene on behalf of research participants for their benefit? This chapter examines a number of such ethical dilemmas that arose during the course of conducting field research designed to identify microcontextual risk factors for HIV infection among injection drug users (IDUs).

The need to examine researchers' responsibilities in conducting descriptive research is prominent these days for a number of reasons, including heightened public concerns about possible ethical lapses in the conduct of health research and voiced concerns from researchers about the need for greater guidance. It is particularly salient because of a growing hesitancy on the part of institutional review boards (IRBs) to approve research with high-risk populations because of fears of legal liabilities (Mello, Studdert, & Brennan, 2003; Resnik, 2004). To guide researchers, Emanuel, Wendler, and Grady (2000) and Emanuel, Wendler, Killen, and Grady (2004) conducted a major review and synthesis of the most historically significant documents and ethical codes promulgated to date and identified eight requirements that must be met to ensure that research is conducted ethically (see the Introduction to this book).

In reviewing these standards, this chapter focuses on the fourth requirement, determining a favorable risk–benefit ratio. In particular, I discuss three key issues that have received insufficient attention in previous analyses of the ethical obligations of researchers in conducting nonintervention descriptive research: (a) novel problems in failing to protect confidentiality, (b) novel and unanticipated potential harms to participants, and (c) potential harms to third parties. The central thesis of the chapter is that the conceptualization of risks and benefits deemed ethically relevant in determining the ethical propriety of health research must be broadened. A comprehensive analysis must take into account not only the risks and benefits to the research participants themselves, but also the risks and benefits to the population at large. On the basis of this analysis, the chapter highlights two key areas in which new policies must be developed to provide additional guidance to researchers conducting investigations with high-risk populations; these areas focus on the needs for classifying the severity of collateral risks and for assessing the likelihood of their occurrence.

BACKGROUND

Although the potential for harm in medical experiments involving human subjects has received extensive attention, the issue of researcher responsibilities in responding to threats of harm that may arise while conducting descriptive social scientific research has been largely overlooked. Relative to experimental research (e.g., clinical trials of new cancer treatments), descriptive studies have generally been considered minimal risk. Most previous analyses have found that the greatest potential harm associated with nonexperimental, descriptive research lies in violations of confidentiality, wherein information that is potentially damaging to the subject's interests is disclosed (Abrams, 1986; Gold, 1996).

The principle of protecting confidentiality can be traced back to the tenets of the Hippocratic Oath and its admonition

> What I may see or hear in the course of the treatment or even outside of the treatment in regard to the life of men, which on no account one must spread abroad, I will keep to myself, holding such things shameful to be spoken about.

The Hippocratic Oath established a fiduciary duty of fidelity to the individual patient and proscribed any form of divided loyalties in which physicians might act as agents on behalf of anyone other than their patient. As the field of bioethics evolved, it drew heavily on the principles originally articulated in the Hippocratic Oath, and hence the preponderance of ethical analyses of descriptive research has concluded that the primary threat to the research participants lies in disclosures of personal information. Revealing confidential information can be highly traumatic, causing emotional distress to the point to which individuals might even contemplate suicide (Gutheil, 2001; Huprich, Fuller, & Schneider, 2003). Inadvertent or intentional disclosures might also embarrass them, stigmatize them, or directly damage their welfare through loss of housing, job, children, health insurance, or other adverse consequences. On the basis of these concerns, ethical attention has focused predominantly on protecting confidentiality and, consequently, on developing detailed procedures for storing and managing data safely and securely.

Although the principle of protecting confidentiality had been well established for centuries, its precedence was formally challenged in 1976 by the case of *Tarasoff v. the Regents of University of California* (see the Introduction, this volume). At its most basic level, the justification for breaching confidentiality is that all moral agents are held to have a duty to rescue those in need, as long as it does not imperil their own life (Richardson & Belsky, 2004). The reason for making the information known is that it could stop the harm from happening.

The issue of researcher responsibilities with respect to a duty to protect not directly related to the research procedures themselves has more recently come to the forefront of public and scientific attention in the controversial court decision by the Maryland Court of Appeals in *Grimes v. the Kennedy Krieger Institute, Inc.* (2001). In the Kennedy Krieger Institute case, the researchers sought to test low-cost lead abatement procedures in public housing in inner-city Baltimore (Pollak, 2002). In citing the *Tarasoff* case, the judges ruled that because of their "special relationship" with the participants, the researchers had a duty to protect the research participants from potential harm, in this case exposure to lead paint in the environment. Because both the Belmont Report (National Commission, 1979) and the Common Rule (Protection of Human Subjects, 2005) are silent on the issue of the ancillary duties of researchers to prevent harms that are not the direct result of the research, there is an urgent need to address researcher responsibilities in these situations. The specific types of concerns that need to be addressed are well illustrated in the research that we conducted with IDUs.[1]

THE SYRINGE ACCESS, USE, AND DISCARD PROJECT: FIELD RESEARCH WITH INJECTION DRUG USERS TO REDUCE HIV RISK

The Syringe Access, Use, and Discard (SAUD): Context in AIDS Risk project used ethnographic, survey questionnaire, and bioassay methods to identify risk factors for contracting HIV among IDUs at the individual, neighborhood, and city level. The project was conducted in New Haven, Connecticut; Hartford, Connecticut; and Springfield, Massachusetts, from 1999 to 2002. The research had four objectives: (a) to identify social and environmental factors that increase HIV risk with regard to the acquisition of syringes, (b) to identify social and environmental influences on patterns of syringe use, (c) to identify risky patterns of syringe discard, and (d) to test hypotheses regarding identified social and environmental factors and HIV and hepatitis risk. The primary hypothesis of the research examined whether the presence of needle-exchange programs or over-the-counter pharmacy sales of sterile syringes in local neighborhoods reduced risk of infection. In New Haven and Hartford, there were eight targeted neighborhoods: two that had both a pharmacy and a needle-exchange program, two that had just a pharmacy, two that had just a needle-exchange program, and two that had none. Springfield served as a control site because it had neither needle-exchange programs nor pharmacy access.

The research combined quantitative and qualitative research methods (Singer, Stopka, et al., 2000). On the quantitative side, we conducted structured interviews with a total of 989 IDUs (roughly 320 from each site, 40 from each neighborhood) regarding syringe acquisition, use, and discard practices, using a modified AIDS Risk Assessment instrument. Qualitative methods included (a) ethnographic field observations of syringe acquisition, (b) field observations of drug injection, (c) field observations of syringe discard sites, (d) "day visits" with IDUs, and (e) IDU diaries. Because these methods are germane to the discussion, a brief description of each follows.

[1]The research described in this paper is supported by the National Institute on Drug Abuse, grant #R01 DA12569, Merrill Singer, Principal Investigator.

The first objective of the SAUD research addressed syringe acquisition. To achieve this objective, an ethnographer and an outreach worker in each city went out with IDUs and asked them to use their normal process for acquiring syringes. The field staff asked participants, "How do you usually acquire syringes? Show us how." They then went with the research participants to the locations at which they normally purchased or acquired their syringes. In Springfield, for example, we found that the most common source for buying syringes was people with diabetes, who sold their legally obtained prescription treatment equipment.

We also conducted observations of people injecting themselves, sometimes in injection locales ("shooting galleries"), but more often in their apartments. It is worth noting that this process was never totally naturalistic, obviously, because the researchers and participants prearranged these meetings and the participants, quite atypically, had researchers observing them. We also collected discarded syringes from shooting galleries, which we took to the project's lab, where they were tested to determine the presence of HIV or hepatitis.

In addition, we conducted day visits with IDUs, in which we would arrange to hang out with a research participant for about 6 hours on a given day, with the aim of gaining a better understanding of the routine flow of activities during a typical day. Finally, we collected daily diaries. In these diaries, we asked participants to write down their activities over a 5-day period. We gave them a pen and a notebook and asked them to jot down every hour the place they were and what they were doing. We met with them every day to go over what they had done the previous 24 hours.

It is important to note that a completed Form 441 describing the research methods was duly submitted to and approved by three independent IRBs presiding at each collaborating institution. Following federal guidelines and ample precedent, the primary concern of the researchers and the respective IRBs was that research procedures adhere to strict protocols for storing all data collected from participants to protect their confidentiality. Typical of these procedures, the research protocols included written, informed, and signed consent; voluntary participation (including the right to refuse to answer any questions at any time during any phase of the research); the use of arbitrarily constructed subject identification codes on all questionnaires and interviews; storage of raw data in locked filing cabinets; the expunging of any individually identifiable information from all data files; strict password-protected and limited access to the computerized databases; the storage of master identification lists in separate locked facilities; and so on. Following these procedures, we were confident that the data management procedures would scrupulously protect the privacy and confidentiality of the participants.

In the event, however, we encountered many circumstances that caused us to reconsider the adequacy of these assurances.

During the course of collecting these data, we ran into a number of unanticipated problems that posed ethical dilemmas with respect to the proper course of action, as we sought to strike the right balance between protecting the research participant—and others outside of the immediate research context—and achieving the research objectives. The types of problems encountered fell into three categories: (a) novel problems in failing to protect confidentiality, (b) novel and unanticipated potential harms to participants, and (c) potential harms to third parties. These concerns came up on multiple occasions.

Novel Problems in Failing to Protect Confidentiality

As noted, although protecting confidentiality is generally considered the most salient ethical concern in descriptive research, most prior analyses have focused on developing procedures for data coding, encryption, storage, and management to minimize the potential for inadvertent breaches of confidentiality. There is now, however, a growing body of literature that has begun to identify other threats to the confidentiality of participants (Buchanan, Shaw, Stopka, Khooshnood, & Singer, 2002; Singer et al., 1999; Singer, Huertas, & Scott, 2000; Singer, Simmons, Duke, & Broomhall, 2001). The following examples contribute to the growing set of case studies that can be used to sensitize the research community to new ethical concerns that may arise in conducting this type of research. The first several examples focus on potential breaches of confidentiality that are the result of field data collection.

In Springfield, on the basis of our community collaborators' advice, we carefully chose a community health center and a neighborhood community center as places to conduct the structured interviews. These locations are high-traffic areas, they have lots of different programs, and they have private rooms in which we could conduct the interviews with the mutual expectation that the participant's confidentiality would be protected.

One problem that we encountered, however, concerns the obligations of the researchers to ensure that the participants do not accidentally run into someone they know. As a case in point, in the community center a guard was posted in the front lobby where everyone must sign in on entering and exiting the building. The guard was a long-time resident of the neighborhood who was well acquainted with the majority of people who used the building. He had grown up with and knew very well almost all of the drug addicts from the neighborhood, greeting most by name. He was aware of most who struggled with addiction, but, as we learned, he did not know them all. After signing in, as we entered the interview room, 1 participant became clearly agitated because he was afraid that the guard would say something to his neighbors, family, or others about his drug habit. Because these are illegal behaviors, the participant feared that he faced the threat of losing his job, his children, and his housing if word was to get out.

In another example, the director of one of our collaborating agencies objected to providing cash payments to the participants in return for their participation because she believed that it enabled their addiction. The issue of paying participants has received considerable attention in the bioethics literature, but it has most frequently been addressed in terms of its potential for coercion, unduly influencing the participant's decision to enlist in the research (Grady, 2001; Miller & Shorr, 1999). In contrast, in our experience, the use of incentives brought up an unexpected problem with regard to confidentiality protections.

To address the agency director's concerns, we brokered a deal with a local neighborhood bodega whereby we purchased money orders that could be used only to buy food at this store. We gave the money orders to the research participants to compensate them for their time and effort in lieu of cash payments. Not unexpectedly, we found that many participants sold the money orders. What we did not anticipate was that our attempt to resolve one problem would create another. The money orders were unique transactions, the first time that they had been used at this market. As a result, when participants presented the money orders to purchase groceries, we heard reports that the cashiers commented, "Where did you get that? How come you have this? Are you on drugs?" Again, it appeared that we had failed to protect the participants' confidentiality adequately.

The final example of novel breaches of confidentiality illustrates the threat of harm to the participants more directly. To achieve one of our primary research objectives, we asked active drug users to take us with them when they acquired syringes from their usual sources. Our purpose in this part of the research was to collect and test newly acquired syringes to determine whether they had been used (on the basis of the presence of human DNA). Going out with the research staff, however, was conspicuous. In Springfield, for example, the White ethnographer worked in predominantly African American and Puerto Rican neighborhoods. As we found, cooperating with the research staff elicited increased attention from the police, as the company the participants kept fell outside the scope of normal traffic in the neighborhood and the police assumed that any dubious-looking minority person with a White person must be purchasing drugs for them. In one instance, the police stopped and frisked both the research participant and the ethnographer. Fortunately, this happened on the way to the buy, and no one had any paraphernalia or drugs on them. However, if it had happened on the way back, the research participant and staff member could have been arrested.

Novel Harms to Participants

Although breaches of confidentiality have generally been considered to pose the greatest threat of harm to participants in nonexperimental, descriptive research, we discovered other novel threats of harm during our field research with IDUs.

As part of the data-gathering process, we collected syringes found in injection locales—indoor and outdoor sites where IDUs use drugs, either individually or in small groups. The research objective was to test these syringes to determine whether they contained antibodies for HIV, thereby indicating that they had been used by an infected individual. The research methods called for retrieving syringes off the ground or wherever else they might be found (using safe procedures), depositing them in sharps safety containers, and transporting them to the lab for testing.

In this work, we soon discovered that we found not only syringes that had been discarded (because they were worn out or otherwise malfunctioning), but also syringes that had been carefully stored for later use. Because carrying a syringe puts IDUs at risk of arrest, many leave their syringes hidden at the site where they inject. Unlike discarded syringes thrown on the ground, it is generally easy to tell when syringes are still in use because they are typically not in plain sight; rather, they are usually tucked away on top of a rafter or under something and often wrapped in plastic bags with the rest of the user's "works" (i.e., cotton, cookers). The ethical dilemma here turns on what researchers should do when they find syringes that are still in use: Should they leave them where they are, or collect them for testing? This dilemma was pointedly brought to the attention of our field staff by an IDU who protested that the project had "stolen" his needle and that he wanted us to buy him a new one.

Although there are several different aspects of this situation that merit attention, the first issue is that collecting syringes without replacing them could put IDUs at higher risk. They expected to find their syringe where they had left it. If it was not there, the worry was that they might resort to using some other syringe more likely to have been used by others in this unexpected emergency situation. For example, they might share or purchase a syringe from other users who happened to be there at the time or they might obtain a syringe as expeditiously as possible off of the street instead of going to their usual supplier. On the basis of our experience, it seemed apparent that the failure to replace stashed syringes increased the chances that someone would inject with a used and potentially infected needle.

The general concern with breaching confidentiality in this context is that it will lead to social or legal sanctions associated with engaging in deviant or illegal behaviors relative to the dominant norms of society. We found that it can also create problems with respect to the behavior itself. During the course of conducting syringe acquisitions, we set out to gain a better understanding of the process that people use to purchase syringes. Often, this involved going up to rooms in low-rent apartment complexes to make a purchase. On one occasion, the syringe seller immediately barked out, "Who the heck are you? I'm not selling to you guys, I don't sell, and don't ever come back here again." Over time, we learned that participants were equally, if not more, concerned that their suppliers would notice that they were accompanied by the research staff as they were about being spotted by the police. As happened in this instance, several participants expressed fears that their source would assume that they were collaborating with the police ("snitches") and hence refuse to make transactions with them any longer. The problem was that if their usual supplier refused to do business with them, then the participants might be forced to turn to alternative sources. As we learned in this research, the disruption of access to their usual source (e.g., as when their dealer is arrested by the police) puts IDUs at higher risk of obtaining adulterated equipment.

Harms to Third Parties

The final topic for discussion is the issue of harms to third parties. This issue concerns researcher responsibilities to protect innocent third parties, on the basis of the precedents set by the *Tarasoff* (1976) case and echoed in the *Grimes v. Kennedy-Krieger* (2001) lead abatement trial. It regards the conditions for invoking a researcher's duty to warn.

In the SAUD project, participants were asked to write daily diary entries that described their syringe access, use, and discard practices. Participants were asked to make note of the locales where they bought and used heroin and anything else that would help us to understand the nature of the risks they face. To assist in this process, participants commonly wrote entries about their "running buddies" and the street names of drug dealers. Unfortunately, 1 participant was arrested while in possession of his diary, which contained entries from several previous days. When booked at the local jail, the participant's possessions were taken from him, according to standard police procedure. The arresting officer found the pocket-sized notebook diary and began flipping through it, saying, "Wow, this looks interesting, I wonder what we could find out in here." Although it turned out the officer was joking and ultimately did not pay too much attention to it, the experience raised concern about our duties to warn in situations in which the participant had written entries that read, "Scored at this address" or "Saw so-and-so," including the potential for violence if third parties learned their name had been disclosed to the police.

Conducting this research not only posed risks to the participants but also to the research staff. In another facet of the scenario described earlier, we decided to replace any syringes that we found at injection locales that appeared still to be in use with sterile syringes, to reduce the risk to the participants. It is, however, against the law to be in possession of syringes in Massachusetts. Collecting syringes from discard sites thus put our research staff in direct violation of Massachusetts law. We met with the local police department, but they politely informed us that their hands were tied, the law is the law, and they would arrest us if they caught us in possession. We requested a license from the Massachusetts State Department of Public Health so that we could possess syringes legally, but they denied our request, stating that the research was not covered by the intent of the law, as codified in Massachusetts General Law. However, public health advocates were urging us to get arrested to test the provisions of a statewide pilot needle-exchange program.

As is common in this type of research, the SAUD outreach workers were people in recovery who had a long history of unhappy interactions with the police. They were deeply concerned about carrying syringes because they feared they would be harassed, if not jailed, by the police. Of even greater concern, state law held that if the police detected the residue of any illegal drugs in the syringes, they could charge that person with possession of narcotics, over and above any charges relating to syringe possession. It was not uncommon for us to pick up between 20 and 30 discarded syringes per site; the likelihood that 1 or more had trace amounts of heroin was high. Thus, the issue was whether we could ethically ask our field staff to put themselves at risk of arrest, even if it was most likely that the case would be thrown out of court. In the end, to reduce the risk to the research staff, we resolved that either the ethnographer or the site director, who were less likely to be harassed by the police because of their social status, would be responsible for replacing the sterile syringes. (It is important to note that we obtained them from a needle-exchange program, provided free of charge to the project, using no government funds.)

In another unanticipated twist, problems analogous to breaching confidentiality came up with respect to one of our outreach workers. A relative spotted one of our team members in the field going out with a participant to acquire syringes. She then erroneously reported to her extended family that their cousin (our outreach worker) had relapsed and was back "in the mix." His family promptly told him that he was no longer welcome at Thanksgiving dinner. She also told his employer, who insisted that he get a urine test, even after we vouched for him. It was a humiliating experience.

The last example concerns the problem of observing HIV-discordant couples. From our interviews, we knew the HIV status of each participant. During the course of conducting a field observation of "typical" injection practices, the ethnographer was invited to the participants' apartment and saw that the male HIV-positive partner was about to share his needle with his female HIV-negative lover. What are the researcher's responsibilities in this situation? Do researchers have a duty to warn the third party that she is in danger of being infected? How should considerations of the ethnographer's own safety weigh in the decision, on the spot, at that moment? In these types of situations, should researchers feel obligated to breach confidentiality, abandon the research methods, and warn the third party?

DISCUSSION AND CONCLUSION

In most prior analyses of the risk–benefit ratio in health research, an ethical standard has been established that assesses the risks and the benefits to the individual research participant on the basis of the model of clinical trials (Emanuel et al., 2000). Drawing on the concept of equipoise, a long tradition in health care research has claimed that clinical trials can be conducted ethically if and only if the intervention under investigation is hypothesized to offer the prospect of benefits to the individual patient–participant equal to the current standard of care (Freedman, 1987; Fried, 1974). If the individual participant does not stand an equal chance of benefiting from the intervention under investigation, relative to the comparison condition, then the risks cannot be justified and the trial is considered ethically unacceptable. But how is this model supposed to be applied to nonexperimental, descriptive research? What are the ostensible benefits to the participants that are supposed to counterbalance and outweigh the risks of participation?

Descriptive research has historically been justified by the perception of minimal risk to the participants, which is considered to be outweighed by the social benefits of the research—not by the benefits to the individual participant per se but by the value of the knowledge to be gained, which can then be used to prevent similar problems in future generations. Although it is not uncommon for researchers to suggest that the participants might benefit (e.g., from assistance with referrals into drug treatment programs), IRBs have traditionally been quite cautious about allowing investigators to make claims about the purported benefits of participation in this context, generally viewing such assertions as potentially undue inducements.

As the SAUD research has demonstrated, however, in conducting descriptive field research there are many novel risks to the participants and risks to third parties that cannot be ignored. To provide an adequate ethical foundation for assessing the merits and acceptability of descriptive research, it is, therefore, critically important to acknowledge a broader conceptualization of risks and benefits that should be considered ethically relevant, beyond the risk and benefits to the individual participants. A more satisfactory analysis must take into account not only the risks and benefits to the research participants themselves, but also those to the population at large.

On the basis of a more comprehensive account, descriptive research on high-risk populations is justified by the benefits to be achieved, namely, developing the capacity to prevent harm and reduce the toll of these widespread health problems on society. The most ethically sound position with respect to the foregoing issues, then, is that because of the important social value of the research, confidentiality protections should be overridden and research suspended only when the situation warrants it for compelling reasons (Kagle & Kopels, 1994). Researchers should be obligated to act on a duty to protect and breach the promise of protecting confidentiality if and only if (a) the potential harm is sufficiently serious and (b) they judge that the harm is more likely to occur than not.

To justify breaching confidentiality, there must be harmful consequences of serious magnitude at stake (Macklin, 1991). Harm is commonly defined in three dimensions: severity, extent (number of people affected), and duration. This chapter has highlighted many novel types of harm. To meet the requirements for the ethical conduct of this type of research, then, the first issue that must be addressed is codifying the range and types of potential harms that may occur during the course of data collection with high-risk populations. These events range from life-threatening and serious injuries, such as battering and child abuse, which are unmistakably severe harms that merit immediate action, to less consequential problems, such as revealing a third party's moral or legal transgressions or threats of property damage, wherein the obligation to intervene is less certain. To assist researchers, IRBs, and community advisory boards in determining whether the research should be suspended, it is imperative that the research community develop standardized criteria for assessing the magnitude of different possible harms that may arise in conducting descriptive research.

In clinical trials, for example, an analogous problem arose with respect to the side effects of different experimental cancer treatments. Starting in 1982, the research community developed an evolving set of Common Toxicity Criteria to classify and rank the severity of different types of potential adverse events in clinical cancer trials. These criteria recognize that certain harms, such as death, are more serious—and therefore, merit immediate action, such as stopping the research—than other possible occurrences, such as edema. Such events are graded on a 0 to 5 scale, ranging from nonoccurrence to mild, moderate, severe, life threatening, and death. These criteria have periodically been revised and updated, as the state of the science evolves. To address the potential for harm in descriptive studies, a comparable consensus process needs to be initiated in the social scientific research community.

The second critical issue involves assessing the probability that the harm will actually occur. To breach confidentiality, the researcher must determine that there is a clear and imminent danger, wherein the research participant has revealed a credible intention to inflict serious harm. If there is only a remote chance that harm will result, then breaching confidentiality is unwarranted. Unlike developing a list of potential adverse events, however, assessments of likelihood of harm are largely dependent on situation-specific contingencies, which are difficult to specify fully in advance, as this chapter has suggested.

For example, faced with an HIV-discordant couple about to share a needle, what should the researcher do, breach confidentiality or not? I am skeptical about the idea that it is possible at this point in time to develop standardized guidelines that recognize all possible contingencies to govern how researchers should act in such situations. There are many complex dynamics involved: the researcher's safety, the researcher's knowledge of and relationship with the participants, fluency in communication (e.g., speaking Spanish), the setting, back-up by other staff, the field worker's training and experience in dealing with these types of situations, and so on. Although standardized instruments for assessing specific threats, such as suicide, are improving, it appears that accurate assessments of the chances of a serious harm occurring will in the near future necessarily rely on the researcher's judgment of the situation at hand. These concerns may thus be best addressed by developing and implementing casuistical (case-based) training programs (Jonsen & Toulmin, 1988).

In the scenario described here, for example, it would be unconscionable for the researcher simply to ignore the threat of infection, merely for the sake of data collection. In this case, the researcher has a moral obligation to prevent harm, because it is serious and likely, but it might be fulfilled in ways other than breaching confidentiality. For instance, with better training programs, field staff may be better prepared to discuss and to demonstrate safer drug injection practices, as part of any responsible HIV/AIDS education campaign, without jumping immediately to disclosure of the partner's HIV status. Afterward, the researcher can take the HIV-positive partner aside, provide him with additional information, encourage him to seek counseling, advise him that the researcher feels compelled to warn the HIV-negative partner if his behavior does not change, and then, only as a last resort, break confidentiality and warn the third party.

In this analysis, determining the likelihood of a serious harm actually occurring in the situation at hand entails an irreducible element of judgment (Taylor, 1988, 1995). It is impossible to specify in advance adequate guidelines or regulations to prescribe what one should do, given the broad range of circumstances and contingencies that must be considered. Researchers can improve their capacity for exercising judgment and making the right decision in the face of morally complex events through experience and reflection on case studies (Jonsen & Toulmin, 1988). Therefore, it is essential to produce and compile case studies on these issues; they can be used to inform enhanced mandatory ethics training programs for social scientific researchers. The purpose of such training programs would be to improve the researchers' judgment in determining when a particular harm is more likely than not to occur (Ferris et al., 1998).

To wrap up this discussion, two final issues—IRB approval and informed consent—need to be addressed. Faced with fears of legal liability, there are reports of a growing reluctance on the part of IRBs to approve research with high-risk populations (Mello et al., 2003; Resnik, 2004). In response, Appelbaum and Rosenbaum (1989) have reasoned that IRBs should know and apply the same standards as the courts. Over the past 30 years, interpretations of the duty to warn by the courts and state legislatures have evolved through several stages, which have been characterized as expansion, diversification, and retreat (Felthous, 2001). More recent legal rulings and state statutes regarding *Tarasoff*-like situations have begun to limit significantly the circumstances in which a duty to protect would attach (Walcott, Cerundolo, & Beck, 2001). Many observers have pointed out that the ability of psychiatrists to predict a violent episode by a patient is poor (Beck, 1998; Monahan et al., 2005; Skeem et al., 2005). If therapists with a long and intimate relationship with an individual cannot diagnose the potential for violence accurately, then many argue there is virtually nothing to be gained in seeking to hold those with less in-depth knowledge accountable for averting the threat of harm. Gutheil (2001) has suggested that the retreat from *Tarasoff* (1976) in court opinion reflects a growing recognition that warning third parties might be the least effective and most noxious means of mitigating risk: The only visible effect of issuing warnings has been to increase the potential victim's state of anxiety. Thus, in contrast to the apparent drift of IRBs, the courts are moving in the direction of limiting responsibilities to increasingly narrow circumstances. On the basis of the swings in court opinion, one reasonable approach is to stake out a middle ground of intermediary steps that researchers could take, with IRB approval, that would defuse the likelihood of violence, like those suggested in field research with IDUs. More strongly, if the research design calls for sustained, in-depth contact with the participants, then it is reasonable for an IRB to ask the researcher to include one of the increasing number of tools now becoming available that exhibit satisfactory validity in predicting certain types of violence (Monahan et al., 2006; Walcott et al., 2001). In these cases, researchers would need to make provisions for warning third parties in anticipation of times when the protocol would trigger disclosure.

Regarding informed consent, federal regulations require that participants be informed of any limitations that apply to confidentiality, but fully describing these limitations is not a simple matter. Most IRBs recognize that it is futile to try to develop an informed consent form that spells out every conceivable situation and describes precisely how researchers plan to respond in any and all such instances (Richardson & Belsky, 2004). Because many discoveries cannot be anticipated, judgment and discretion will always be necessary, despite whatever assurances may have been provided in the informed consent process. However, if threats of harm can be reasonably anticipated, advance warning is necessary and appropriate. In research with high-risk populations using methods that enable reliable determinations of true threats, the participants' right to be informed of potential disclosures must take precedence over the researchers' interest in recruiting subjects. Although it is likely that such disclosures will have a detrimental effect on recruitment, especially on research that directly examines interpersonal violence, researchers in these situations have an obligation to inform the participants that certain information must be disclosed. Child abuse is an indisputable example of a situation that must be reported.

In conclusion, there are three possible resolutions of the question of researcher responsibilities with respect to a duty to protect: It could be considered morally obligatory, prohibited, or permissible (Macklin, 1991). I have argued that the third option is the most sensible and sound position for two reasons: It enables the realization of an important, socially valued good—that is, knowledge to improve prevention efforts—while providing appropriate protections for research participants and, because of the in-principle limitless range of possible scenarios, predetermined prescriptions about what one must do are virtually impossible. The third option allows the individual researcher considerable discretion, and it thus carries the greatest burden for making on-the-spot decisions in specific circumstances. Because of this significant burden, a panel on physician responsibilities concluded that mandatory standards were preferable because it is less taxing and more clear-cut to require warnings than it is to leave it to individual discretion (Ferris et al., 1998). In contrast, on the basis of the examples presented in this chapter, the broad range of ambiguous and unpredictable situations encountered in the course of conducting field research with high-risk populations make unconditional requirements of a duty to protect confidentiality—or, conversely, a duty to intervene to prevent harm—unwarranted. Further research is urgently needed to document and classify the range of possible harms that may arise during the course of conducting descriptive studies, and better training programs are needed to enhance researchers' capacity for evaluating when a duty to warn may be warranted in the particular circumstances at hand.

REFERENCES

Abrams, N. (1986). Ethics and public policy in high-risk research. In L. Tancredi (Ed.), *Ethical issues in epidemiological research* (pp. 47-63). New Brunswick, NJ: Rutgers University Press.

Appelbaum, P. S., & Rosenbaum, A. (1989). Tarasoff and the researcher: Does the duty to protect apply in the research setting? *American Psychologist, 44*, 885–894.

Beck, J. C. (1998). Legal and ethical duties of the clinician treating a patient who is liable to be impulsively violent. *Behavioral Sciences & the Law, 16*, 375–389.

Buchanan, D., Shaw, S., Stopka, T., Khooshnood, K., & Singer, M. (2002). Ethical dilemmas created by the criminalization of status behaviors: Case examples from ethnographic research with injection drug users. *Health Education and Behavior, 29*, 30–42.

Emanuel, E., Wendler, D., & Grady, C. (2000, May 24). What makes clinical research ethical. *JAMA, 283*, 2701–2711.

Emanuel, E. J., Wendler, D., Killen, J., & Grady, C. (2004). What makes clinical research in developing countries ethical? The benchmarks of ethical research. *Journal of Infectious Diseases, 189*, 930–937.

Felthous, A. R. (2001). The clinician's duty to warn or protect. *Behavioral Sciences & the Law, 19*, 321–324.

Ferris, L. E., Barkun, H., Carlisle, J., Hoffman, B., Katz, C., & Silverman, M. (1998). Defining the physician's duty to warn: Consensus statement of Ontario's medical expert panel on duty to inform. *Canadian Medical Association Journal, 158*, 1473–1479.

Freedman, B. (1987, July 16). Equipoise and the ethics of clinical research. *New England Journal of Medicine, 317*, 141–145.

Fried, C. (1974). *Medical experimentation: Personal integrity and social policy*. Amsterdam: North-Holland.

Gold, E. B. (1996). Confidentiality and privacy protection in epidemiological research. In S. Coughlin & T. Beauchamp (Eds.), *Ethics and epidemiology* (pp. 128–142). New York: Oxford University Press.

Grady, C. (2001). Money for research participation: Does it jeopardize informed consent? *American Journal of Bioethics, 1*(2), 40–44.

Grimes v. Kennedy Krieger Institute, Inc., 366 Md. 29 782A 2d 807 (2001). Retrieved September 29, 2008, from http://www.courts.state.md.us/opinions/ coa/2001/128a00

Gutheil, T. G. (2001). Moral justification for Tarasoff-type warnings and breach of confidentiality: A clinician's perspective. *Behavioral Sciences & the Law, 19*, 345–353.

Huprich, S. K., Fuller, K. M., & Schneider, R. B. (2003). Divergent ethical perspectives on the duty-to-warn principle with HIV patients. *Ethics & Behavior, 13*, 263–278.

Jonsen, A. R, & Toulmin, S. (1988). *The abuse of casuistry: A history of moral reasoning*. Berkeley: University of California Press.

Kagle, J. D., & Kopels, S. (1994). Confidentiality after Tarasoff. *Health and Social Work, 19*, 217–222.

Macklin, R. (1991). HIV-infected psychiatric patients: Beyond confidentiality. *Ethics & Behavior, 1*, 3–20.

Mello, M. M., Studdert, D. M., & Brennan, T. A. (2003). The rise of litigation in human subjects research. *Annals of Internal Medicine, 139*, 40–45.

Miller, F. G., & Shorr, A. F. (1999). Advertising for clinical research. *IRB, 21*(5), 1–4.

Monahan, J., Steadman, H. J., Appelbaum, P. S., Grisso, T, Mulvey, E. P., Roth, L. H., et al. (2006). The classification of violence risk. *Behavioral Sciences & the Law, 24*, 721–730.

Monahan, J., Steadman, H. J., Robbins, P. C., Appelbaum, P., Banks, S., Grisso, T., et al. (2005). An actuarial model of violence risk assessment for persons with mental disorders. *Psychiatric Services, 56*, 810–815.

National Commission for the Protection of Human Subjects of Biomedical and Behavioral Research. (1979). *Belmont Report: Ethical principles and guidelines for the protection of human subjects of research*. Washington, DC: U.S. Government Printing Office.

Pollak, J. (2002). The lead-based paint abatement repair and maintenance study in Baltimore: Historic framework and study design. *Journal of Health Care Law & Policy*, 6, 89–108.

Protection of Human Subjects, 45 C.F.R. § 46 (2005).

Resnik, D. B. (2004). Liability for institutional review boards. *Journal of Legal Medicine*, *25*, 131–184.

Richardson, H. S., & Belsky, L. (2004). The ancillary-care responsibilities of medical researchers: An ethical framework for thinking about the clinical care that researchers owe their subjects. *Hastings Center Report*, *34*, 25–33.

Singer, M., Huertas, E., & Scott, G. (2000). Am I my brother's keeper: A case study of the responsibilities of research. *Human Organization*, 59, 389–400.

Singer, M., Marshall, P., Trotter, R., Schensul, J., Weeks, M., Simmons, J., & Radda, K. (1999). Ethics, ethnography, drug use and AIDS: Dilemmas and standards in federally funded research. In P. Marshall, M. Singer, & M. Clatts (Eds.), *Integrating cultural, observational, and epidemiological approaches in the prevention of drug abuse and HIV/AIDS: Current status and future prospects* (GPO 017-024-01652-7, pp. 198–219). Bethesda, MD: National Institute on Drug Abuse.

Singer, M., Simmons, J., Duke, M., & Broomhall, L. (2001). The challenges of street research on drug use, violence, and AIDS risk. *Addiction Research & Theory*, 9, 365–402.

Singer, M., Stopka, T., Siano, C., Springer, K., Barton, G., Khoshnood, K., et al. (2000). The social geography of AIDS and hepatitis risk: Qualitative approaches for assessing local differences in sterile syringe access among injection drug users. *American Journal of Public Health*, 90, 1049–1056.

Skeem, J. L., Miller, J. D., Mulvey, E., Tiemann, J., & Monahan, J. (2005). Using a five-factor lens to explore the relation between personality traits and violence in psychiatric patients. *Journal of Consulting and Clinical Psychology*, *73*, 454–465.

Tarasoff v. Regents of the University of California, 551 P.2d 334 (1976).

Taylor, C. (1988). Critical notice. *Canadian Journal of Philosophy*, *18*, 805–814.

Taylor, C. (1995). Explanation and practical reason. In C. Taylor, *Philosophical arguments* (pp. 34-60). Cambridge, MA: Harvard University Press.

Walcott, D. M., Cerundolo, P., & Beck, J. C. (2001). Current analysis of the Tarasoff duty: An evolution towards the limitation of the duty to protect. *Behavioral Sciences & the Law*, *19*, 325–343.

8

ETHICAL AND LEGAL ISSUES IN CONDUCTING TREATMENT RESEARCH WITH POTENTIALLY VIOLENT INDIVIDUALS

BARRY ROSENFELD AND DEBBIE GREEN

Researchers who conduct research with potentially violent persons face many ethical and legal issues. Dilemmas arise in attempting to maintain the rights of research participants while simultaneously ensuring the safety of research personnel and the community at large. This chapter addresses a range of ethical and legal issues that arise when conducting mental health treatment research with potentially violent persons, including risks to third parties and research personnel, and highlights steps that can minimize these risks. Although there are many clinical research settings in which potentially violent persons may be the focus, this chapter addresses those issues that arise in clinical intervention studies because this setting typically raises the broadest range of ethical and legal issues. In addition, because many, if not most, violent individuals are encountered in criminal justice settings, this context serves as the central focal point of this chapter.

TREATMENT RESEARCH WITH CRIMINAL OFFENDERS

Case Vignette

> Trevor was convicted for the second time of domestic violence against his common-law girlfriend Jennifer. He was sentenced to a 3-year term of probation, and an order of protection barred him from being within 100 feet of Jennifer. In addition, his probation officer ordered him to participate in mental health treatment. When he contacted the treatment program, Trevor was offered participation in a 6-month research study that involved outpatient mental health treatment for men with a history of violence. During informed consent, Trevor was informed of the limits of confidentiality, including the fact that his communications in the treatment program could be disclosed if he was perceived to be a threat to himself or anyone else. Outside of these circumstances, only information verifying his attendance (or failure to attend) would be shared with his probation officer. During treatment, Trevor admitted that despite the order of protection he continued to go to Jennifer's house almost every week, sometimes at her request and other times uninvited. He denied any violence during these visits but readily acknowledged that he had frequently assaulted Jennifer in the past, particularly when intoxicated. Because the informed consent process only specified risk of harm to himself or others as the reasons for breaching his confidentiality, the clinician struggled with the decision as to what, if anything, to convey to Trevor's probation officer. Despite his discomfort, it was not until Trevor acknowledged that he had resumed drinking and had recently had an argument with Jennifer in which he grabbed her by the shoulders and "shook" her that the clinician informed him that he would be notifying his probation officer. He explained the basis for his decision and requested that Trevor actually inform his probation officer himself. Trevor initially resisted this request, but eventually acquiesced. His probation officer, impressed with Trevor's willingness to take responsibility for his actions, decided not to terminate his probation and instead added the requirement of outpatient substance abuse treatment to his existing regimen. In addition, the probation officer contacted Jennifer, explained to her the concerns, and requested that Jennifer contact her if any further problems arose. Trevor completed the remainder of his probation period, including the 6-month domestic violence treatment program, without incident and has not been rearrested since.

This vignette raises several issues that plague clinicians who work with violent individuals, including navigating the boundaries of confidentiality and determining whether, when, and how to disclose potentially dangerous behavior. The circumstances in which illegal behavior can and must be disclosed are often unclear, in both clinical and research settings. In this section, we address these and other issues that directly affect potentially violent individuals who participate in treatment research, including the importance of voluntariness. The requirement of voluntary participation in research can become clouded when participants are referred by the legal system, and researchers must be especially vigilant to ensure that participants do not feel coerced into participating in a research study. Additionally, researchers must determine how and when to maintain the confidentiality of participants, which is often complicated when participants are required to answer to third parties (i.e., the court) and by the reality that research study participants may engage in conduct that researchers are compelled to report. Finally, researchers should be aware of how to screen participants' level of dangerousness to self and others to determine what level of violence risk can be managed within a particular setting. Because important differences exist depending on whether potentially violent individuals are incarcerated, these settings are discussed separately.

Anticipating and Minimizing Coercion

Research Within Prisons

Until the late 1970s, prisoners were viewed as ideal research participants given their confined status and relative stability and the constant routine of institutional environments. Additionally, because prison wages were lower than the minimum wage, incentives for participation could likewise be reduced. In 1978, federal regulations specifically protecting prisoners in biomedical and behavioral research were adopted and stipulated that offenders in correctional institutions must be excluded from study if the only rationale for their inclusion is convenience (Additional Protections Pertaining to Biomedical and Behavioral Research Involving Prisoners as Subjects, 1978). Subpart C has remained unchanged. Regulation 46.306a of federal regulations Subpart C restricts research with prisoners to four domains of study. The first two domains of study are only permissible if the research presents no more than minimal risk or inconvenience to participants (a) to study the causes, effects, and processes of incarceration and of criminal behavior and (b) to further knowledge of prisons as institutional structures or prisoners as incarcerated persons. The second two domains focus on (a) conditions particularly affecting prisoners as a class (e.g., hepatitis, sexual assault, drug addiction) or (b) research on practices likely to enhance the health or well-being of participants. Research conducted within these latter two domains may present participants with greater than minimal risk but requires approval by the Secretary of the U.S. Department of Health and Human Services, following consultation with experts in penology and other relevant fields. Subpart C of the federal regulations further protect prisoners from potential coercion by requiring institutional review boards (IRBs) reviewing research involving prisoners to include on the IRB at least one member who is a prisoner or prisoner advocate.

In addition to limiting the type of research in which prisoners can participate, federal regulation 46.305a explicitly prohibits research incentives of a magnitude that would compromise prospective participants' abilities to weigh the risks of research against the value of such advantages in the limited-choice environment of prison. This is relevant because offenders are recognized to be especially vulnerable to coercion given the constraints of incarceration. Coercion includes obvious acts of forced participation, such as direct pressure applied by prison staff, and prisoners' fear of punishment should they refuse (Moser et al., 2004). Additionally, allowing or causing a prisoner to believe that his or her participation will be considered by parole boards is also considered inherently coercive (U.S. Department of Health and Human Services, 2006). Moreover, in institutions in which conditions are poor or medical access is inadequate, even modest incentives offered by researchers may be coercive, although less obviously so. For example, if access to medical care, better food, relocation to special units, opportunities to earn money, and even increased contact with noncorrectional staff or other inmates lead prisoners to participate in studies that they would not have otherwise consented to, then the issue of coercion and extent of voluntary consent arises.

One form of incentive that has been particularly contentious is whether incarcerated participants should receive financial payment and, if so, in what form. For participants outside of correctional institutions, monetary compensation is permitted provided it is commensurate with any discomfort and inconvenience endured. On one hand, however, because wages available in prisons are considerably lower than in the community, offering prisoners the same monetary incentive as would be given to community participants may be unduly enticing and therefore potentially coercive. On the other hand, to compensate prisoners at a lower rate than individuals outside of institutions may be perceived as unjust or exploitive. One approach to navigating this dilemma is to offer prisoners incentives equal to what is offered community participants, but rather than directly compensate the prisoner, deposit credit into a general fund to be distributed to all inmates (e.g., in the form of educational supplies or other benefits to be shared by the entire ward or unit). Alternatively, researchers might place the funds into an account that the prisoner would receive on release or transfer the funds directly to family members (U.S. Department of Health and Human Services, 2006). Although numerous other strategies exist for ensuring that research with prisoners complies with legal and ethical standards, all such research requires considerable vigilance on the part of the researcher (Gostin, Vanchieri, & Pope, 2006).

Research in the Community

Violent offenders outside of correctional facilities are also susceptible to coercion in intervention research. For example, experimental interventions are likely to be offered at no cost or for a nominal rate. Individuals with low income (i.e., the majority of persons on probation or parole) may not actually be able to afford alternative noninvestigative programs, therefore increasing the likelihood of their consent to a research intervention. Some individuals may seek treatment from an experimental program before their trial or sentencing with the hope that doing so will appear more favorable to the courts (e.g., an individual arrested on charges of child molestation may attempt to evade jail or prison by entering treatment). Despite the strong external incentives to enter an experimental treatment program, prisoners are not unique in this situation. Patients with cancer and individuals with schizophrenia often choose to participate in randomized clinical trials for economic reasons or for new and innovative treatments not available in the community. Although potentially coercive incentives are almost invariably present in research offering the prospect of direct benefit, researchers are expected to anticipate and minimize these potential sources of coercion. Perhaps most important, it is incumbent on the researcher to clearly explain, during the informed consent process, the potential risks of participation, including the possibility that because the treatment has not been demonstrated to be an effective intervention, it may not be effective or accepted by those in the legal system.

Court-Mandated Participation

The issue of voluntary participation becomes an even greater concern when individuals are court mandated to attend an experimental or untested treatment program that is part of a research study. Because there may not be an established treatment program that is appropriate for a particular type of offender other than the program offered through an experimental intervention study, courts may seek to mandate individuals directly into the research program. Mandated participation in a research trial may reflect judges succumbing to the "therapeutic misconception," or the erroneous belief that like practitioner-initiated treatment, all aspects of a clinical trial are designed to benefit participants directly rather than to test whether the treatment works (Appelbaum, Roth, & Lidz, 1982). Such arrangements with a court or probation department should be avoided whenever possible to ensure that participants have the opportunity to refuse the experimental treatment program without repercussions. Although offenders may still be forced to choose among entering an inappropriate program, entering one that is still under investigation, or risking violating the conditions imposed by the courts by rejecting both options, this choice should belong to the offender rather than be predetermined by the court.

The American Psychological Association's (APA) "Ethical Principles of Psychologists and Code of Conduct" (2002; hereafter referred to as the Ethics Code) requires that psychologists conducting intervention research involving the use of experimental treatments not only clarify the experimental nature of the treatment but inform prospective participants of available treatment alternatives if an individual does not wish to participate in the research or withdraws once a study has begun (Fisher, 2003). To comply with this standard, psychologists conducting research involving persons mandated to undergo treatment can and must minimize the possibility of coercion by clearly outlining, during informed consent, what other treatments are available in lieu of the proposed research intervention and ensuring, to the extent feasible, that these options are equally viable. In addition, some researchers may opt to provide their own nonresearch alternative intervention, enabling them to provide a no- (or low-) cost alternative that does not involve participating in a research study.

In addition to concerns about entering an experimental intervention, offenders mandated to undergo treatment often feel that their decision to remain in, versus prematurely terminate from, treatment is not truly voluntary. This also poses an ethical dilemma for researchers because although informed consent must include an assurance to participants that the investigator will impose no negative consequences for withdrawing from a study, the actions of the court after participant withdrawal are not under investigator control. Participants who are court mandated to treatment are often placed in the position of determining whether to terminate their participation with the awareness that dropping out might be considered a violation of court-imposed conditions. As with the disclosure of alternative treatments during informed consent, participants who express a desire to terminate their participation before a study ends should be informed about alternative programs. In practice, a large proportion of research study dropouts do so without warning, simply refusing to return to the program and ignoring outreach on the part of the research team, making such disclosures impossible. Nevertheless, anticipating the possibility of an individual's refusal to complete a research study and separating this decision from that of whether to continue treatment is critical to minimizing both real and perceived coercion.

Finally, in instances in which participation in a research intervention is used by a participant to fulfill an order for court-mandated treatment, investigators will have to provide some documentation to the court that the individual attended treatment. This process should also be clarified during informed consent. In addition, participants must also be informed, if relevant, that the court will have to be notified if they withdraw from the study. In these situations, it is particularly important to have identified alternative treatments readily available to the participant to avoid imposing unnecessary coercion on the participant.

Court mandates to attend experimental treatment programs are actually quite common in many settings, such as domestic violence and child abuse, sex offenses, and substance abuse. Such interventions may range in the degree to which they are truly "experimental," with some programs merely requiring ongoing data collection to evaluate treatment outcome (sometimes framing this "research" as program evaluation, to avoid consent and coercion issues) and others in which each individual will be randomly assigned to one of several interventions. For example, if a university professor receives a large research grant to study a novel child abuse intervention program and seeks to compare this program with a "typical" parenting support intervention, family court judges may seek to refer parents directly to this experimental treatment in hopes that some portion of the referrals will receive a more intensive, and they hope more effective, intervention. In such a case, it is incumbent on the researcher to clearly explain the research element of the intervention to the judges who make referrals and to provide an opportunity to the individual parents who are referred to refuse study participation without jeopardizing their ability to participate in treatment. In this scenario, researchers might facilitate referral to the "usual" treatment program for parents who refuse to participate in the research study.

Labeling Research as "Treatment"

Institutions or courts that mandate violent incarcerated or community-dwelling persons to treatment seek programs that have a high likelihood of effectively reducing future violence. Although clinical researchers hope for the same outcome, they face an ethical dilemma in attempting to develop and validate an innovative approach. Experimental programs are conducted because their efficacy may be unknown. To validate an approach, a sufficient number of participants must complete the treatment and demonstrate observable benefits. As with established treatments, it is possible that an experimental treatment will not be beneficial and participants will remain at the same (or greater) level of risk of violence or recidivism as when they began the treatment. Yet, for researchers to successfully recruit participants, there may be an incentive to present unproven programs as "treatment," downplaying the experimental nature because it is less likely that unproven interventions will generate adequate referrals. Not only might this temptation lead some researchers to misrepresent their research intervention and violate both federal regulations and the APA (2002) Ethics Code, but it can result in even greater difficulties for both participant and investigator if an individual reoffends or engages in further violence after beginning or completing treatment.

In instances in which there is no established treatment for a particular problem, the need to identify possible treatments may outweigh the risks of potential failure, provided both referring parties and potential participants are informed of this additional risk (that treatment may not be successful). However, when alternative treatment approaches do exist, researchers must be able to adequately communicate to referring institutions and courts, and to prospective participants, the limitations of the experimental alternative approach.

Confidentiality of Research Data

Perhaps the most common ethical issue that arises in the conduct of treatment research with violent individuals concerns confidentiality. Given the possibility that violent individuals will commit subsequent violent or criminal behavior, either during the course of a study or after its completion, researchers must consider how and when to protect the confidentiality of research participants and when to disclose such information. For example, in research with violent populations, it is more likely than with other classes of participants that research records may be subpoenaed by the court to demonstrate continued risk of violence, lack of treatment response, or simply the extent of any individual's psychopathy or unrecorded criminal behavior. Even if researchers are not officially asked to provide information about known offenses to the court, probation or parole officers may ask about treatment progress or the content of statements made during treatment.

Violent persons involved in research are entitled to the same confidentiality protections as nonviolent participants. This right becomes particularly important in research with violent persons given the sensitivity of information that is collected and the potential negative effect on participants if this information is disclosed. Of course, researchers typically use standard procedures to ensure confidentiality, such as separating the names of participants from study data and securing any linkage between the data and participant identities. For some participants, even their involvement in a study can have negative consequences if revealed (e.g., a pedophile who has never acted on his impulses but seeks treatment to prevent the occurrence of any illegal or inappropriate sexual behavior). Thus, protecting both the identity of study participants and the content of their disclosures is paramount, albeit subject to limitations (discussed further subsequently).

By detailing these limitations during the consent process, researchers enable potential participants to make informed decisions about whether to participate and aware of what areas they are free to discuss and which they may choose not to discuss to maintain their confidentiality. In actuality, limits to confidentiality may have little impact on a participant's willingness to self-disclose (Kalichman, Brosig, & Kalichman, 1994). Additionally, for court-mandated participants, treatment may seem like little more than an extension of their probation or parole conditions, and they may therefore already be hesitant to honestly divulge information (even when some limited confidentiality has been assured). In such cases, discourse about confidentiality may actually serve to educate and potentially build therapeutic alliance (Rosenfeld, Fava, & Galietta, 2008).

Researchers who focus on violent behavior have also developed a number of innovative methods to maintain the confidentiality of their participants. Israel (2004) described a study in which researchers asked participants to complete questionnaires regarding instances of child abuse and neglect and then had them seal their responses, ensuring that their answers and identity could never be linked. Alternatively, participants in treatment studies might be instructed by researchers to avoid providing specific information, such as the identity or details of previous offenses that they have not been charged with, as well as details about future offenses they intend to commit.

Certificate of Confidentiality

As with many ethical and clinical dilemmas, concerns about confidentiality are best managed by anticipating possible problems and taking steps to avoid problematic situations before they arise. For example, when the possibility of court interference exists, researchers should consider seeking a Certificate of Confidentiality (Public Health Service Act, 1988; discussed in more detail in chap. 2, this volume), issued by the National Institutes of Health specifically to protect research records. A Certificate of Confidentiality applies to research settings in which sensitive information—such as about sexual attitudes, preferences, and practices; use of illicit substances; and illegal activities—is likely to be revealed and the possibility of future legal action or economic or other harms exists. The certificate protects participants by protecting researchers from being compelled to reveal information gathered in the course of a study that might cause harm to identified individuals. In other words, researchers who obtain a certificate are permitted to refuse to disclose any information that would arguably harm a participant's finances, employability, or legal status. To qualify for such protection, the researcher must demonstrate that the risk of harm to the participant or to the integrity of a study outweighs the importance of such disclosures. The certificate does not, however, protect researchers from being required to report child and elder abuse, risk of self-harm, or explicit threats against an individual that fall under federal and state regulations (Fisher, Hoagwood, & Jensen, 1996; discussed subsequently in further detail). Moreover, even when a Certificate of Confidentiality has been granted, limits exist as to how and when confidentiality can be maintained.

Disclosure of Confidential Information

The Certificate of Confidentiality (Public Health Services Act, 1988) protects investigators from forced disclosure of information, but it does not prohibit them from disclosing such information for a valid purpose (Fisher, 2003). As discussed later in the chapter, the APA (2002) Ethics Code permits psychologists providing treatment to disclose information without the participant's consent if the purpose is to provide needed professional services or protect the participant or others from harm, as long as such disclosures are mandated or permitted by law. Investigators working with violent persons participating in intervention research are likely to confront issues of disclosure more frequently than other investigators. On one hand, effective treatment typically requires an open and trusting relationship; clinicians often insist that offenders admit to past acts of violence before they can be considered to have successfully completed treatment (Kalichman et al., 1994). On the other hand, depending on the content of such admissions, researchers may feel compelled to report this information to the authorities. For example, a man in treatment for violence against his spouse may acknowledge similar aggression against his children, requiring the researcher to file a report with the state office of child protective services. Although mandated reporting requirements may make violent individuals reluctant to disclose such information, disclosures do occur and are often a great source of stress for clinicians (as described in the opening vignette).

Although concern about disclosures may risk reducing the reliability of research data and impede the conduct of some types of research altogether, to guarantee participants full confidentiality when disclosures are possible and in some cases probable is a clear violation of participants' rights (Zinger, Wichmann, & Gendreau, 2001). During the consent process, researchers must explicitly detail the information that they may be compelled to report, such as child and elder abuse and threat of harm to self or others (Zinger et al., 2001), as well as information that they are not compelled to report but will (e.g., if substance abuse or nonattendance is to be reported to the court). Researchers who study clinical interventions with potentially violent individuals also face a dilemma as to how to encourage full disclosure from participants while remaining bound to limits of confidentiality and mandated reporting laws.

Clinical Management of Potentially Violent Participants

Advance consideration of ethical and legal issues helps facilitate research with violent persons, but it is naïve to presume that a research study can accommodate all violent offenders. Some individuals will simply be too dangerous to be managed within a research (or treatment) setting. It would be unethical to include in a study individuals at risk of directly harming themselves in reaction to experimental procedures or those for whom the intervention has virtually no likelihood of effectively reducing harm to others. The latter risk not only jeopardizes the safety of society, but also enhances the likelihood that a participant will be (re)incarcerated. Therefore, appropriate screening for potentially high-risk individuals is necessary in any clinical research setting, both to assess the likelihood of violence posed by a prospective study participant and to monitor this risk on an ongoing basis.

Numerous approaches to evaluating violence risk exist across a large number of settings and populations (e.g., domestic violence, psychiatric patients, juvenile offenders). A review of this literature is beyond the scope of this chapter, but comprehensive summaries are readily available (e.g., Monahan, 2008). In this chapter, we highlight a number of critical issues that cut across different clinical research settings without regard to how violence risk is actually assessed, although we would caution that an adequate and empirically grounded risk assessment is critical.

Risk Assessment

One element of violence risk assessment that is particularly important in clinical research settings is the need to obtain as much information as possible before the initial contact with prospective study participants. Because of the possibility that a high-risk individual will be referred to a research study, clinical researchers must take steps to anticipate possible problems before they arise. In extreme cases, researchers may need to take precautions before even scheduling an initial appointment, such as when the individual in question has a history of severe violence. Probation officers may be able to provide details about previous convictions, violations of probation, and the nature of prior offenses (e.g., whether victims were targeted acquaintances or random strangers and whether weapons were used), all of which can help the study coordinator determine (a) whether to accept the referral and (b) what, if any, precautions should be taken. Of course, access to such information may be restricted, because of either institutional or governmental regulations (e.g., prohibiting the release of reports prepared by the Department of Probation or Health Insurance Portability and Accountability Act of 1996 regulations that preclude disclosure of protected health information by health care providers), forcing the researcher to obtain a signed release of information from the prospective participant in advance of study screening procedures.

Having some background information before interviewing potential participants will allow researchers to make a rough determination as to violence risk before even beginning the informed consent process and may help researchers challenge the distorted reports that many offenders provide. Of course, formal (or informal) risk assessment data are precisely the type of information that might become problematic if a treatment study participant engages in violence and records are subpoenaed (emphasizing the benefits of a Certificate of Confidentiality). Nevertheless, clinical necessity often dictates the need for both initial screening and ongoing risk assessment.

Inclusion and Exclusion Criteria

Researchers must also determine, in advance of beginning a study, what level of violence risk can be tolerated within the study. This decision will, of course, hinge on the study setting because treatment programs housed within secure facilities (e.g., psychiatric hospital or correctional institution) may be able to manage individuals who pose an extremely high risk of violence, whereas outpatient or community-based treatment studies often cannot. Treatment research studies should include explicit policies as to how to manage an individual who is identified as posing too great a risk, whether in advance or during the course of treatment, as well as how such risks are to be evaluated. Researchers may consider establishing policies such as referring individuals directly into treatment rather than randomly assigning them to one of several treatment arms (particularly if one alternative is no treatment or a waiting list). Although this approach can compromise the ecological validity of a research study and should therefore be avoided whenever possible, when high-risk patients cannot be safely managed within a research protocol it is critical for the researcher to ensure that this bias in the treatment assignment does not adversely affect the validity of study results for other participants. For example, individuals who cannot be managed in the research setting might be referred to a separate or different intervention altogether, avoiding the problem of having one treatment arm made up of much more refractory or high-risk patients (which provides a much more difficult treatment milieu for research study subjects). In addition, participants should be explicitly informed, if applicable, about whether their participation can be terminated if the investigator decides that the risk of violence is too great.

PROTECTION OF THIRD PARTIES

Case Vignette

> After he was arrested for a third nonviolent sexual offense, Jose was referred to a sex offender treatment program in his community as a condition of parole. The treatment program offered to enroll Jose in a new treatment study comparing an innovative cognitive–behavioral treatment program with a treatment-as-usual condition (i.e., the same individual outpatient psychotherapy they typically provided). During his initial intake evaluation, Jose revealed that he had harbored fantasies about molesting a young child in his neighborhood. Although he insisted that he had no intention of acting on this fantasy, the research investigator was extremely concerned about his risk to this child. Moreover, a formal risk assessment administered as part of the research protocol supported the clinician's intuition, identifying Jose as posing a very high risk of harm. Not only were clinical staff members concerned about their ability to manage Jose in the outpatient treatment study, but questions were raised about whether to warn the identified potential victim.

Despite ethical obligations to maintain participants' confidentiality, as noted previously, there are circumstances in which clinicians are compelled to report information disclosed. Section 4.05(b) of the APA (2002) Ethics Code stipulates that confidentiality may be broken without an individual's consent when required by law, including "to protect the client/patient, psychologist, or others from harm" (p. 1066). In many jurisdictions, clinicians are required to report known or suspected instances of child abuse, elder abuse, and risk of harm to patient's self and to other third parties. Although researchers are typically not specified as mandated reporters in state statutes, research settings that provide clinical interventions differ little from nonresearch clinical contexts (Appelbaum & Rosenbaum, 1989) and thus are presumably held to the same standards of practice. Furthermore, researchers engaged in clinical intervention studies may have both clinical and research relationships with the patient–participant, complicating the applicability of reporting requirements. Finally, IRBs tend to require that researchers report known risks, even when researchers may not be mandated by law to do so.

Duty to Protect

The seminal case mandating a practitioner's duty to protect potential victims from a client–patient's violent actions is Tarasoff v. Regents of the University of California (1976). This case is described in detail elsewhere (see the Introduction to this volume) and is not reviewed again here. What is particularly relevant, however, is that in response to this seminal decision, many state and regional governments in the United States and Canada introduced their own duty-to-protect statutes modeled after the *Tarasoff* ruling. Some of these statutes have copied the *Tarasoff* decision verbatim, and others have broadened or modified the scope of professional responsibility (Truscott, Evans, & Mansell, 1995). For example, California law stipulates that only when a patient has identified a specific plan and an identifiable intended victim is the clinician liable for failing to report this risk. However, some jurisdictions have stipulated that clinicians must take actions to protect third parties even when there is no victim explicitly identified.

Jurisdictions also differ in whether clinicians have a duty to warn versus a duty to protect. Although *Tarasoff* (1976) has often been misinterpreted as a mandate for mental health providers to warn potential victims, jurisdictions vary with regard to what actions are required on the part of the clinician. As a result, some courts mandate a duty to warn, whereas other courts adopted the actual intention of the courts in the *Tarasoff* ruling: a duty to protect through whatever means necessary (Quattrocchi & Schopp, 2005). Steps to protect potential victims may include increasing the frequency of therapy, prescribing psychotropic medications, requiring psychiatric hospitalization, notifying law enforcement authorities, or warning potential victims (Appelbaum & Rosenbaum, 1989). However, under the constraints of a research protocol, some of these options may not be feasible. For example, it may be outside the research protocol to increase the intensity of an intervention for an individual who has made an unanticipated threat against a third party. An investigator who terminates the individual's participation in the study may be implicated in future violent actions the former participant takes against the third party. Additionally, in some research protocols, the treating staff may not be instructed to seek or maintain information about the identity or contact information for persons potentially at risk of harm. In such circumstances, the head of the research team may also be liable for the participant's subsequent violent acts.

In the wake of the *Tarasoff* (1976) decision, investigators studying violent individuals in treatment programs should build into their research protocols criteria for treatment staff to identify, document, and take appropriate action when participants threaten actions against a third party (Fisher et al., 1996). Particularly when research is conducted on an outpatient basis, researchers should have readily available the names and phone numbers of probation or parole officers, police, or other legal system personnel (e.g., the judge or district attorney) to enable rapid communication about potentially violent participants. Because the variations in legal standards and requirements are too numerous to cover here, researchers are advised to familiarize themselves with the relevant statutes in their particular regions (for examples of state judicial rulings, see Quattrocchi & Schopp, 2005, and Rosenfeld & Galietta, 2004).

Mandated Child and Elder Abuse Reporting Laws

Since the 1976 Child Abuse Prevention and Treatment Act, all 50 states have enacted statutes mandating the reporting of suspected child abuse or neglect for mental health professionals and in many states researchers, as members of the general citizenry (Fisher et al., 1996). In the vignette described earlier, issues of mandated reporting are likely to be in the forefront of research design considerations. However, cases are likely to arise in which requirements are far less obvious (e.g., a domestic violence offender who has children in the home). Child abuse is defined as acts of physical, emotional, or sexual abuse, as well as neglect (e.g., depriving a child of schooling, medical care, adequate food, or supervision; Kalichman et al., 1994). The federal Child Abuse Prevention and Treatment Act (last reauthorized and amended in 2003) provides the minimum standards for what defines child maltreatment; individual states stipulate their own standards that satisfy or exceed these federal minimums.

Just as jurisdictions vary in their specific requirements for reporting third-party risk, the specific wording for when mandated reporters must submit a report of child abuse varies. Most states require that practitioners make reports when they "suspect or [have] reason to believe" that abuse or neglect is occurring; however, the standard is higher in some states, requiring that a reporter must have "knowledge of or observes a child being subjected to conditions that would reasonably result in harm to the child" (Child Abuse Protection and Treatment Act, 2003). In short, there is discrepancy between whether researchers should act on suspicion versus evidence of a child's being at risk. Each state also stipulates different processes regarding how to file a report (i.e., which agency processes reports and the allowable time frames in which to submit a report). Researchers must familiarize themselves with the relevant statutes that apply to the circumstances in which they will be conducting treatment research. Researchers who fail to report acts of child maltreatment are liable both ethically and legally and therefore must determine in advance what steps will be taken if they are provided evidence that is required to be reported, as well as how they will prepare participants for limitations in confidentiality.

In addition to knowing the mandated laws aimed at protecting the safety of children, researchers should be familiar with state laws protecting elderly persons. Mandated reporters are specified in almost every state, and in the vast majority, mental health professionals are included in the list of entities required to report elder abuse (Welfel, Danzinger, & Santoro, 2000). Elder abuse is typically defined as acts of physical abuse, neglect, psychological abuse, financial exploitation, and violation of rights, although the precise wording varies across jurisdictions. States also differ in how they define the age that constitutes "elderly" and whether reporting is required only for those elderly people who are of a particular health or competency status. For example, in New York and New Jersey, mental health professionals are required to report suspected abuse perpetrated against elders only when the elder lives in an institutional setting, and therefore not for those who reside in the community. The ethical considerations that support reporting elder abuse, however, do not vary according to venue.

Taking Proactive Steps

The nature of treatment research with potentially violent persons inevitably raises the likelihood that researchers will be faced with learning about participants' past, present, or future acts or threats of harm. As detailed earlier, some of these threats may require the researcher to warn or protect potential victims or inform authorities of suspected harm, whereas others may be managed through the clinical intervention under investigation. In either case, laws prioritize the rights of third parties over maintenance of confidentiality. Therefore, to enable research to contribute to the understanding and decrease of violence, investigators should take proactive measures to inform participants of the circumstances in which confidentiality will be breached, such as if they reveal directly or raise suspicion that children or elderly people are at risk or that they intend to cause serious harm to a third party. Additionally, because statutes are worded to indicate a likelihood or suspicion of violence, as opposed to a certainty, researchers should be aware of how to probe for such factors as violence history, availability of the victim, access to weapons, substance use, and present stressors (Truscott et al., 1995) and should learn the laws relevant in their state.

PROTECTION OF RESEARCH PERSONNEL

Case Vignette

> Susan participated in an experimental treatment program for adolescent girls who engaged in violent behavior that was developed by a university faculty member and implemented by university graduate students. The program was operated in rented office space near the university, and the researchers hired off-duty police officers to provide security during clinic hours. The security officer used a metal detector to scan incoming participants to ensure that they were not carrying weapons and was responsible for intervening if any participants became violent. Some of the participants, particularly Susan, perceived the security officer to be disrespectful, and Susan complained frequently in group that she was "made to feel like a criminal every week." One evening, Susan arrived at the program extremely agitated after she had been accused of shoplifting on her way to the program. When the security officer asked her to remove her jacket, Susan refused and pushed her way into the clinic, walking directly into the group. The security officer did not follow because there were other participants attempting to enter the building. When two of the researchers approached Susan and asked her to return to the security desk, she became even more agitated, cursing and accusing the researchers of not understanding what it was like to be disrespected. She refused to follow their instructions and paced around the room, frightening the research staff and other group members. When the security officer finally returned to intervene, he discovered that Susan had a large knife in her coat pocket.

Clinicians and researchers who treat violent individuals invariably place themselves at some degree of risk. Participants may harbor hostility toward the clinicians, particularly if they perceive the demands of the intervention as excessive or unreasonable. Participants who are court mandated may react negatively to the threat of being terminated from a study or to confrontations regarding their behavior. In addition, as described in the vignette, some individuals may lack sufficient coping skills or react angrily to stressors extraneous to the research intervention. Concerns about violence risk are heightened when graduate students participate in the research program, whether as treatment providers or in another research capacity (e.g., conducting intake or follow-up interviews). The young age of many trainees and their relative inexperience in managing difficult clients requires that researchers take extensive steps to provide adequate training and security for treatment staff.

Although there is no recipe to guarantee successful management of violent patients, several steps can be implemented that minimize the likelihood of harm to research personnel and other treatment program participants. These include decisions about the most appropriate setting in which to conduct the proposed research intervention, who the treatment and research staff should be, how they are trained to recognize and contain aggressive behaviors, and, in extreme cases, perhaps even protecting the identity of research staff.

Determining the Appropriate Research Setting

Deciding where a study will be conducted encompasses a number of factors including not only convenience and cost (which are often paramount for many researchers, particularly when funding is limited) but also determining what level of security is required and what, if any, measures need to be taken to modify the environment. Within correctional institutions, the risk of harm to researchers and other participants may be minimized by the ready access to correctional or safety officers. Nevertheless, researchers are often advised to select a location that is easily visible to others (e.g., with Plexiglas walls or in open areas) and/or that contains security phones. Researchers should always avoid areas with objects that could be used as potential weapons (e.g., office supplies, kitchenware, medical instruments).

Although clinicians may presume that an institutional environment eliminates the risk of participants bringing a weapon to the treatment site, such an assumption is naïve and potentially dangerous. Inmates and forensic patients often create or obtain shanks or other homemade weapons, and the potential harm inflicted by such instruments can be severe. Moreover, unlike community settings, in which participants may be routinely required to pass through a metal detector and/or have their possessions searched, institutional environments may not require such procedures. Thus, clinicians must be no less mindful when implementing clinical research interventions in an institutional setting than they would be in a community-based environment. For example, demanding that adequate security be available and nearby may require considerable advance negotiation but is critical to ensuring the safety of research staff. Participants should also be informed about any security measures that may affect them such as being observed by security or supervisory personnel or being searched or "wanded" (for metal detection). Community-based settings also raise a number of additional issues that are often more easily managed in institutional settings. When the risk of violence posed by study participants is high, researchers might consider seeking space within a secure setting such as probation offices or a court.

Although security may already exist in these settings, increasing the convenience and decreasing the expenses (which can be particularly important for studies with limited funding), this advantage needs to be weighed against potentially adverse effects. For example, research and treatment personnel may become associated with legal entities and elevate participant concerns about confidentiality even more than is already inherent. In addition, such associations may actually heighten the risk of harm to research personnel, as participants may feel pressured to participate in treatment for fear of reprisal (despite any assertions to the contrary made during the informed consent process). In less secure settings, such as on a university campus or in rented office space, researchers should consider contracting with a private security company or providing their own security personnel (e.g., purchasing metal detector wands, which can be obtained quite inexpensively) to minimize the likelihood of participants bringing weapons into the study setting or becoming aggressive during treatment.

In addition to the setting chosen, several considerations pertain to the physical layout of the treatment space. For example, researchers should consider and address questions such as the following: Have rooms been set up to enable researchers to easily escape if need be? If the intervention involves individual treatment, are other researchers within close proximity? Have researchers considered items that might potentially be used as weapons? For example, using weighted chairs might be preferable to light chairs, which are easier to lift and throw or swing. Researchers are advised to scan the environment before each interaction with a potentially violent participant to minimize risk.

Additional Protective Measures

Security may also be enhanced by ensuring that research is conducted by at least two researchers in tandem. This model is common in clinical practice and ensures that one person will be available to get needed help while the other person can try to deescalate any violence potential. Additionally, researchers should establish protocols for responding to a participant who becomes potentially violent, for example, determining who will obtain help and from where and what means will be used to separate the participant from other participants. Obviously, researchers should avoid any physical confrontations with participants. Instead, there are various verbal and nonverbal techniques that can assist in deescalating an agitated participant, such as dropping one's voice, validating an individual's experience, and asking questions.

In addition to ensuring immediate physical safety, researchers need to be cognizant of their safety outside of the treatment. For example, with some offenders (e.g., stalking offenders, rapists) it may be especially important to ensure that steps are taken to protect personally identifying information. To do so, researchers might avoid use of their last names. Of course, research publications and treatment program advertisements must consider this issue because Internet access is hardly uncommon, and many high-risk individuals could search the Internet for the treatment program name, thus discovering the names of researchers and graduate student coauthors. In our own research, we have occasionally omitted the name of the treatment program from published materials to minimize the risk that an individual who searches for information on the program will discover the names of treatment staff. In addition to these steps, study participants and referring personnel may choose to use a contact phone number that is reserved for the study (e.g., a cell phone) and cannot be linked to any individual staff member. Under no circumstances do we recommend providing personal contact information to research program participants (e.g., personal cell or home phone number).

CONCLUSION

The challenges faced by clinical researchers working with potentially violent individuals are numerous, but they are balanced by the critical importance of continuing to develop appropriate and efficacious interventions for this challenging population. This chapter should serve as a starting point, but it by no means provides an exhaustive summary of all of the issues that may arise in any particular study. In addition to the general guidelines described here, consultation with experienced clinicians and researchers can often help to identify issues and risks that are unique to a particular setting or population that are simply too numerous or idiosyncratic to be included in this brief overview.

As evidenced by the breadth of this chapter, treatment research with individuals known or suspected of posing a significant risk of violence poses a number of legal, ethical, and practical challenges. Researchers are obligated to address these issues on multiple levels, including protecting the rights of research participants while maintaining the integrity of their study methods. In addition, protecting the safety of research staff and other study participants is critical to the success of treatment research, particularly for those researchers who use graduate students in their research setting. Only with vigilance to all of these issues can clinical researchers avoid the many potential pitfalls that exist in this challenging research area.

REFERENCES

Additional Protections Pertaining to Biomedical and Behavioral Research Involving Prisoners as Subjects, 43 Fed. Reg. 53,655 (Nov. 16, 1978) (to be codified at 45 C.F.R. pt. 46).

American Psychological Association. (2002). Ethical principles of psychologists and code of conduct. *American Psychologist, 57,* 1060–1073.

Appelbaum, P. S., & Rosenbaum, A. (1989). Tarasoff and the researcher: Does the duty to protect apply in the research setting? *American Psychologist, 44,* 885–894.

Appelbaum, P. S., Roth, L. H., & Lidz, C. (1982). The therapeutic misconception: Informed consent in psychiatric research. *International Journal of Law and Psychiatry, 5,* 319–329.

Child Abuse Prevention and Treatment Act, 42 U. S. C. 5116 et seq., as amended, Pub. L. 104-235. Retrieved February 10, 2007, from http://www.acf.hhs.gov/programs/cb/laws_policies/cblaws/capta03/index.htm

Fisher, C. B. (2003). *Decoding the Ethics Code: A practical guide for psychologists*. Thousand Oaks, CA: Sage.

Fisher, C. B., Hoagwood, K., & Jensen, P. (1996). Casebook on ethical issues in research with children and adolescents with mental disorders. In K. Hoagwood, P. Jensen, & C. B. Fisher (Eds.), *Ethical issues in research with children and adolescents with mental disorders* (pp. 135–238). Hillsdale, NJ: Erlbaum.

Gostin, L. O., Vanchieri, C., & Pope, A. (2006). *Ethical considerations for research involving prisoners*. Washington, DC: National Academies Press.

Health Insurance Portability and Accountability Act of 1996, Pub. L. No. 104-191, 110 Stat. 1936 (1996).

Israel, M. (2004). Strictly confidential? Integrity and disclosure of criminological and socio-legal research. *British Journal of Criminology*, *44*, 715–744.

Kalichman, S. C., Brosig, C. L., & Kalichman, M. O. (1994). Mandatory child abuse reporting laws: Issues and implications for treating offenders. *Journal of Offender Rehabilitation*, *21*(1–2), 27–43.

Monahan, J. (2008). Actuarial risk assessment of violence. In R. I. Simon & K. Tardiff (Eds.), *Textbook of violence assessment and management* (pp. 17–34). Washington, DC: American Psychiatric Press.

Moser, D. J., Arndt, S., Kanz, J., Benjamin, M. L., Bayless, J. D., Reese, R. L., et al. (2004). Coercion and informed consent in research involving prisoners. *Comprehensive Psychiatry*, *45*, 1–9.

Public Health Service Act § 301(d), 42 U.S.C. 241(d), as amended by Pub. L. No. 100-607 § 163 (1988).

Quattrocchi, M. R., & Schopp, R. F. (2005). Tarasaurus rex: A standard of care that could not adapt. *Psychology, Public Policy, and Law*, *11*, 109–137.

Rosenfeld, B., Fava, J., & Galietta, M. (2008). Treatment of the stalking offender: Considerations for risk assessment and intervention. In J. Werth, E. R. Welful, & G. A. H. Benjamin (Eds.), *The duty to protect: Ethical, legal, and professional considerations for mental health professionals* (pp. 157–173). Washington, DC: American Psychological Association.

Rosenfeld, B., & Galietta, M. (2004). Clinical and ethical issues in the treatment of potentially violent individuals. In T. L. Jackson & L. VandeCreek (Eds.), *Innovations in clinical practice: Focus on violence treatment and prevention* (pp. 165–176). Sarasota, FL: Professional Resource Press.

Tarasoff v. Regents of the University of California, 551 P.2d 334 (1976).

Truscott, D., Evans, J., & Mansell, S. (1995). Outpatient psychotherapy with dangerous clients: A model for clinical decision making. *Professional Psychology: Research and Practice*, *26*, 484–490.

U.S. Department of Health and Human Services. (2006). *Institutional review board guidebook: Chapter VI special classes of subjects*. Retrieved January 31, 2007, from http://www.hhs.gov/ohrp/irb/irb_chapter6.htm

Welfel, E. R., Danzinger, P. R., & Santoro, S. (2000). Mandated reporting of abuse/maltreatment of older adults: A primer for counselors. *Journal of Counseling & Development*, *78*, 284–292.

Zinger, I., Wichmann, C., & Gendreau, P. (2001). Legal and ethical obligations in social research: The limited confidentiality requirement. *Canadian Journal of Criminology, 43*, 269–274.

9

DO DRUG ABUSE RESEARCHERS HAVE A DUTY TO PROTECT THIRD PARTIES FROM HIV TRANSMISSION? MORAL PERSPECTIVES OF STREET DRUG USERS

CELIA B. FISHER, MATTHEW ORANSKY, MEENA MAHADEVAN, MERRILL SINGER, GREGORY MIRHEJ, AND G. DERRICK HODGE

The intertwining effects of illicit drug use and HIV have created a public health crisis, especially in minority communities, in which the poorest and most vulnerable are at risk of HIV transmission through sharing or reusing syringes and other drug paraphernalia and through unprotected sex (Centers for Disease Control and Prevention [CDC], 2005; National Institute on Drug Abuse, 2000; Sanders-Phillips & Schoenbaum, 2001; Singer, 1994). Few studies have spoken to the social norms surrounding or perceived responsibility for HIV transmission among illicit drug users (but see Deren, Beardsley, Coyle, & Singer, 1998). However, in an effort to create innovative HIV prevention programming among drug users, researchers have begun to investigate the prevailing ethics and social norms regarding HIV transmission in illicit drug-using populations (Fisher et al., 2008). Such research may present unique questions of research ethics. Indeed, social scientists conducting ethnographic and field research are often involved in long-term professional relationships with HIV-infected active drug users involving exploration of participants' intimate thoughts and private behaviors. In such contexts, investigators often become aware of participants' sexual or needle-sharing practices that increase the risk of HIV transmission to noninfected third parties (Loue, 2000; Singer et al., 1999). In such situations, do investigators have an ethical obligation to protect third parties from harm? When, if ever, does a responsibility to intervene in HIV transmission supersede obligations to protect participant confidentiality?

Confidentiality is particularly important in ethnographic and field research with vulnerable populations. Active drug users living with and at risk of HIV often fear social stigma, community rejection, and economic discrimination. Disclosure of such confidential information by researchers can make these fears a reality and may also discourage others from research participation. At the same time, the community context in which such research takes place often means that the investigator may have an ongoing relationship with both the participant who is HIV infected and his or her noninfected drug or sexual partner.

HIV-RELATED RESEARCH AND THE DUTY TO PROTECT

To address the question of the extent of researcher responsibility to intervene to prevent possible HIV transmission from a research participant to another person, some have looked for theoretical parallels and distinctions between the research context and the legal duty to protect imposed on psychologists, psychiatrists, and other health care professionals after the landmark 1976 *Tarasoff v. Regents of the University of California* (Appelbaum & Rosenbaum, 1989; Fisher, 2004; see also the Introduction to this volume).

Since *Tarasoff* (1976), there have been numerous and conflicting decisions in state and federal rulings on the application of *Tarasoff's* mandate that health professionals must warn third parties of potential violence. In particular, there has been substantial debate about whether knowledge of a person's intent to transmit HIV fits within this violence framework. The validity of the analogy between using a weapon to murder someone and knowingly transmitting the HIV virus was heatedly debated in the beginning of the HIV epidemic when there were no treatments for the fatal disease (*Reisner v. Regents of the University of California*, 1995). However, with today's treatment options and available public knowledge about steps to protect oneself from HIV transmission, the analogy is more tenuous (Ainslie, 1999). There is also the question of whether intent to have sex without protection can be read as intent to transmit HIV.

Although there is as yet no case law addressing a researcher's duty to protect third parties—and such law might not include HIV transmission as a category within the duty to protect—the issue remains a moral one for drug-use ethnographers and other researchers. In this respect, the three criteria for the duty to protect outlined by the *Tarasoff* (1976) doctrine may provide a useful conceptual model within which to frame the ethical questions of concern (Appelbaum & Rosenbaum, 1989; Levmore, 1986); namely, does the researcher have a "special relationship" to the participant that places the investigator in a position to prevent harm (HIV transmission) to another? Does the researcher have the ability to predict that harm (HIV transmission) will occur (Singer, Huertas, & Scott, 2001)? Does the researcher know the identity of the potential victim?

SCOPE OF THIS CHAPTER

To address these three criteria, we present recent research that sought the perspective of HIV-positive and HIV-negative drug users regarding the moral obligations among researchers, HIV-positive research participants, and the participants' HIV-negative partners. Too often, bioethicists and the research community have deliberated the duty-to-protect obligation without taking into account the moral values of the participants who would be affected by any actions taken or not taken (Ainslie, 1999; Fisher, 1999, 2002, 2003, 2004; Melton, Levine, Koocher, Rosenthal, & Thompson, 1988; Singer, 1993). To explore these perspectives, we used the focus group method to gain the emic, or insider, perspective with current and recent street drug users. Focus group discussions on the issue of duty to protect were stimulated by a brief videotaped presentation of a "research vignette" that was carefully designed to present participants with a visual example of an ethnographic study that contained all three *Tarasoff* criteria.

METHOD

Data for this study were collected as part of a larger National Institute on Drug Abuse–sponsored project exploring participant perspectives on ethical issues in drug use and HIV-related research (Fisher et al., 2008; Singer et al., 2008). Eleven focus groups were conducted (6 in New York City and 5 in Hartford, Connecticut). Groups were homogeneous with respect to ethnicity and gender (African American men and women, Hispanic men and women, non-Hispanic White men and women). In addition, two groups composed of mixed-ethnicity men who have sex with men (MSM) were held in New York City. Focus groups with Hispanic participants were conducted in Spanish. All focus group sessions were conducted in meeting rooms provided by Housing Works in New York City or the Hispanic Health Council in Hartford. The study was approved by the institutional review boards at each site, and all participants gave written informed consent.

Participants and Recruitment

One hundred self-described active or recent drug users (68% male; 22–70 years old, M age = 43 years) were recruited through street outreach in Hartford and agency referral in New York City. Participants were excluded if they showed signs of mental disorder or cognitive impairment. Participants self-identified as African American (33%), Hispanic (37%), non-Hispanic White (22%), and other (8%); 24%, as MSM; and 39%, as HIV positive. Most participants (61%) were unemployed and reported welfare or social security benefits as their only income; 32% reported disabilities that interfered with full-time employment; 79% had no more than a high school education; 75% had participated in research on drugs, alcohol, or HIV; and 43% had participated in a treatment study for these disorders.

Data Collection and Analysis

As noted, discussions were stimulated by three 4-minute videotaped vignettes in English and Spanish depicting drug research scenarios with "participants" portrayed by ethnically diverse professional actors. Each focus group watched videos in which the participant was the same gender as the members of the group and the investigator was of the opposite gender. In total, three vignettes on different research methods were shown to participants. Here we report on data generated by the "ethnographic" vignette. Discussions were tape recorded. To protect confidentiality, the investigators acquired a Certificate of Confidentiality (Public Health Service Act, 1988), and participant pseudonyms were used. Participants were paid a $25 incentive plus transportation costs. An advisory board of drug abuse advocates, social workers, and addicts assisted in deciding on fair compensation and final content and format of the informed consent and video scripts. A codebook was developed integrating themes emerging from the participants' own words and themes on the basis of the bioethics literature. The final set of codes was catalogued in a software program (Atlas.ti, ©2002–2008—ATLAS.ti Scientific Software Development GmbH) that was then used to recode the transcripts and generate the final themes and subthemes.

The Vignette

The vignette of interest for this analysis depicted a meeting between an ethnographic researcher and a participant with whom the researcher had been working for several months. The researcher and participant appeared to be on friendly terms—the interaction began with the researcher giving the participant a sandwich and something to drink. As the interview progressed, however, a major ethical dilemma regarding HIV confidentiality and disclosure emerged. The participant, who had previously told the investigator that she (he) was HIV positive, casually mentions that she (he) is having regular unprotected sex with a third party (Chris) who is HIV negative and unaware of the participant's HIV status. The participant had recommended that Chris also be part of the ethnographic study, and the investigator had conducted an initial interview with Chris and had scheduled another. Hearing that the participant and Chris are an HIV-discordant couple engaged in unprotected sex, the ethnographer raises the issue of informing Chris of the participant's HIV status, to which the participant strongly objects. In describing his or her responsibility to disclose the participant's HIV status to the naïve partner, the ethnographer reminds the participant that this requirement was discussed during the informed consent process. The participant angrily responds, "I gave you permission to write stuff down I talk about, but I didn't give you permission to ruin my sex life."

The vignette met all *Tarasoff* (1976) criteria: (a) The investigator had a "special relationship" (symbolized by the gift of food) in which he (she) could possibly prevent HIV transmission by informing Chris of the participant's HIV status; (b) the HIV transmission was foreseeable on the basis of information the participant provided; and (c) because Chris was also a participant, the potential "victim" was identifiable and locatable. The vignette also addressed contextual issues by noting that the limits of confidentiality had been explicitly mentioned during informed consent and that the participant refused to disclose her (his) HIV status to her (his) partner. Key subsequent focus group discussions included the following issues: (a) the obligation of a researcher to warn a third party of the participant's harmful behavior; (b) the researcher's compromising his or her relationship with the participant to warn the third party of this behavior; (c) the obligation of the participant to take responsibility for her or his own harmful behavior; (d) the researcher's responsibility to the overall welfare of the community he or she is researching; (e) the right of the participant to self-govern and maintain a private life; and (f) the limits to confidentiality being clearly communicated through the consent procedures.

PARTICIPANT PERSPECTIVES

In this section we give voice to participants' moral beliefs about investigator and participant obligations in response to the *Tarasoff*-type vignette. We organize our presentation of these beliefs through the following themes: Researchers as moral agents with responsibilities to personal conscience and community; pragmatics of ethical decision-making in high risk contexts; participants/drug users as moral agent; informed consent as contractual obligations; and instances when prior agreements regarding confidentiality may have been unclear.

Researcher as Moral Agent

Our research team was struck by the regularity of focus group participants' interpretations. They nearly universally viewed the vignette through the lens of an obligation to protect others from harm. Given the privileged status that confidentiality has had in bioethics, we had anticipated that the group's first response would be to object to any violation of confidentiality. Although confidentiality was certainly important to the participants, as we describe later, the majority of focus group members cast ethnographic researchers as moral agents who were responsible for taking action when it was within their capacity to prevent a harm committed by someone else.

"There Is Some Obligation There to Say Something"

A foundational claim made by many focus group members was that researchers have a moral imperative to interfere with an individual's destructive behavior to protect another person from harm. As a Black woman asserted, "The bottom line is that he [investigator] can stop her [infected participant] right now, because she can spread this around." Similar to the third criteria of the *Tarasoff* (1976) doctrine, knowing the identity of a potential victim was a deciding factor, as indicated by the following comment by a focus group participant: "If you know who they are, then I would think that there is an obligation to tell those people that they're at risk" (White woman).

"It's in His Job Description"

In assigning moral agency to the researcher, it is evident that some focus group members viewed the researcher as a professional whose duties involved acting in the best interests of the community. They argued that in the words of one Black woman, "the job that he's doing is to protect someone, not hurt them." Indeed, when asked whether the researcher should warn a participant's sexual or drug partner about his or her risk of HIV infection, one participant responded, "That is his [the researcher's] job. His job to tell him that the other person is positive" (Hispanic woman). Likewise, a Hispanic male participant asserted that "she [the researcher] needs to tell; she needs to tell that girl. She needs to be professional and do her job." Finally, another participant argued that

> He [the researcher] took the job and he knows there are certain things he's gonna face, he's going up against . . . okay? He's get trained for that job first off, to know what he's gonna cop up on. So he's already ready for whatever. (Black woman)

For some participants, their views on the researcher's professional obligations stemmed from their experience with the reporting obligations of health care providers. One White woman stated, "Don't you have to disclosure that information being, you know, being a psychologist or sociologist, don't you have to disclose that?" Another participant asserted, "She [the researcher] has a legal obligation under the statute to tell . . . inform the girl that . . . he's HIV positive. Just like when you tell a shrink you're gonna commit suicide, he has a legal obligation to report it to the authorities" (Black man).

"How Is the Researcher Going to Feel Later On?"

To some, the duty to protect was an obligation of personal conscience, perhaps causing a negligent investigator to be haunted with guilt if he or she failed to follow through. As described by the following participant,

> For me, I think he [the researcher] has to say it because in his [conscience] he is going to think that he should have told, like, "Take care and protect yourself." Because if he doesn't say it, how is the researcher going to feel later on? (Hispanic woman)

In the eyes of other participants, a researcher who did not disclose the participant's HIV status to his or her unknowing partner became an "accomplice" to the "crime." One Hispanic woman argued that "it is like the researcher is covering [for] the participant but is killing the boyfriend." Furthermore, as described by another participant,

> He [the researcher] really can't hide that, because if anything was to happen to that man it would be on his head, because he already knows and, um, the job that he's doing is to protect someone, not hurt them, so it would really be on his head. (Black woman)

"She Has a Responsibility Overall to the Community"

According to focus group members, the moral urgency to protect identified third parties from HIV transmission goes beyond the individual and reflects fears about the potential ripple effect of HIV transmission throughout the community. One Black female participant, speaking metaphorically, likened this process to "dropping a bomb" in the community. Another Black female participant noted, "Because if [the third party] doesn't know, he can infect the next person, and the next person. [The participant is] endangering a lot of lives . . . She may have already endangered a lot of lives." A Black male participant echoed this sentiment, stating,

> "She [the investigator] has a responsibility overall to the community. Where she has to disclose . . . if she knows that he's hurting or putting someone at risk to be hurt then she has to disclose, she has to disclose."

Common wisdom among ethnographic and field researchers tells us that researchers must work to protect participant confidentiality so as to gain the trust of the community to enable effective research. Although some focus group members thought that the community would, in the words of one Black woman, "probably be thanking" the researcher, most others recognized that these actions might indeed jeopardize the research. From a moral perspective, however, as 1 Black female participant expressed it, this was "a chance he [the investigator] gonna have to take." This duality of research risk and responsibility was illustrated in comments among members in one of the MSM groups. Although some thought that the researcher might be "riding a thin line" or "messing with her credibility in the neighborhood with the drug addicts," other focus group members were quick to point out that "there are going to be other people that are going to be glad that you told because they won't mess around with that person either."

People Are Responsible for Themselves: "I Should Be the One Who Protects Myself"

Not all focus group members thought that the investigator had a moral responsibility to alert a third party to the dangers of HIV transmission. Some argued that each individual should be responsible for his or her own well-being, and if individuals have unprotected sex or share needles, they put themselves in harm's way.

> I don't think she [the researcher] should [tell Chris, the third party]. I think that Chris knows what he's getting into. Look, if you're gonna have sex with somebody, you know what's out there now. Everyone knows about AIDS. You put a rubber on. If you don't put a rubber on when you're having sex, that means you know what you're planning . . . you're taking your chances and that's that. It's as simple as that. If you don't want to catch something, you protect yourself. Even if someone said yes, they were negative, you still should put [a condom] on because you don't know. So it's really up to him. It's not up to her [the researcher] to tell somebody else's business. (Black man)
>
> I personally think that being in this environment, it's nothing new, that I should be the one who protects myself because nobody else out there is gonna to protect me from any kind of disease or anything. So I should be the one who's responsible for protecting myself. (White woman)

A few participants argued, in the words of 1 Black male participant, that "a relationship means to ask the person from the beginning, like we need to go ahead and discuss it if you're thinking about having sex with me." An HIV-negative partner who does not take this precaution, in the eyes of another Black male participant, "is actually harming himself."

Pragmatic Approaches to the Dilemma

Some male participants advocated a middle-of-the-road approach to the dilemma. Although they recognized the obligation of the researcher to protect the third party, they also recognized issues of investigator safety and research participant privacy.

"He Could Have Killed Her for That"

Several focus group participants did not base their decisions on a sense of right or wrong. Instead, they were more practical, asserting that the researcher may be putting him- or herself in physical danger if he or she discloses the participant's HIV status.

> He [the participant] could have killed her [the researcher], and she put herself in a precarious position by threatening him to tell his girlfriend. He doesn't know . . . how much value there is first of all in that relationship, what it is. If it was very, very valuable, she [the researcher] could have been hurt. (Black man)
>
> When she [the researcher] said to him [the participant] that she was obligated to say to the other person that he was infected, otherwise he is going to hurt his partner. And how about if the guy loses his mind and hurts her right there? (Hispanic man)

"Saying It Without Saying It"

Focus group members suggested creative ways in which the researcher could fulfill her obligation to protect both the third party and herself. As a Hispanic male participant stated, "She has to find a way of talking to him so that she is not gonna have to convince him but she can say to him that the three of them can talk together." Other participants agreed,

> I guess what she [the researcher] should have did, instead of saying it to him [the participant], she should be trying to make Chris take a HIV test. That's what she should be doing. . . . She could say, well, you know that you've been doing and have . . . she could ask him have you been having unprotected sex? Something like that, and then working to you're using drugs and having a lot of unprotected sex, you really should seriously think about taking the HIV test. Something like that. That way she doesn't get into his personal business with the other person. (Black man)
>
> What she could tell her is that, you know what, when was the last time you got tested? "Don't you think it's time you got tested for HIV? Since your boyfriend is getting high, whatever." That is one way to bring it up. (MSM, unknown ethnicity)

The Participant (Drug User) as Moral Agent

Many focus group members believed that both the researcher and the HIV-infected participant were morally responsible to take action to protect a third party from HIV transmission; they also judged the HIV-infected participant as being morally responsible to warn or protect his or her partner.

"Taking Your Responsibility"

Some focus group participants felt that revealing one's status is ethically justified because it stems the tide of the AIDS epidemic in their neighborhoods. Accordingly, 1 White woman stated, "Knowledge is power: So if you know, at least you can stop yourself from spreading it and giving it to someone else."

> [Sharing HIV status] should be done before any sexual contact, period. I know it's hard for everyone. Today, look at what's going on with all the dealing, all the deal information going on, look at the results in your neighborhood. So you gotta look at the overall good and the fact that, look, let's stop the bullshit. People are dying who have nothing to do with what you did sexually, and you're bringing it back to someone who is totally innocent, like the mother with children. You're taking a mother away from [her] children. You're ruining people's lives. And that overrides all that other stuff about I don't want to tell because I'm gonna lose them. (MSM, unknown ethnicity)

Others constructed moral responsibility as relational. Having a caring and intimate relationship with someone creates an ethical responsibility to be honest with him or her and to protect him or her from harm.

For example, 1 Black male participant claimed that "beyond the simple fact that he [the participant] wasn't thinking about Chris. Because if he was and he really cared for Chris, he would have told him from the jump." Echoing this relational ethics, a Hispanic female participant argued that "because they are both living that together; they are involved with each other. And if she has HIV, he has to know that, he has to know that she is infected." Additionally, another participant asserted,

> Then I would say, too, somebody . . . you're putting another person at risk because I believe . . . that if you're HIV positive and you're involved in a relationship, and the minute that it becomes a little bit more intimate and you know you're going down that route and become sexually involved, or plan to be in a long-term relationship, I think it's the other person's obligation, who is positive, to tell. (MSM, unknown ethnicity)

Some pointed out the vulnerability of partners who are trusting, and others noted that one could still maintain an intimate relationship with a partner who knows about his or her HIV status.

> In the relationship there should be trust and if there isn't, well, that is too bad. But that is like what happened to my brother . . . that a friend of his who had HIV invited him and my brother was so desperate that he shared needles with him; he couldn't say "no" to some friends, you know. He's been dead now for 18 years. (Hispanic woman)
>
> There's people out there that know that, you know, they still can have a relationship even though they have the virus . . . he don't have to worry about not being able to meet somebody else, because there are people out there that can handle it and know how to protect themselves. (Black woman)

"It's Fair, You Know Why? 'Cause He Lied"

For a number of focus group participants, ethical justification for the investigator's intervention in the participant's spreading of HIV was laced with contempt for the participant and in some cases was motivated by the desire for distributive justice; as 1 Black woman noted, "She [the participant] was showing him no love for herself. And, therefore, if you ain't showing for yourself, you don't care about no one else." This sentiment was particularly characteristic of the views of the MSM group members: "He's a liar and he's infecting people and, yeah, she shouldn't do that without telling him, yes. Even if it's not professional or anything, but, just because of that" (MSM, unknown ethnicity).

> You know, the same thing happens to me. That's why I'm telling you that it's not fair for them to not tell you because this nurse that I used to know he never told me. I was 21 years old, still naive, I didn't know very much, I was coming from a place that I didn't know this big city was like the way it is and he never told me he have HIV and I have sex with him one time. One time. I wasn't using drugs. It wasn't drugs related, it wasn't nothing related like that. And that guy gave me HIV, you understand? I don't think it's fair, and now I'm fine, but back then it was hell for me. Try and understand why people can be out there infecting people and not telling them. (MSM, unknown ethnicity)

"That's Killing Somebody"

Focus group participants' disregard for the consequences of disclosure for the HIV-infected participant was notable and appeared rooted in contempt for an individual who was knowingly spreading HIV. Indeed, a person who was spreading HIV was seen, by many focus group participants, as committing murder. These views are of particular interest because medical advances in treating HIV have made HIV infection less of a death sentence. The interpretation that knowing transmission of HIV is a crime is evidenced in the following dialogues among members of a Black female and a White female focus group, respectively:

Participant 1: If you knew that you are positive and you don't tell nobody and you get. . . . I felt like that should be a crime.

Participant 2: Yeah . . . should be a crime.

Participant 1: It should be a crime, 'cause you're killing them.

Participant 2: It is attempted murder.

Participant 1: Yeah, that's how I feel.

Participant 3: She's hurting her boyfriend.

Participant 2: If they did pass away, and you gave somebody HIV intentionally. . . .

Participant 3: That's killing somebody

Similar sentiments were voiced by MSM participants, with 1 group member stating, "To me you're just taking another person's life away, and that's not fair to you or to them. And I've seen it happen, where people just went around giving it." Another argued, "This day and time, you do something like that you go to jail. Because it is putting at risk another life of a human being and they can prosecute you for that."

Informed Consent and Following the Rules

An influential factor in many focus group members' opinions about investigator and participant responsibilities was the fact that the limits of confidentiality had been included in the original research consent discussion (Researcher: "Remember I told you that I might have to tell someone if I learned you were going to hurt them").

"She Should Enforce the Rules on Him"

Many focus group members argued that the researcher should report a participant's HIV status to his or her unknowing partner if doing so followed the guidelines as outlined in the consent form. Participants emphasized what they believed were "contractual" obligations, forged during informed consent. In this situation, respondents saw the researcher's "allegiance to a set of rules" as holding greater moral suasion than his or her ongoing relationship with the participant or the participant's preferences. As 1 White male group member asserted, "They sign consent forms at the beginning of the interview. They should follow whatever the consent forms say, doesn't matter who it is." A Black male participant stated, "Actually, she [the researcher] had no allegiance [to the participant] really. She had allegiance to a set of rules, of policy. None of the interviewees were who she's working for." These sentiments were echoed throughout the focus groups:

> I think she [the researcher] should tell him [Chris] because she already explained to him the rules and regulations at the beginning. If she felt that you were hurting somebody, it's the rules and regulations that I have to take part and tell this other person that doesn't know. And she let him know that from the beginning. It doesn't matter what he says. She should enforce the rules on him. (MSM, unknown ethnicity)
>
> He [the researcher] did state it to her [the participant] up front, if anything that could, that's gonna hurt someone, he has to tell, and she's still not trying to hear him. And she signed that consent, that he's gonna do that, you know? Anything that's hurting the next person, he has to report that. (Black woman)
>
> She [the researcher] said it loud and clear. Because you signed this paper, I have to let you know if someone wants to hurt you. The same way, if you are going to hurt someone, I have to let that person know. She was clear to him. (Hispanic man)

One participant thought that on the basis of the informed consent information, the participant had the responsibility not to tell the researcher anything that she or he knew the researcher might have to disclose:

> She shouldn't have never said it. She shouldn't have said it to him. Because he signed a paper saying that if she found out something . . . she have him sign there, so it doesn't matter if you want it or not, I'm gonna tell that person professionally because I'm gonna save someone out there. (MSM, unknown ethnicity)

When Limits to Confidentiality Are Unclear

Focus group members had mixed opinions about investigator responsibilities when the limits of confidentiality were not made clear to the participant during informed consent or when consent capacity was compromised because of drug use or drug cravings.

"It Would Be an Illegal Action"

Members in one of the Black male groups argued that a researcher does not have the right to disclose a participant's HIV status if the right to do so was not explicitly stated in the consent procedures. They asserted that the right to disclose HIV status "must be under contract" and that the researcher must "present and show him the signature on the contract" each time he or she comes into contact with the participant. As one group member noted,

> It is illegal to reveal any information that you don't sign a paper telling that you want to release information. Without a paper for you to sign, it would be illegal to any company or person that you are doing a study with to reveal anything about your life, name, anything. (Black man)

"It Has to Be Reported Under Any Circumstances"

For other participants, the researcher's moral obligation to intervene in the spread of HIV took precedent over the contractual arrangement as understood by the research participant. When asked whether the researcher should warn the third-party individual of his or her HIV risk—even if this limitation to confidentiality was not stated in the informed consent—one focus group composed of Black women emphatically argued that the researcher is still "going to have to tell." Indeed, in response to this question, these individuals stated that the researcher is still responsible to the third party even if consent procedures do not make this clear: "She'd still be taking a life, whether he put it in [the consent form] or not, so he has to tell."

For some participants, the duty to protect trumped instances in which the participant failed to read or was too high to understand the informed consent information. As a Black female participant stated, "It's fair because he gave it to her to read, saying that he could do it." Another participant noted,

I don't care if you're high. Always read things before you sign it. That way you know what you are signing and what you're getting yourself into. Don't go to a group, a focus group, and be like okay if I go here it's $50 or $60, there's $4 on a MetroCard, and it's like, okay, sign, boom, boom, boom, and not read the guidelines because you're more concerned about the money, like he said, or I was high, blah, blah, blah. Well, look, you was high but did you ever take time to really read it? (MSM, unknown ethnicity)

CONCLUSION

The moral perspectives of drug users expand understanding of the ethical issues involved in a researcher's duty to protect. Focus group participants, for the most part, positioned research investigators as moral agents whose role includes intervening to prevent harmful activities perpetrated by those participating in their studies. Although debate was evident among focus group members, their perspectives bolster and support research ethicists' assertions that in some contexts researchers have the same *Tarasoff*-like moral obligation as mental health practitioners. Active and recent drug users couched their moral arguments for and against duty to protect third parties from HIV transmission within the same criteria as those underlying the *Tarasoff* (1976) doctrine. The fact that the investigator had a special relationship with both the participant and the victim, making it feasible for him or her to prevent harm, was salient to many group members' justifications for disclosure. Similarly, the fact that the victim was identifiable to the researcher played a crucial role in decision making. Even within the present-day context of safer sex techniques and effective treatments for HIV, focus group members thought sexual transmission of HIV was a foreseeable and life-threatening harm.

As HIV awareness grows, the percentage of individuals who know their seropositive status has steadily increased (Heimer, Grau, Curtin, Khoshnood, & Singer, 2007). Research has shown that up to 70% of those diagnosed with HIV continue to engage in sexual relationships (Crepaz & Marks, 2002). Of those who continue to be sexually active, research has estimated that approximately 30% to 50% do not confide their HIV-infected status to sexual partners, perhaps fearing rejection and stigma or feeling overburdened by the obligation to make sure that others act responsibly (Marks, Burris, & Peterman, 1999; Singer et al., 2006).

HIV intervention literature has suggested that HIV risk behaviors are embedded in community norms. People do not necessarily make individual morally guided choices about risk behaviors but act in line with local community ethics. Research investigating the customs and social norms among high-risk HIV populations has found that in some circles, drug sharing and sexual norms directly conflict with HIV prevention practices (Latkin & Knowlton, 2005; Singer, Scott, Wilson, Easton, & Weeks, 2001). For example, in some communities at high risk of HIV infection, insisting that a sexual partner use protection demonstrates a lack of trust or implies promiscuity or infidelity, making safe sex an unlikely occurrence (Muller, 1996). Other reasons for nondisclosure may be fear of domestic abuse or abandonment by loved ones. Innovative intervention programs aim to alter social mores such that safe and responsible sex and drug practices become the socially acceptable norm. These strategies underlie the success of peer education intervention techniques (Latkin & Knowlton, 2005; Weeks et al., 2001).

Through interview research, Plumridge and Chetwynd (1998) observed that young injection drug users (IDUs) for the most part view themselves as socially responsible actors within needle-sharing and drug use contexts. Although the IDUs they interviewed all acknowledged the danger of sharing unclean needles, they rationalized their decisions to either borrow or lend unclean injection equipment. When lending equipment to others, Plumridge and Chetwynd's subjects insisted that they were not acting unethically because each person has the responsibility to look out for him- or herself. When borrowing unclean injection equipment, they exonerated themselves from acting irresponsibly by citing uncontrollable drug cravings. In either case, this research suggests that IDUs feel an ethical commitment to protect others from behaviors that would put them at risk of HIV infection.

Our focus group data are consistent with the moral foundations that are implicit in the responsible attitudes of the IDUs that Plumridge and Chetwynd (1998) observed. A majority of recent and current drug users in our study, at least one third of whom knew they were HIV infected, believed that HIV-infected drug users have a responsibility to protect sexual and needle-sharing partners from HIV transmission—with special concern about the snowball effect of HIV transmission on a community. Some thought it was the responsibility of all community members to protect themselves against HIV transmission irrespective of disclosures made by their partners. When drug users fail to fulfill their moral obligation, focus group members believed it becomes the responsibility of an informed researcher to protect a third party from harm. This obligation was particularly binding when the limits of confidentiality had been discussed during informed consent. We titled this chapter "Do Drug Abuse Researchers Have a Duty to Protect Third Parties From HIV Transmission?" The moral perspectives of drug users in our sample answer this question in the affirmative. Additionally, we found that drug users generally feel the same way about their own moral obligations. These findings call into question a popular conception of drug users as thoughtless prisoners of their addictions, whose cravings render them unable to contemplate moral obligations to themselves and to others.

REFERENCES

Ainslie, D. C. (1999). Questioning bioethics, AIDS, sexual ethics, and the duty to warn. *Hastings Center Report, 29*, 26–35.

Appelbaum, P. S., & Rosenbaum, A. (1989). Tarasoff and the researcher: Does the duty to protect apply in the research setting? *American Psychologist*, *44*, 885–894.

Center for Disease Control and Prevention (CDC). (2005). *HIV/AIDS Surveillance Report, 2004. Vol. 16.* Atlanta, GA: U.S. Department of Health and Human Services, Centers for Disease Control and Prevention.

Crepaz, N., & Marks, G. (2002). Toward an understanding of sexual risk behavior in people living with HIV: A review of social psychological, and medical findings. *AIDS*, *16*, 135–149.

Deren, S., Beardsley, M., Coyle, S., & Singer, M. (1998). HIV serostatus and risk behaviors in a multi-site sample of drug users. *Journal of Psychoactive Drugs*, *30*, 239–246.

Fisher, C. B. (1999). Relational ethics and research with vulnerable populations. In *Research involving persons with mental disorders that may affect decision making capacity: Vol. II: Commissioned papers by the National Bioethics Advisory Commission* (pp. 29–49). Rockville, MD: National Bioethics Advisory Commission. Retrieved February 14, 2007, from http://www.bioethics.gov/reports/past_commissions/nbac_mental2.pdf

Fisher, C. B. (2002). Participant consultation: Ethical insights into parental permission and confidentiality procedures for policy relevant research with youth. In R. M. Lerner, F. Jacobs, & D. Wertlieb (Eds.), *Handbook of applied developmental science* (Vol. 4, pp. 371–396). Thousand Oaks, CA: Sage.

Fisher, C. B. (2003). Adolescent and parent perspectives on ethical issues in youth drug use and suicide survey research. *Ethics & Behavior*, *13*, 302–331.

Fisher, C. B. (2004). Ethics in drug abuse and related HIV risk research. *Applied Developmental Science*, 8, 91–103.

Fisher, C. B., Oransky, M., Mahadevan, M., Singer, M., Mirhej, G., & Hodge, G. D. (2008). Marginalized populations and drug addiction research: Realism, mistrust, and misconception. *IRB: Ethics & Human Research*, *30*, 1–9.

Heimer, R., Grau, G., Curtin, E., Khoshnood, K., & Singer, M. (2007). Assessment of HIV testing of urban injection drug users: Implications for expansion of HIV testing and prevention efforts. *American Journal of Public Health*, 97,110–116.

Latkin, C. A., & Knowlton, A. R. (2005). Micro-social structural approaches to HIV prevention: A social ecological perspective. *AIDS Care*, *17*(Suppl. 1), 102–113.

Levmore, S., (1986). Waiting for rescue: An essay on the evolution and incentive structure of the law of affirmative obligations. *Virginia Law Review*, *72*, 879-941.

Loue, S. (2000). Ethical issues of behavioral interventions for HIV prevention. In J. L. Peterson & R. J. DiClemente (Eds.), *Handbook of HIV prevention* (pp. 297–310). New York: Kluwer Academic/Plenum.

Marks, G., Burris, S., & Peterman, T. A. (1999). Reducing sexual transmission of HIV from those who know they are infected: The need for personal and collective responsibility. *AIDS*, *13*, 297–306.

Melton, G. B., Levine, R. J., Koocher, G. P., Rosenthal, R., & Thompson, W. C. (1988). Community consultation in socially sensitive research: Lessons from clinical trials of treatments for AIDS. *American Psychologist, 43*, 573–581.

Muller, B. M. (1996). "Don't ask for trouble": Women who do sex and drugs. *Family and Community Health, 19*(3), 35–48.

National Institute on Drug Abuse. (2000, May 9). *The makings of a public health epidemic: Drug abuse, HIV/AIDS and hepatitis* C [NIDA News Release]. Bethesda, MD: Author.

Plumridge, E., & Chetwynd, J. (1998). The moral universe of injecting drug users in the era of AIDS: Sharing injecting equipment and the protection of moral standing. *AIDS Care, 10*, 723–733.

Public Health Service Act § 301(d), 42 U.S.C. 241(d), as amended by Pub. L. No. 100-607 § 163 (1988).

Reisner v. Regents of University of California, 31 Cal. App. 4th 1195, 37 Cal. Rptr. 2d 518 (Cal. App. 1995)

Sanders-Phillips, K., & Schoenbaum, E. (2001, April). *Gender differences and the dynamics of HIV/AIDS among racial and ethnic populations.* Panel presentation at the Differential Drug Use, HIV/AIDS, and Related Health Outcomes Among Racial and Ethnics Populations: A Knowledge Assessment Workshop, National Institute on Drug Abuse, Bethesda, MD.

Singer, M. (1993). Knowledge for use: Anthropology and community-centered substance abuse research. *Social Science & Medicine, 37*, 15–25.

Singer, M. (1994). AIDS and the health crises of the U.S. urban poor: The perspective of critical medical anthropology. *Social Science & Medicine, 39*, 931–948.

Singer, M., Erickson, P., Badiane, L., Diaz, R., Ortiz, D., Abraham, T., et al. (2006). Syndemics, sex and the city: Understanding sexually transmitted disease in social and cultural context. *Social Science & Medicine, 63*, 2010–2021.

Singer, M., Huertas, E., & Scott, G. (2000). Am I my brother's keeper: A case study of the responsibilities of research. *Human Organization, 59*, 389–400.

Singer, M., Marshall, P. L., Trotter, R. T., II, Schensul, J. J., Weeks, M. R., Simmons, J. E., & Radda, K. E. (1999). Ethics, ethnography, drug use, and AIDS: Dilemmas and standards in federally funded research. In *Integrating cultural, observational, and epidemiological approaches in the prevention of drug abuse and HIV/AIDS* (NIH Pub. No. 99-4565, pp. 198–222). Rockville, MD: National Institute on Drug Abuse.

Singer, M., Mirhej, G., Hodge, D., Saleheen, H., Fisher, C. B., & Mahadevan, M. (2008). Ethical issues in research with Hispanic drug users: Participant perspectives on risks and benefits. *Journal of Drug Issues, 38*, 351-372.

Singer, M., Scott, G., Wilson, S., Easton, D., & Weeks, M. (2001). "War stories": AIDS prevention and the street narratives of drug users. *Qualitative Health Research, 11*, 589–611.

Tarasoff v. Regents of the University of California, 17 Cal. 3d 425 (1976).

Weeks, M., Clair, S., Singer, M., Radda, K., Schensul, J., Wilson, S., et al. (2001). High risk drug use sites, meaning and practice. *Journal of Drug Issues, 31*, 781–808.

10

ETHICAL AND LEGAL DILEMMAS IN ETHNOGRAPHIC FIELD RESEARCH: THREE CASE STUDIES OF DISTRESSED INNER-CITY FAMILIES

ELOISE DUNLAP, BRUCE D. JOHNSON, AND DORIS RANDOLPH

The examination of ethical issues in this chapter is intended to illustrate real-life dilemmas that arise when one is doing research among hidden populations who often engage in illegal behaviors. Ethnographic methods necessitate spending extended periods of time developing deep rapport and trust with respondents so they will open up and provide rich information about their lives and thereby illuminate the subcultural patterns being studied, but at the same time, the researcher often encounters ethical dilemmas. The dilemmas described here were encountered by Eloise Dunlap during five ethnographic research projects between 1989 and 2005 in New York City

This research was funded by National Institute on Drug Abuse (NIDA) Grants 5R01 DA 013690, 5 R01 DA09056, T32 DA07233, 1R01 DA 05126, R01 DA021783-02, and 1 R01 DA021783-01 as well as a National Institute on Alcohol Abuse and Alcoholism/NIDA Minority Research Supplemental Award. The ideas or points of view in this paper do not represent the official position of the U.S. Government, NIDA, or National Development and Research Institutes, Inc. We thank Ellen Benoit, Deborah Murray, and Beverly Jones-Squall for their contributions to this manuscript.

and fall into three major categories: legal, ethical, and professional. The cases cut across these categories and cannot be disentangled because real-life phenomena do not fit such categories precisely. Legal and professional codes offer some insight and guidelines, but the ethical dilemmas faced by the ethnographer often remain problematic.

These case studies are told in first person throughout this chapter by Eloise Dunlap. Although all persons in this chapter are real, their identities have been protected by giving them pseudonyms and altering names of particular places. I had distinct emotional reactions to these cases that were often as important as the professional, legal, and ethical issues raised. These emotional reactions have now dissipated somewhat, but my personal values and standards condemn the behaviors reported. I came very close to reporting these events to child abuse hotlines or to the police but did not do so for reasons discussed in each case. In addition, the purposes of ethnographic research and professional relationships with the participants required a sympathetic understanding of their situations, lifestyles, and problems. Thus, even though I do not condone the behaviors (e.g., child sexual abuse, homicide), I understand why the individuals acted according to the street subcultural norms in which their lives were embedded.

LEGAL AND ETHICAL ISSUES

The focus of this chapter and the three case studies contained within is to discuss the challenges I have faced in my research when balancing my need and obligation to assure confidentiality with my legal and ethical responsibility to report crime. In the following section, I explore some of the common issues faced by research staff when conducting research in the field.

For all of my research, I have obtained a federal Certificate of Confidentiality from the National Institute on Drug Abuse of the National Institutes of Health that protects respondents and me from revealing most crimes to authorities. This certificate means that I cannot be compelled by a court or administrative hearing to provide information from the protected research about an individual's drug use or illegal behavior. This protection, plus the promises of confidentiality given in the informed consent process, means that I do not have to report such behaviors, and I feel a professional obligation not to reveal to legal authorities most of what I find in the research. Because the majority of my research deals with issues pertaining to illegal drug use and sales, most participants in my research are regular drug users and sometimes sellers. The Certificate of Confidentiality protects what they reveal about their drug use, drug dealing, and other illegal activities (see chap. 2, this volume).

This certificate does not cover certain classes of information that may come to light in the course of conducting research. For example, the certificate does not cover observation or suspicion of child sexual abuse and neglect. Human service workers, including researchers, are mandated to report suspicion of sexual abuse, neglect, and statutory rape (when an adult age 18 or older has sexual intercourse with a person under the age of 15 and is punishable by law even if the adolescent victim consents; see, e.g., New York State Penal Code, 2001).[1] It is important to note that human service workers and ethnographers are not required to report suspected child sexual abuse to police or prosecutors—only to child abuse hotlines or child protective services. In addition, New York State law (each state has its own laws that require specific responses) requires researchers and human service workers to report to legal authorities (those specified by law as reporting agents, generally child welfare agents and agencies) instances when a respondent reports future plans to assault or kill someone, but these workers are not required to do so for past instances of assault or homicide.

Ethnographic researchers also have to keep in mind that culture plays an important part in defining neglect or abuse. For example, a research subject of mine (a 30-year-old female) has three children ages 4, 7, and 12. It is common for her to curse at her children. It is simply the way she talks. Such language as "Get your funky ass here and sit down"; "Shut the fuck up"; and "Bitch, I am going to kick your ass" may be considered abusive of the child in the dominant culture, but in the street subculture, such cursing is ordinary language (Dunlap, Johnson, & Rath, 1996). Even statutory rape may look different when examined within the framework of subcultural norms, as the first case study in this chapter will demonstrate.

Another ethical problem presented by ethnographic study involves minors and informed consent. A special set of issues emerges for potential subjects who are under age 16 when parental consent must be obtained. Parents may be willing to sign an informed consent form giving permission for the researcher to study their family and their children. The researcher may then discover possible forms of neglect, such as the parent's being aware that the teenager is engaging in illegal or dangerous behavior—smoking marijuana, not attending school or attending only periodically, or having a sexual affair with an older person—and doing nothing to stop the behavior or even condemn it. In cases involving teenagers smoking marijuana and skipping school, teenagers are often willing to take part in the study but want assurances from the researcher that their parents will not be told of these behaviors—otherwise, they may be unwilling to ask their parents to sign the parental consent form and cannot become respondents. This situation presents researchers with a question of whether legally or ethically they are responsible for informing unsuspecting parents of, for example, their child's drug use. Cases of sexual behavior present a somewhat different dilemma for the researcher in that the sexual behavior could constitute statutory rape, be considered abusive, and be subject to mandatory reporting.

---

[1]Although age 18 is the legal age limit for defining statutory rape in most states, the age does differ by state. South Carolina, for example, has set the age at 14 (see http://www.coolnurse.com/consent.htm).

The informed consent requirements also present researchers with another dilemma. It is nearly impossible to make field observations of a focal subject who has given their informed consent without also observing what is taking place around them. For example, an informant may take the researcher to a location such as a crack house so the researcher can see what takes place there. It is impossible to gain the informed consent of every person who comes into that location to acquire drugs, take drugs, or simply hang out. It is also impossible to acquire informed consent when hanging out with a drug dealer standing on a corner selling drugs or in a park where people are constantly coming and going. In addition, the researcher observes who comes to buy the drug, how much they purchase, the patterns of concealment, and other things that may happen in the field. This raises an important question: Because informed consent has not been obtained from everyone in the local scene, is it ethically permissible for the researcher to record what takes place around the focal subject who has signed the informed consent form?

For instance, in my early studies of poor households, I was required to gain the informed consent only of the head of the household. This was generally a single female with children or other family members living in the household. Prior to 2003, the National Development and Research Institutes' (NDRI) Institutional Review Board had accepted that the informed consent of the household head also granted permission to record information about other household members. When another household member was approached for a personal interview, staff would initiate a full informed consent discussion. Frequently, other members of the household would agree to become a part of the research project once they realized that it was safe. In 2003, however, the Office for Protection of Risks to Human Subjects of the U.S. Department of Health and Human Services began requiring ethnographers to cease recording information about any household members who had not given their individual consent (for more information on this office, see http://www.hhs.gov/ohrp). National Institutes of Health funding for one of my research projects was held up for almost 6 months until an agreement was reached that only the person who had given the permission to participate in the study could be recorded and information documented about that person. Other members and individuals in the household when the ethnographer was there could not be observed nor field notes written about them unless they gave their informed consent/assent. All persons in the house and those entering the house had to give their informed consent in order for the ethnographer to be able to record anything about them. As a result, valuable ethnographic observations have been lost. Ethnographers now seek to obtain the informed consent of other household members soon after entry, even when waiting until later allows a level of trust to develop and it becomes more comfortable and successful to approach other members.

It is critically important to understand the subculture in which these investigations occur. Understanding the lifestyle, thinking, and conduct norms followed by the people being studied enables the researcher to acquire deep rapport and trust and to obtain data that reflect the truth of what takes place rather than what people want others to see. In general, as an ethnographer I aim to penetrate and document hidden information. I have been able to conduct observations in public settings and households, recruit and gain informed consent, and conduct interviews over several years with many drug users and sellers. The following section includes three case studies that emerged during my years of conducting research that raised important legal, moral, and ethical issues. They provide concrete examples of the professional and ethical quandaries that field study can present researchers.

STREET SUBCULTURE

Street subculture has three main attributes: drug use and sales of drugs, sexual activity, and violence. In the "street," all three merge, and common behavior patterns and norms are generated by specific activities. For individuals to survive in street subculture, they must learn the norms of street life and know what is expected under certain conditions and in specific situations. Most research on subcultures has rarely elaborated on the content of subcultures or, especially important, the content of specific values and conduct norms. Participation in street life initially can appear exciting: Persons can pretend to be what they want to be, and the bright lights, parties, and numerous acquaintances may be alluring at first. However, eventually the harshness of the street—the violence, the drugs, the sex—becomes limiting and leaves "nowhere to go." For many, unfortunately, it is the only life they know.

Subcultures are organized around specific behaviors (e.g., in the case of street life, the drug use and sales, sexual activities, and violence mentioned earlier; Dunlap, Johnson, Golub, & Wesley, 2002). A specific behavior is largely defined by the specific conduct norms associated with the behavior. The conduct norms both prescribe what participants must do, proscribe what must not be done, and define appropriate sanctions for violations of these norms. Conduct norms and subcultures have an existence independent of the persons who practice the behaviors (Dunlap & Johnson, 1999). Individuals may follow the conduct norms of a subculture for a while and then cease such involvement, but the conduct norms and subculture exist as long as other persons continue to follow these standards.

Individuals may take such behavior patterns and conduct norms into their households and influence behavior patterns there (Dunlap et al., 1996). Subcultural conduct norms and related behaviors then become intertwined with family life. In addition, changes in subcultural behavior (e.g., initiating drug use) may change behavior patterns. For example, crack addicts' intense and frequent binges require different behavior patterns than heroin addicts, who generally require a specific number of hits a day in order to operate normally. These variances in behavior have differing effects on family life (Dunlap, 1992, 1995; Dunlap & Johnson, 1996). Both crack and heroin, however, require participation in other aspects of street subculture that call for similar conduct norms and behavior patterns. New techniques of consumption or performance connected with new or different drugs necessitate the construction of new and different social conduct norms and behaviors but at the same time tap into old norms of street subculture (Dunlap & Johnson, 1999). It is important to understand both that these changing street cultural norms exist and also that they affect those within the subculture in profound ways. Responsible researchers must be sure to consider cultural differences in weighing the legal and ethical issues that arise from close observation of street subculture.

INTRODUCTION TO THE CASE STUDIES

The three case studies presented here describe a child I call Fruit Loops and two adult male drug dealers I call John and Borace. Fruit Loops was 12 years old when I first met her while conducting a research project titled "Violence in Crack User/Seller Households: An Ethnography." Fruit Loops's mother was a crack user who gave her informed consent to participate in the research project. She also gave her consent for me to ask her children to participate in the research project, and subsequently, Fruit Loops also gave her consent to participate. John and Borace initially were not primary research subjects; both were introduced to me through another subject, Ross, who was their supplier. Borace eventually became a research respondent but John did not.

Though the cases of Fruit Loops, Borace, and John have different legal ramifications, all three cases were handled in the most appropriate professional manner. Professionalism, however, does not resolve the ethical issues that these cases raise. Although legal and professional codes of conduct that govern field research were carefully upheld, what emerged in the field is not addressed by those guidelines. The ethical and legal issues with respect to Fruit Loops are discussed first, Borace's death second, and John's report of killing someone last.

Fruit Loops and Family

The case of Fruit Loops involves my suspicion of sexual abuse, which would qualify as statutory rape if brought to the attention of legal authorities. This case also shows the normative behavior among subpopulations of crack users, especially girls and women, and reveals the role of subcultural patterns in early sexual intercourse that are common in street subcultures (Dunlap, 1992; Dunlap, Golub, & Johnson, 2003a). The fundamental moral and legal dilemma confronted in this street and drug subcultural norm involved my responsibility to fulfill mandatory reporting of child abuse and sexual abuse under state law.

I met Fruit Loops when I recruited her mother Ricochet, a crack user and sex worker for the 1992 research project mentioned previously. At age 32, Ricochet had four children; her oldest daughter Tushay was 14 years old, and her second daughter was 12-year-old Fruit Loops. At that time, Ricochet was living with her children in a welfare-subsidized apartment. In addition to welfare support, Ricochet received crack or money for crack from various partners who stayed in her house for short periods of time. Her pattern of behavior was one of *transactional sex*, exchanging sexual relationships for goods, services, and often drugs. Many poor, drug-using women like Ricochet have a relatively stable pool of sex partners. The women may have sexual relations with as many as 5 to 10 men in exchange for money, services, goods, or drugs. The men typically have little money to offer; thus, most transactions involve exchanges of goods, including drugs. It is necessary to keep in mind the street/drug subcultural normative behavior patterns in order to understand the ethical dilemma I encountered in Fruit Loops's situation.

From inner-city women's perspective, transactional sex does not constitute prostitution because they see prostitutes as "streetwalkers" who take money from men with whom they have no other relationship. In contrast, the women engaged in transactional sex whom I have studied report sexual relationships with men with whom they have ongoing relationships, so the men are not considered johns. In fact, it is not uncommon for the women to have children by such men at various points in their lives. In many cases, the women may not be clear which man is the father of which child. It is also not unusual for females in inner-city street/drug subculture to report having their initial sexual experiences with adult men soon after puberty (Dunlap et al., 2003a; Dunlap, Golub, & Johnson, 2003b).

Initially, after getting to know Ricochet's family, I came to suspect that Fruit Loops was being sexually abused by one or a number of older men in her life. At the time of the research, my information was only from a third party who was also in the study and a sex worker. Indeed, Fruit Loops consistently denied such sexual exchanges to me and all other authorities. Fruit Loops's experience also happened to her older sister, Tushay, who was 14 years old at the beginning of the research. Furthermore, although other third parties reported Fruit Loops to the local bureau of child welfare (BCW), and several foster care placements occurred, at no time did BCW or legal guardians ever refer these cases to the police for prosecution under statutory rape statutes.

This is a story of how the initiation to transactional sex practices begins in childhood. As indicated previously, such patterns are common among the families being studied, and their normative patterns do not fit well with state laws regarding statutory rape, which are often ignored by the BCW, guardians, and other adults who may be knowledgeable or involved.

The many ethical and legal issues we encountered in Fruit Loops's family have been encountered in numerous other poor households; the details of the stories vary only modestly from household to household. Many adolescent girls are socialized into the same behavioral norms, and these norms appear to have been transmitted across several generations (Dunlap et al., 2002).

The major concern, in this case, is the issue of informed consent and the professional obligation to protect confidentiality and not report illegal behaviors to the authorities, except child abuse. As mentioned earlier, when I first recruited Ricochet, I obtained her informed consent to talk to her and to her two oldest daughters, Fruit Loops and Tushay. I also acquired the informed assent of Fruit Loops (then age 13) and Tushay (then age 15) 1 year after meeting them. The information obtained clearly fell under the guidelines of the Certificate of Confidentiality. I had carefully explained to Ricochet and each daughter that the Certificate of Confidentiality did not cover physical or sexual abuse and that instances of child abuse would have to be reported to the appropriate authorities. They knew in advance that if they revealed certain information, especially sexual activity, Ricochet would be in jeopardy of losing her children, and the daughters knew they would be placed in foster care.

In the beginning, these women treated me like other authorities, such as the BCW. It took time and repeated interviews to build a level of rapport that would penetrate the protective shield that they presented to others. Fruit Loops concealed her relations with men and sexual activities from me and denied what was happening. This denial is an example of a consistent pattern found among children in many households. The fear of breaking up the family and being placed in foster care causes them to endure much abuse, refuse to report, and consistently deny any wrongdoing. What they encounter in family life, in their minds, is never as bad as being separated from their family. Many fear what would happen to them in foster care. A number have experienced the foster care system and prefer family life to that system. Fruit Loops and Tushay experienced several placements in foster care; each time they ran away and returned to their mother, Ricochet.

At age 16, Fruit Loops reported that her sexual involvement with adult men was consensual and not forced. During the course of the investigation, Ricochet revealed one day while high that Wilson, an older male, had raped Fruit Loops. In an attempt to learn from Fruit Loops what had taken place, I began to uncover the conduct norms associated with initiation into transactional sex and the subsequent behavior patterns of street subculture. The following interview is an example of this.

Interviewer: When I first met you, they were talking something about a 34-year-old man had raped you.

Fruit Loops: He didn't rape me . . . I used to like go to the store. When I was walking to the store, this man was like, "Oh you so pretty, you so pretty." I used to be like, "Okay, okay, okay." . . . Okay, one day he was like, "You know I been watching you a long time." I was like, "Everybody got eyes, right?" He said, "Yeah." So then we started going together . . . like boyfriend and girlfriend.

Interviewer: Okay, and how old is he?

Fruit Loops: Thirty-four.

Interviewer: And how old were you then, you were 12 then?

Fruit Loops: Uh-huh.

Interviewer: Now "going together" meant what for you?

Fruit Loops: Well he didn't know my age.

Interviewer: How old did he think you were?

Fruit Loops: Sixteen.

Interviewer: You told him you were 16?

Fruit Loops: Yeah.

Interviewer: You liked him? What did you like about him?

Fruit Loops: He was cute. . . . He had money, but when I left, he couldn't touch me. . . . He was burned. . . . Gonorrhea.

Interviewer: Gonorrhea and he gave it to you?

Fruit Loops: Yeah.

Interviewer: Did ya'll ever go places together? Did he ever take you anywhere? Did he ever buy you things?

Fruit Loops: Yeah, he buy me things. . . . He bought me a TV before . . . he buy me like stupid stuff . . . like stuffed animals and stuff like that.

Interviewer: Okay, you got another man that you like now?

Fruit Loops: Yeah . . . he says he's 25. But he's not. One boy said he's 41. His mother said no, he's just 2 years older than his mother.

Interviewer: Oh, cause the boy's mother is 39?

Fruit Loops: Uh-huh.

Interviewer: This guy is 2 years older. Is he a Jamaican guy?

Fruit Loops: Yeah.

Interviewer: This guy here, what do you like about him?

Fruit Loops: I used to mess with him. . . . No, before my mother said I can't go with him no more . . . I used to mess with him. . . . Everybody talking about you and him, you not going with him no more. So I was like uh-huh that's what she thinks. So one lady told her

> [Fruit Loops's mother] why don't you let him talk to her because if you don't, you just making her run away. You gonna make her run away and sneak and do it. So [my mother] thought about it, and she said I could talk to him; but she told me I can't talk to him in front of her face. . . . I was like okay then; fine with me. . . . He bought me clothes and stuff.

To summarize, Fruit Loops has explained that Wilson was selling drugs on the corner when he began to flirt with her, telling her how "pretty" she was, when she went to the corner store. Eventually, after he convinced her to have sex with him, she saw him as her "boyfriend" and their relationship as "going together." Sex became a regular occurrence until she (and her sister Tushay) contracted a sexually transmitted disease from him.

I subsequently learned that even after being hospitalized for an advanced stage of the disease, she continued to have sex with him. No criminal charges were ever filed against him. Moreover, Fruit Loops's mother, Ricochet, alternated between threatening to report Wilson and encouraging the relationship in order to receive benefits, primarily crack and money, from Wilson for Fruit Loops's favors.

In time, both Ricochet and Tushay related that Wilson had raped Fruit Loops. He sold drugs, wined and dined her, bought her marijuana, and gave her mother crack to accept the relationship. Fruit Loops, however, consistently denied the charges, claiming that he was her "boyfriend" and that they had a "relationship."

At age 14, Fruit Loops began a sexual relationship with a 21-year-old man, Ennis, who she claimed was the father of her oldest son, Shakie. While pushing her baby in a stroller, she met Peter, who was in his mid-40s, and began another sexual relationship that continues to the present time. Peter was working two jobs and living with his legally married wife. Peter began to spend money on Fruit Loops, have sex with her, and was most likely the father of her next three sons. Her mother condoned the relations when they were beneficial to her.

In the following excerpt, Fruit Loops and Ricochet talk about what her grandmother thinks about Fruit Loops going out with older men. Note how comfortable the mother is with the situation, appearing to have no objections to the affair between her adolescent daughter and a 45-year-old man.

Interviewer: What does your grandmother say about Peter and you, Fruit Loops?

Fruit Loops: "You ain't got no money, and laying up there with that old-ass man. He can't give you no money? Let me tell you what to do when y'all come back from the hotel. You take his ass shopping. That's what you do. You take him to shopping." Grandma, I ain't got no money. You ain't got no money! Grandma, I just told you I ain't got no money.

Ricochet: "All them worms in your ass [sexually transmitted diseases]." That's what she's sayin'.

Fruit Loops: She [grandmother] saying, "Come here, Fruit Loops. What? Now, you know that you're too young to be messing with that old-ass man [with] that worm." She call my name any more, I'm gonna run out the house.

Ricochet: She says, "Old-ass man, with that belly full of worms."

Fruit Loops: "All you got is worms."

An intergenerational process of socialization can be inferred from this conversation (Dunlap et al., 2002). Fruit Loops is being socialized to interact with men as goods providers; the older women stress that the point is to get the man to go shopping and buy things for Fruit Loops. What the mother and grandmother do not tell Fruit Loops about relations with the older man is significant; a genuine male–female relationship is not mentioned. This lays the groundwork for transactional sex. Fruit Loops reports that the grandmother thinks that she should not be going out with the older man because he will give her "worms." At the same time, she tells Fruit Loops that as soon as they leave the hotel, the man should take her shopping.

This socialization process continued when Fruit Loops became pregnant, probably by her second significant sexual partner, Ennis. At this time Fruit Loops is also still "dating" Peter, who is married and living with his wife. In the following conversation, Fruit Loops and her mother discuss what her grandmother believes should be done about the new baby, which she believes is Peter's.

Ricochet: I was laughing at her [Fruit Loops's grandmother] that day. I did, when she said "adotion" [*sic*, meaning "abortion"], I got up and started dancing. She told Fruit Loops get rid of that baby. Peter didn't come over to the house for a long time.

Fruit Loops: I didn't see him to let him know I still is. Supposed to be 6 months. But when it is time to take that sonogram, I ain't gonna be no 6 months.

Ricochet: You better go to the hospital and see if somebody got a sonogram thing, paper, bring it out and show it. You know how you go to GYN, you always see somebody's sonogram paper; you better just roll it off.

Interviewer: Oh, you are pregnant.

Fruit Loops: Now.

Interviewer: Right, but why were you telling him you were pregnant before?

Fruit Loops: Because I wasn't gonna tell him I lost the baby. Plus that's what he wants, a baby.

Interviewer: He doesn't have any children?

Fruit Loops: No.

Interviewer: Maybe he can't have any, all these years [he has been married].

Fruit Loops: Right, right.

Ricochet: And I told her that. She said something wrong with the dick. You can look and tell, because it's got a hunka nuts in his pants.

Because Peter is a married man, the grandmother feels that Fruit Loops should have an abortion. Rather than responding to this rather serious suggestion, Ricochet makes fun of the way the grandmother pronounces *abortion* and emphasizes Peter's sexual organs.

When she was 15, Fruit Loops had her first child, a son. Fruit Loops said that she believed the baby belonged to Ennis, but she was not really sure. She reported also having had sex with a man named Eventor and also with Wilson—although the latter was in prison doing 4 years when the child was born. Although Ennis gave her a little money when he first learned that she was pregnant, he eventually stopped giving her help of any kind. With this pregnancy, the BCW removed Fruit Loops from her mother's household and placed her in a Catholic home for pregnant teens. One month later, she had a fight and left, she said, under pressure.

She was next placed in a foster home. Although she had been removed from her mother's household, she spent much of her time at her mother's house until one day she did not return to the foster home. Pregnant with her second child at the age of 17, Fruit Loops decided to tell Peter the baby was his child even though she believed Ennis was the father. Peter was seen as stable because he had a wife and a legal job. When Fruit Loops turned 18, she became pregnant with her third son. Fruit Loops considered Peter the father, but Ricochet said that the child was not fathered by Peter. At 19, she had her fourth child, a son, also attributed to Peter. Peter continued to deceive his wife, telling her he was staying with his "sister" while he lived part time with Fruit Loops and provided money for her and the children. No one in Fruit Loops's family saw any problems with this arrangement. By this time, Ricochet had lost all her children to the BCW. Fruit Loops, however, had acquired an apartment for herself and her children, for which Peter paid the rent. So Ricochet moved in with Fruit Loops even while she fought frequently with Peter over money.

Fruit Loops's sexual relationships had been reported to the authorities twice. The first time was by a neighbor who used crack and was angry at Ricochet. When questioned, Fruit Loops denied the rape charges. In the second instance, both Fruit Loops and Tushay were hospitalized for an advanced sexually transmitted disease and were reported to the BCW by the hospital. They were taken from Ricochet but eventually returned. Ricochet claimed that they were uncontrollable. She tried to keep them from running the streets at night, but it was hard to do.

I never actually saw Wilson and Ennis with Fruit Loops but saw presents that they had given to her. They could not be reported because there was no evidence of rape or molestation taking place. All three, Ricochet, Tushay, and Fruit Loops, would deny that it was rape or molestation.

My moral dilemma was how to balance conducting the research, following guidelines of child protection laws, and providing information to help Fruit Loops and Tushay. The informed consent process and Certificate of Confidentiality do not prevent investigators from releasing information in instances of clear and present danger to the subject or when there are serious thoughts of suicide, current or future child abuse, assault, or similar crimes. This responsibility does not apply to past incidents, and it does not resolve such ethical issues faced by researchers as whether to report a 13-year-old suspected of having relations with numerous older males in years past. What is the ethnographer's role in reporting, especially when such incidents have been reported to the BCW and the children have been removed from the household and returned? In addition, when reported, the girls concealed and denied their sexual affairs, ran away from foster care and returned to their mother's household, and continued their behavior patterns.

Fruit Loops had been taken from her mother because of acquiring a sexually transmitted disease from an older male. She also had been reported to BCW as being raped by the older male but had denied it. In reporting abuse, there has to be a concrete basis for substantiating the claim. The "say so" of a third party is not valid for reporting sexual abuse. If the mother and Fruit Loops had previously denied the abuse, then it was likely they would deny any sexual abuse that I might report. Moreover, Fruit Loops was socialized into the street drug subculture and saw her behavior as normal. Her relations with these men were not perceived as sexual abuse or rape by either herself or her mother. In the meantime, although Ricochet would threaten to report these older men to police for statutory rape in order to secure the benefits (money or crack) that she needed at the time, for as long as I have known her, she has never contacted the police—this would be a serious violation of street codes against snitching.

Several interesting conversations among Ricochet's family involved disputes about the paternity of a given child. In the following conversation, Fruit Loops talked about planning a christening for her first child:

Fruit Loops: Shakie [baby] getting christened . . . Peter, he act like he my father.

Interviewer: That's the African guy?

Ricochet: No. That's Joseph.

Fruit Loops: No, he's not like my father.

Interviewer: He's supposed to be your father. Wasn't one of you going with him?

Fruit Loops: I was.

Interviewer: You still having sex with him?

Fruit Loops: No.

Interviewer: But he's going to take care of the baby's christening?

Fruit Loops: That's his church . . . he got to pay for it.

Ricochet: And [Shakie's] . . . godfather is Peter and . . .George.

Interviewer: Who is he?

Fruit Loops: It's a guy I'm messing with. He's sexy.

Interviewer: How you have all your different men there?

Fruit Loops: What different men?

Interviewer: Is Peter going to be there?

Fruit Loops: Right. He's the only one I'm messing with.

Interviewer: And Easy?

Fruit Loops: Easy, please; that's like my daddy.

Interviewer: Right, but I'm saying he's an old boyfriend, or whatever. But then, Alloo,[2] you say you mess with him.

Fruit Loops: Right. Only two, Alloo and Peter.

Interviewer: Yeah, so you're going to have them in the same setting?

Fruit Loops: Right.

Interviewer: What you think supposed to happen, I mean . . .

Fruit Loops: Nothing.

Here, Fruit Loops names five men as sex partners. Ricochet is well aware of these men in her life. Fruit Loops was planning to include all her male sexual partners in the christening activities. However, this talk turned out to be just conversation because the christening never happened.

In this next excerpt, Fruit Loops reveals that males may act violently toward her, raises a question about the father of the baby, and mentions yet another male with whom she had a sexual relation.

[2]Alloo went with Ricochet first, then went with Fruit Loops after Ricochet told him to get a younger girl. After the breakup with Fruit Loops and spending a period of time in jail, he started going with Ricochet again. While living with the family, Alloo tried to rape Tushay while she lay in bed with her kids. He was arrested and lost his job.

Fruit Loops: Ooh, Peter will get violent when he want to. I was in the car the other night; I was talking to Shay. I was like, oh, right, that's why I killed your motherfucking baby [had an abortion]. I was just ahh-ahh.

Ricochet: Why do you say that to him, knowing that he will kill you for that?

Fruit Loops: So what? I'm letting him know, nigger, if it don't be no baby eventually, I'm telling you the truth . . . now, before the time come and you want to hit me.

Interviewer: You told him you had an abortion? Or you didn't tell him yet?

Fruit Loops: I keep telling him I had an abortion.

Interviewer: Right, but in the meantime, are you pregnant?

Fruit Loops: Now.

Ricochet: Now he gonna figure it out.

Fruit Loops: Right.

Ricochet: And it still ain't his baby. What the fuck!

Fruit Loops: The first time it was his baby. I killed it [had an abortion]. I wasn't having sex with Ennis the first time.

Interviewer: Uh-huh. So you don't know if it was Ennis's or his.

Fruit Loops: It was his, the first time. And this time, it's Ennis.

Interviewer: You sure it's Ennis?

Fruit Loops: Ennis the only one I fucked without a condom.

Interviewer: What about Alloo?

Ricochet: Alloo . . . you know better. He African, too . . . he a good-looking motherfucking African.

Fruit Loops: I met him on the train. Yeah, he's nice looking. . . . Supposed to give me the money for the baby's suit.

Ricochet: Everybody's trying to buy the baby's [clothes]. . . . Shakie's gonna have about five different outfits.

Family Situation in 2006

At age 40, Ricochet had lost all of her six children to the BCW, lost welfare support, and was homeless unless she stayed with Fruit Loops. Fruit Loops and Tushay reported having had several abortions and miscarriages. Tushay had six children by age 25 and lost custody of all six to protective services because of an assault on a male partner. At age 22, Fruit Loops was the most stable and competent family member, maintaining an apartment for Ricochet, herself, and four children. She also tolerated a revolving set of other persons in her home (Peter, other male partners, Tushay and her six children). I counted 11 persons living at the same time in Fruit Loops's two-bedroom apartment.

Summary

The dilemmas this case presented for me could not be understood without looking at Fruit Loops within her family life and how that family was influenced by the inner-city street/drug subculture. Parental modeling of male–female relationships, bearing children, parenting, and a number of other social skills that followed the street/drug subculture were observed as damaging to women and their offspring.

The interrelationship between street/drug subculture and poor inner-city households is clear: They feed into one another. Some inner-city poor children are socialized into street/drug subculture; further, street/drug subculture codes are modeled in these households. This is an ongoing process that reproduces drug use and sales, prostitution, crime, deviant behavior, and so on, across generations. Seeing young girls being socialized into prostitution and showing disregard and disrespect for themselves was very stressful for me. Yet, I made the difficult decision to not report any of what I witnessed or was described in part to protect the women and their privacy and in part to protect the rapport I had built up with them.

HOMICIDES AMONG DRUG DEALERS

During ethnographic research examining the exchange of sex for crack in 1988, I met a crack prostitute named Naomi, who introduced me into her family. Naomi lived with her mother, Island, and brother, Ross, who was a crack dealer (Dunlap, 1995). More than 20 years earlier, a drug-addicted mother had given her son Allen as a baby to Island to raise, so Island considered Allen her son. Because Ross had witnessed the research process through his sister's participation in the crack prostitution study, he agreed to participate in the "Natural History of Crack Distribution" (1989–1998) research project, which focused on the structure and functioning of crack dealing (Dunlap & Johnson, 1992, 1996; Johnson, Dunlap, & Tourigny, 2000). After administering an informed consent, I had several long interviews with Ross (although the veracity of his self-reports was often suspect).

Ross was my key introduction to a group of crack sellers. Ross sponsored me as trustworthy among his network. Ross had carefully read the Certificate of Confidentiality and showed it to his comrades before he introduced me to others. I had to forge independent relationships with each seller, and I always explained that I was not a cop and would not report what I learned to the police. Ross vouched for my honesty in this regard. He sometimes helped me interview other crack sellers and guarded my personal safety in the dangerous streets. Ross introduced me to Allen, Borace, and John. Ross appeared to be the supplier and informal trainer for a generation of young crack sellers, many of whom were killed during the 1990s. His sellers worked out of the park where I often visited and observed their distribution activities.

Beginning at the peak of the crack epidemic, our research goal was to describe changes in drug distribution groups. As an ethnographer, I met many drug dealers during this study and was often a neutral observer of unpleasant and vicious episodes. The killings associated with Borace and John (reported later in this chapter) occurred in 1991–1992. Homicides peaked during these years in cities across the United States (e.g., in New York City, there were around 2,300 per year; Blumstein, 2006; Blumstein & Wallman, 2006) and were associated with a nationwide pattern of crack distributors gunning down other distributors (Blumstein, 2006; Blumstein & Wallman, 2006). They involve what Goldstein (1985) called *systemic violence*.

The episodes of violence in this study again had overlapping legal, professional, and ethical implications. I was confronted by three difficult dilemmas: (a) What actions should I take (or not) about reporting homicides and potential perpetrators to police? (b) How could I avoid being seriously maimed or killed myself if I reported to the police? (c) How could I maintain a professional stance toward all actors in the midst of severe violence associated with the drug crews being studied?

Borace as a Victim of Homicide

One incident occurred when Borace, an 18-year-old cousin of Ross, came to live in the household. Ross's mother, Island, became the center point for family members and others who needed a place to stay—adolescents aging out of foster care, relatives who had been in prison, users who lost apartments, and so on. All came to Island's household to sleep and live for a while (Dunlap, Johnson, & Tourigny, 2000). Island accepted all but expected them to contribute to the household in whatever way they could (including illegal activities). Ross provided most of them with an opportunity to sell crack. Before Borace arrived, another cousin, Allen (19 years old), who had spent a brief period in jail, had come back to the household to live. He had sold drugs for Ross. Allen and his girlfriend, Tyesha, lived in the back bedroom with their baby boy, David. They lived a more or less normal "street subculture" life together until Allen was shot and killed (the case was never solved).

After his death, Allen's girlfriend Tyesha and the baby David, about 8 months old, continued to live with Island.

About 6 months after Allen was killed, Borace came to live in the household. Borace developed a romantic relationship with Tyesha and began sleeping with her and the baby in the room that Allen had occupied. This disturbed Island, Ross, and Naomi because Allen had been Island's favorite nephew. Because of violent incidents that began taking place, Tyesha left the household and returned to her mother's household, leaving the baby with Island. This pleased Island, who felt that David was her grandson. Tyesha and Borace continued their relationship together and made plans to get an apartment of their own and take the baby with them. None of the household members liked this; they objected vehemently. Not only did they not like Borace having a romantic relationship with Tyesha, but Tyesha and Borace's plan to take David and get an apartment together felt to Island, Ross, and Naomi like this couple was killing Allen all over again.

One afternoon, Ross, Borace, Island, and the baby were sitting on the stoop of the building; Ross suggested that Island take the baby across the street to the park. He said to her that it was going to "get hot" in the neighborhood and she did not need to be there. She went to the park.

About an hour after Island left, Borace was shot and killed on the front stoop of the building. The story that Ross told the police investigators was that he and his friends and Borace were sitting on the stoop laughing and joking. Borace was sitting on the railing of the stoop when three guys ran up, argued with Borace, shot him, and ran. Ross said that it happened so fast that they did not have time to see who the guys were, and they did not know them. Because they were trying to get Borace to talk to them while they called the ambulance, they did not see which way the alleged perpetrators ran. By the time the ambulance arrived, Borace was dead.

The story that family members told the authorities changed daily. Island and her daughter Naomi told me what had actually happened. Everyone knew that Ross was the only one on the stoop with Borace. They also knew that Ross knew absolutely everyone in the area and that no one could come into the area and kill without his knowing who it was. In addition, after Borace had been killed, Ross went around singing "just another day in the neighborhood."

I wondered how Ross knew that something was about to go down. I knew that Ross, Island, Borace, and the baby were on the stoop together that afternoon and that Ross had sent Island to the park before the shooting. I knew the problems the family was having with Borace and Tyesha. I knew that the family did not like the fact that Borace and Tyesha were having a romantic relationship. I knew that Tyesha had to leave the household and go back to live with her mother because of problems in this relationship. I knew that the family did not want Tyesha to take the baby from Island. Most important, I knew that the family was violent. All of this had been recorded as part of my data collection (Johnson, Dunlap, & Maher, 1998). Despite my suspicions that Ross had shot Borace, in the end I had no proof. I had no witnesses except Island and Naomi, who would surely not support my accusations if I went to the police.

In addition, if I went to the police and they went back to ask questions about what I had revealed, my life would also be in danger. What to do? The informed consent form clearly states that for "intended assault or similar crimes, such information may be released by the Principal Investigator (or his/her designee) without your consent to the appropriate agency." Nothing in my field notes indicated that Ross intended to shoot Borace, assault him, or commit any crime against him. My moral concern: I was repulsed by what Ross probably had done. The homicide was never solved, and no arrests occurred. The tensions and potential violence surrounding Borace's death were so great that the minister scheduled to lead the funeral service never showed up. I also had to forcefully decline a reporter's request for an interview because I could not reveal what I had promised Ross and other subjects to keep confidential.

John as a Homicide Perpetrator

I wanted to understand the subculture, networks, and patterns of drug dealing. I had gained entrance into a group of freelance crack dealers, but it was a dangerous situation, as Borace's abbreviated life suggests. First, it is not easy gaining access to selling networks (Dunlap & Johnson, 1999). Dealers do not trust people; they have few acquaintances and few people they consider trusted friends. They are suspicious of everyone, so gaining access is a major achievement for a professional researcher. Second, dealers live by street drug subculture norms, which consist of informal, but well-understood, rules of street justice. Because drug dealers are not in a position to take their problems to the police, they have their own codes that govern business. They beat sellers who are short on monies. Going to the police with information about any individual is seen as the same as going to the authorities on all of them.

Over the years, Ross introduced me to many in his network of drug sellers. John was one of the sellers that I met through Ross. I observed John on numerous occasions because he sold in the territory with Ross, and I talked to him about participating in the research. He agreed, but we had not had the opportunity to record his consent on tape and complete his intake interview at the time the events I describe here occurred.

One night, a number of Ross's associates and his sister's and mother's friends came by the apartment. A party ensued. John came by but seemed reserved, with an air of seriousness. He sat for a while, talking and joking a little with the others. Soon, he came over and started talking to me. He asked me to walk outside with him because he had something to tell me.

As we walked together, he said that he had killed someone. He claimed that the victim had pushed him to do it. He wanted to take me to the building where the body was located. He wanted to explain to me how it had happened. Immediately, I knew that John was telling me dangerous information. I knew that I did not want to know more, nor did I want to go with him, but I had to be cautious about turning him down. I had to let him down gently while not appearing judgmental or frightened. Scared people are seen as untrustworthy. They might go to the police because of their fear, so I could not appear afraid. Putting on my most savvy street mannerisms, I told John that I did not want to go to see a dead body, especially in an abandoned building at night. I told him that he could talk to me about it on another day. If the body was dead, it was not going anywhere.

This was a huge ethical dilemma for me. Knowing that John had never given me a formal informed consent form, I worried about whether I should go to the authorities and tell them what had been told to me, whether I should find out more about who it was that had been killed and where the body was located, and how the police would react to what I knew (Blumstein, 2006; Blumenstein & Wallman, 2006). I was also dreadfully afraid of what would happen to me if I went to the police. I was well aware that in point of fact I knew painfully little. I was not prepared to ask John to tell me more or to have him take me to where the body was located. A number of young male dealers in my study had been killed, so I knew that these dealers were dangerous and deadly serious.

Over the years of study, I did not reveal anything about what I had learned to the police. No harm came to the sellers from what they had shared with me, and no one had been arrested. In the end, I decided neither to document what I had learned in field notes nor to meet further with John to discuss what had happened. The next time I saw him I did not bring up the subject. I decided that if John tried to talk to me further about the incident, I would explain to him that I did not want to know more because that would make me an accessory to the crime, and I did not want to be put in such a position. John did not pursue me further to explain what had taken place. We never discussed the matter again. Three months later, a number of bodies were found in an abandoned building that was being torn down.

Several factors were critical in my thinking. First, I expected a great deal of violence in street/drug subculture (Dunlap, Stürzenhofecker, Sanabria, & Johnson, 2004; Johnson, Golub, & Dunlap, 2006). Second, one of the most important norms in drug business is that no one can ever "snitch." People who act as police informants and undercover agents understand that if discovered, they will likely be maimed or killed. Third, I was a professional researcher systematically seeking to stand clear of the many disputes and violence that occur among those I studied. I only learned about events after they occurred. Fourth, what I had learned from John was missing many vital details about who, what, when, and where. In such situations I made a professionally appropriate decision to avoid learning those details. Knowing them would create an ethical obligation to report what I knew to authorities for further investigation. Yet, to know such details and report them would constitute a violation of my promise of confidentiality. It would also appear that I had double-crossed the participants (promising confidentiality and then reporting to police). This would endanger my own personal safety. Finally, any information I provided would be unlikely to make a criminal case if I did not testify at trial, which professionally I felt I could not do under the terms of the Certificate of Confidentiality.

CONCLUSION

This chapter has presented three cases of ethical and legal issues encountered during field research. As was demonstrated, respondents tended to act according to street drug subcultural norms that encourage early sexual experiences and tolerate violence while they systematically concealed and denied behaviors that violated the laws and regulations of larger society.

Both the mother and grandmother of Fruit Loops supported socialization into transactional sexual encounters. The perceived value of the obtained goods, services, money, and illegal drugs overcame (conventional) moral standards—which were poorly modeled by adult guardians. For instance, although the grandmother disapproved of Fruit Loops having sexual relations with an older male, she was adamant that the girl should get something out of the encounter: The man should take her shopping. In the subculture of transactional sexual encounters, Fruit Loops had many male "friends" and was not sure who fathered her children. She also revealed that all of her sexual partners were much older than she was. In fact, she called one male her father because of his age. Witnessing conversations about these events placed me in the tough position of deciding whether to report my well-founded suspicions of sexual misconduct by the males in Fruit Loops's life.

The homicides involving Borace and John presented legal and ethical dilemmas, too. The homicides placed me in a dangerous situation. In both cases, I carefully followed the professional guidelines given in the informed consent, but I also had to recognize the inherent dangers and keep within ethical codes of research. At no time did I have previous knowledge of what was going to happen and therefore could not have reported it.

I had to remain truthful to the research participants and seek to understand their way of reasoning. I had promised them that what I learned would remain confidential, that I would not reveal what I knew to the police, and that the Certificate of Confidentiality protected me from providing information to legal authorities. If John had taken me to see the body and I had recorded the information in my field notes, I could have been in a deeply difficult legal, professional, and ethical situation. Because John had not given me his signed informed consent, I remain uncertain whether the certificate would have protected this information. If the police had stopped me to inquire about a homicide in the neighborhood, I am professionally confident that the Certificate of Confidentiality would have protected me from revealing information about Ross and his dealing comrades or providing information that police would need to formulate a case. Nevertheless, I am glad that I never had any conversations with the police about the illegal behaviors I observed or had described to me.

Despite the legal, professional, and ethical dilemmas reported here, I am fully committed to continuing such research in the future. Following the legal and ethical standards set forth in informed consent discussions and other professional guidelines provides reasonable standards for dealing with difficult situations. It is also important to remember that the professional behaviors of an ethnographer probably will not change the life trajectories of those being studied and prevent these harms from occurring. Finally, it is important to understand the various subcultures into which people are socialized and live out their lives. This chapter has unveiled specific behaviors practiced in many inner-city family lives. The content of specific conduct norms associated with behavior has been examined in the context of this researcher's professional ethics and personal values and standards. I hope that this has demonstrated the complexity involved when a researcher must balance legal and ethical responsibility, especially when studying cultures far outside of his or her own.

REFERENCES

Blumstein, A. (2006). Disaggregating the violence trends. In A. Blumstein & J. Wallman (Eds.), *The crime drop in America* (rev. ed.; pp. 13–44). New York: Cambridge University Press.

Blumstein, A., & Wallman, J. (Eds.). (2006). *The crime drop in America* (rev. ed.). New York: Cambridge University Press.

Dunlap, E. (1992). Impact of drugs on family life and kin networks in the inner-city African-American single parent household. In A. Harrell & G. Peterson (Eds.), *Drugs, crime, and social isolation: Barriers to urban opportunity* (pp. 181–207). Washington, DC: Urban Institute Press.

Dunlap, E. (1995). Inner-city crisis and drug dealing: Portrait of a drug dealer and his household. In S. MacGregor & A. Lipow (Eds.), *The other city: People and politics in New York and London* (pp. 114–131). Atlantic Highlands, NJ: Humanities Press.

Dunlap, E., Golub, A., & Johnson, B. D. (2003a). Girls' sexual development in the inner city: From compelled childhood sexual contact to sex-for-things exchanges. *Journal of Child Sexual Abuse, 12*(2), 73–96.

Dunlap, E., Golub, A., & Johnson, B. D. (2003b). Transient male–female relationships and the violence they bring to girls in the inner-city. *Journal of African American Studies*, *7*(2), 19–37.

Dunlap, E., & Johnson, B. D. (1992). The setting for the crack era: Macro forces, micro consequences (1960–92). *Journal of Psychoactive Drugs*, *24*(3), 307–321.

Dunlap, E., & Johnson, B. D. (1996). Family/resources in the development of a female crack seller career: Case study of a hidden population. *Journal of Drug Issues*, *26*(1), 177–200.

Dunlap, E., & Johnson, B. D. (1999). Gaining access to hidden populations: Strategies for gaining cooperation of sellers/dealers in ethnographic research. *Drugs and Society*, *14*(1–2), 127–149.

Dunlap, E., Johnson, B. D., Golub, A., & Wesley, D. (2002). Intergenerational transmission of conduct norms for drugs, sexual exploitation and violence: A case study. *British Journal of Criminology*, *42*, 1–20.

Dunlap, E., Johnson, B. D., & Rath, J. (1996). Aggression and violence in households of crack sellers/abusers. *Applied Behavioral Science Review*, *4*(2), 191–217.

Dunlap, E., Johnson, B. D., & Tourigny, S. C. (2000). Dead tired and bone weary: Grandmothers as caregivers in drug-affected inner-city households. *Race and Society*, *3*, 143–163.

Dunlap, E., Stürzenhofecker, G., Sanabria, H., & Johnson, B. D. (2004). Mothers and daughters: The intergenerational reproduction of violence and drug use in home and street life. *Journal of Ethnicity and Substance Abuse*, *3*(2), 1–24.

Goldstein, P. (1985). The drugs/crime nexus: A tripartite conceptual framework. *Journal of Drug Issues*, *14*, 493–506.

Johnson, B. D., Dunlap, E., & Maher, L. (1998). Nurturing for careers in drug abuse and crime: Conduct norms for children and juveniles in crack-abusing households. *Substance Use and Misuse*, *33*(7), 1515–1550.

Johnson, B. D., Dunlap, E., & Tourigny, S. C. (2000). Crack distribution and abuse in New York City. In M. Natarajan & M. Hough (Eds.), *Crime prevention studies: Vol. 11. Illegal drug markets: From research to prevention policy* (pp. 19–77). Monsey, NY: Criminal Justice Press.

Johnson, B. D., Golub, A., & Dunlap, E. (2006). The rise and decline of drugs, drug markets, and violence in New York City. In Al. Blumstein & J. Wallman (Eds.), *The crime drop in America* (rev. ed.; pp. 164–206). New York: Cambridge University Press.

New York State Penal Code 2001, Article 130.25. Rape in the Third Degree. Flushing NY: Looseleaf Law Publications.

IV

CONCLUDING THOUGHTS

11

BEST PRACTICES FOR RESPONDING TO THREATS OF VIOLENCE IN RESEARCH ETHICALLY AND LEGALLY

DAVID R. BUCHANAN, LANCE GABLE, AND CELIA B. FISHER

The conduct of research poses many challenges for researchers. The rigors of conducting valid scientific inquiry loom large in the design of studies, and the need to conscientiously uphold ethical and legal requirements in conducting research with human subjects cannot be overstated. Detailed analyses and thinking have gone into elucidating how ethical principles apply to clinical research, and important precedents governing research have been set in law by historically significant court cases and federal regulations. However, as we have explored throughout this book, several inherent legal and ethical challenges remain unresolved in the context of conducting nonintervention research with high-risk populations. The purpose, conduct, and circumstances surrounding these types of studies implicate many of the same ethical and legal considerations as clinical randomized controlled trials, but nonintervention studies also differ in important ways. Moreover, in contrast to prior analyses of descriptive research, the potential for physical harm—to research participants, third parties, and research staff—and the researchers' ethical and legal obligations to address this possibility have been of particular concern in the discussions and examples raised by contributors to this book.

The preceding chapters have identified and examined many complex issues that can arise in the course of conducting nonintervention research with high-risk populations. In our introduction to this volume, we set out the challenge of finding an appropriate balance between protecting human subjects from harm and generating new scientific knowledge that could potentially benefit countless numbers of people at risk for suicide, child abuse, and violence. In this final chapter, we draw key lessons from the preceding discussions and make recommendations to achieve an ethically and legally appropriate balance between allowing the research to proceed and ensuring that every reasonable effort is made to protect the safety and well-being of those involved directly or indirectly with the research.

The chapter opens with a brief synopsis of the social costs of suicide, child abuse, and violence to highlight the implications of failing to seek to learn how they can be prevented. Next, we summarize the major ethical and legal issues identified in the book as guidance for researchers, institutional review boards (IRBs), research participants, and other interested groups. Finally, we lay out an evolving public health ethics framework and set of best practices to guide ethically and legally sound approaches to the design and conduct of research with high-risk populations.

THE SOCIAL SIGNIFICANCE OF NONINTERVENTION RESEARCH INVOLVING HIGH-RISK POPULATIONS

The need for research on suicide, child abuse, and violence is evident in the toll they take on society as seen in the early years of the 21st century. Morbidity and mortality figures associated with violent and health-compromising behaviors demonstrate their significant effects. In 2004, suicide took the lives of 32,439 people and led to an additional 425,650 injuries from self-harm in the United States (Centers for Disease Control and Prevention, 2007). During the same years, more than 20.4 million Americans were classified as substance abusing or substance dependent, and an estimated 25% of inmates convicted of a violent crime reported drug use at the time of their offense (Bureau of Justice Statistics, 2006; Substance Abuse & Mental Health Services Administration, 2007). Between 1998 and 2003 in the United States, there were more than 3.5 million reported cases of domestic violence, and most victims (73%) were women (Bureau of Justice Statistics, 2005). In 2005, approximately 899,000 American children were victims of abuse or neglect (Administration on Children, Youth, & Families, 2007). Drug use, incarceration, domestic violence, and child sexual abuse have all been linked with increased risk of HIV infection and with additional health problems and hospitalizations, costs that are often paid by Medicaid (Rovi, Chen, & Johnson, 2004; Thompson, Kingree, & Desai, 2004). The social burden attributable to these problems includes higher health care costs, increased school drop-out and teen pregnancy rates, reduced job productivity and lost earnings, adjudication and incarceration for criminal behaviors, and increased burdens on the social welfare system.

In response to the epidemic nature of these problems and the paucity of empirical data to guide the development of effective prevention policies and programs, the National Institute on Drug Abuse (NIDA), National Institute of Mental Health, National Institute on Alcoholism and Alcohol Abuse, and other agencies have sought to support research aimed at explaining, preventing, and otherwise reducing the individual, family, and societal costs of these health problems. The urgent need for empirically informed public policies has led social scientists to reexamine their roles and responsibilities in addressing these concerns. As amply demonstrated in this book, however, standard ethical analyses of clinical research designs provide insufficient guidance for investigators in conducting nonintervention studies with participants at high risk of engaging in life-threatening behaviors. The traditional ethical and legal frameworks need to be reevaluated and adapted, and a variety of research strategies, including creative approaches to gathering valid empirical data, as described in this volume, need to be undertaken. Investigators have identified the lack of legal and ethical guidance regarding standards for conducting research on high-risk behaviors as a significant barrier to increasing the volume and scope of research in this arena.

DISTINCT ETHICAL AND LEGAL CONSIDERATIONS

The preceding chapters have identified several distinct and difficult questions that arise in the context of conducting descriptive research with high-risk populations. Many of these questions revolve around the confidential relationship between researchers and research participants in these types of studies. For example, at what point does the need to protect participants from threats of harm, such as suicide, child abuse, or violence, take priority over confidentiality protections? When is the probability or magnitude of harm sufficiently great to justify intentional disclosure of this information? What are the risks and benefits of safeguarding confidentiality in the research context? What ethical reasons or moral justifications support maintaining or abandoning confidentiality in light of a potential threat of harm? To what extent do researchers have obligations beyond individual research participants? When do laws require disclosure of information revealed in the research context in response to a threat to harm to participants, third parties, and staff in nonintervention studies? How can these concerns best be addressed proactively through law and ethics?

The implementation of descriptive research does not expose research participants to the same type of risk of harm inherent in experimental studies. Yet, descriptive research studies may create a risk for harm to participants and others already at high risk because of the nature of the problem under investigation. In focusing on nonintervention research with populations at risk for violent behavior or victimization—that is, research with participants who are likely to be suicidal, to commit acts of violence, or to be traumatized by child abuse or battering—researchers must be well prepared for the possibility of harm befalling the participants themselves or noninvolved third parties during the period of data collection and analysis. Thus, although the widely recognized ethical standards established for conducting clinical research involving human subjects—such as the need for informed consent, protection of confidentiality, and the minimization of harm—must be upheld, their application in the distinct context of descriptive research raises a host of novel and relevant ethical considerations.

Existing bioethical principles provide relevant but inadequate guidance in this context. The Belmont Report (National Commission, 1979) identified three fundamental ethical principles that govern health research: respect for autonomy (which entails protecting a person's confidentiality, among other things), beneficence, and justice in distributing the benefits and burdens of the research. The problem, however, is that these principles and the ensuing federal regulations addressing the protection of human research subjects (Protection of Human Subjects, 2005, also known as the Common Rule) are insufficiently explicit to provide substantive guidance for researchers faced with the wide range of ethical issues that may arise in nonintervention studies with high-risk populations, as documented in the case studies presented here.

Research involving individuals engaged in illegal, violent, and/or health-compromising behaviors, for example, raises questions about confidentiality and reporting responsibilities, about which current federal research regulations and professional codes of ethics are largely silent. Illustrating the point, NIDA typically requires investigators to obtain a Certificate of Confidentiality (Public Health Service Act, 1988). The certificate provides investigators with legal protection against being compelled to disclose confidential data, but obtaining the certificate does not require researchers to withhold such information (Public Health Service Act, 1988). In other words, researchers retain the discretion to disclose confidential information if they deem such disclosures legally or ethically necessary. There is little guidance to help investigators determine the conditions in which it is morally responsible or ethically imperative to reveal self-injurious or threatening behaviors gathered during the course of a study, or about how to inform potential volunteers about these limits on their confidentiality. NIDA has also had a long-standing recommendation that studies involving drug abusers offer HIV counseling (NIDA, 2007). Yet, there are myriad other problems that may be uncovered in such research for which investigators must determine whether counseling or referrals are ethically justified.

Investigators lack sufficient guidance on legal compliance as well. All states have child abuse reporting laws, and some states have *Tarasoff v. Regents of the University of California* (1976) laws requiring professionals to warn prospective victims if they become aware of a substantial threat to their welfare, but most states fail to delineate explicitly the extent to which these laws apply to researchers (Appelbaum & Rosenbaum, 1989; Seiber, 2001).

The import of these gaps and ambiguities has grown increasingly acute over the past decade in the wake of the tragic deaths of two participants in clinical trials, described in the Introduction to this book. As a result, IRBs have become increasingly risk averse in reviewing research proposals (Mello, Studdert, & Brennan, 2003), which now threatens to significantly hinder research on high-risk behaviors. These tensions underscore the importance of providing additional ethical and legal guidance to ensure that this research is carried out responsibly in a timely fashion for the benefit of society.

AN EMERGING PUBLIC HEALTH ETHICS FRAMEWORK

In the Introduction, we presented eight ethical requirements for health research that have been identified in a synthesis of major national and international policy documents historically enacted to monitor health research. These standards are (a) social value, (b) scientific validity, (c) fair subject selection, (d) favorable risk–benefit ratio, (e) independent review, (f) informed consent, (g) respect for enrolled subjects, and (h) community collaboration (Emanuel, Wendler, & Grady, 2000; Emanuel, Wendler, Killen, & Grady, 2004). In a significant extension and reinterpretation of these principles, there has been growing attention to ethics from a public health perspective in recent years. Whereas medicine focuses on individual health, public health seeks to affect the health of the entire population. Thus, in contrast to a fiduciary duty to the individual patient, public health ethics is founded on societal responsibility to protect and promote the health of the population as a whole.

A starting point for reexamining the ethical framework that originated in clinical research (and has since come to govern all health and social scientific research) is to reconsider the issue of social value. As described in the Introduction to this volume, research that will not produce socially valuable knowledge should not be undertaken (Emanuel et al., 2000, 2004), and a study that does not attempt to answer a socially valuable question or hypothesis is not worth conducting because the risks to research participants in studies lacking societal value cannot be justified, making such research unethical. The assessment of social value, however, may be evaluated differently in the context of nonintervention studies than in clinical research. Descriptive nonintervention research may provide the foundational knowledge that is an essential precursor to the development of potentially effective interventions and social policies (Fisher & Lerner, 1994).

A broader public health perspective demands a second look at the role of justice in evaluating the conduct of health research (Buchanan, Sifunda, Naidoo, James, & Reddy, in press; McCarthy, 1998). Many observers have noted a paradigm shift in the evolution of justice concerns in health research, moving from a predominant concern with protecting participants from harm to an emerging interest in improving access to clinical trials (Powers, 1998). In the historical context of public outrage at the egregious misconduct of researchers at Tuskegee and other research scandals, the Belmont Report (National Commission, 1979) concentrated accordingly on justice considerations internal to the research process. Although concerns about distributing the benefits of research fairly in society are presented, the report is largely framed around protecting research participants from harm and exploitation. As Levine (1986) noted, the work of the National Commission has increasingly come under attack for overemphasizing individual rights and failing to recognize and discuss community obligations.

Over time, the weight of public moral concern has shifted from a preoccupation with the risks of participating in research to a greater appreciation of the potential benefits. For example, eligible patients, researchers, and ethicists are reconsidering the potential benefits of participation in Phase 1 cancer treatment trials, which have traditionally been defined and categorized as focusing strictly on toxicity assessments (Joffe & Miller, 2006). Likewise, there are now active debates about the traditional exclusion of "vulnerable" adolescents from "nontherapeutic" HIV vaccine research, given the typical age of initiation of sexual activity and urgent need for more effective prevention measures (Singh et al., 2006; Strode, Slack, Wassenaar, & Singh, 2007). Similarly, the effect of the research on the community as a whole, in terms of its potential risks or opportunity costs as well as growing recognition of the ethical necessity of demonstrating tangible benefits to the community, has received increasing attention in recent years (Brody, McCullough, & Sharp, 2005; Emanuel et al., 2004). These examples point to the paradigm shift that has opened the door to new claims of justice, expanding the range of parties who ought to be considered morally relevant beyond the participants alone in determining the value of the research under consideration.

Following this line of reasoning, Buchanan and Miller (2005, 2006a, 2006b, 2006c) have argued that taking a public health perspective on research ethics involves broadening the conceptualization of risks and benefits deemed ethically relevant in deliberations about approving health research. To ascertain the social value of descriptive research with high-risk populations, a comprehensive analysis must take into account not only the risks and benefits to the research participants themselves, but also to the population as a whole. From a public health perspective, the research community has a binding moral obligation to protect and promote the health of the population, including future potential beneficiaries, as well as the current research participants. A public health perspective on research with high-risk populations entails due recognition of the inherently social purpose of research. In the research context, the decisions of investigators and IRBs have implications for the whole of society. Because the promulgation of policies and programs and prudent use of limited public resources often hang in the balance, the moral consequences of not approving research with high-risk populations, or imposing arduous restrictions, have implications beyond the potential risk faced by individual participants or third parties whom they may threaten. Conversely, failure to give ethical consideration to group stigmatization and depreciation as an unintended consequence of nonintervention research involving socially disenfranchised or disadvantaged groups can also lead to injustices (Buchanan et al., in press; Fisher, 1999). According to Buchanan and Miller (2005, 2006a, 2006b, 2006c), it is therefore appropriate to set a high standard regarding the probability and magnitude of harm to conclude that the risks of the research cannot be justified.

From a public health perspective, the decision to approve research with high-risk populations is justified on grounds that it is in the public's interest to uncover evidence that is essential to the development of new and more effective interventions. Fisher et al. (2002), however, cautioned that any such determination must be tempered with sensitivity to public harms that may emerge when research is focused exclusively on vulnerability to violent behavior and not protective factors with identified populations. A public health perspective recognizes the intrinsic social purpose of conducting research and thus gives greater weight to the risks and benefits of the research (e.g., policy implications) to the population as a whole.

To advance the state of normative analysis, Childress et al. (2002) have articulated five criteria for achieving or maintaining an appropriate ethical balance between the need for protecting the health and welfare of the population as a whole and the social value of minimizing infringements on individual liberty rights: (a) effectiveness, (b) proportionality, (c) necessity, (d) least infringement, and (e) public justification (see Table 11.1). Although originally developed to provide criteria for resolving ethical dilemmas in the context of public health practice, these standards offer a useful framework for thinking about the specific issues involved in nonintervention research.

The justification for conducting research with high-risk populations is based on the increasingly well-recognized importance of practicing evidence-based medicine and evidence-based public health. Public resources are limited. Therefore, these resources must be used prudently and not squandered on ineffective or minimally effective interventions (Emanuel et al., 2000; Jensen, Hoagwood, & Trickett, 1999; Lerner, Fisher, & Weinberg, 2000). The first standard in the Childress et al. (2002) public health ethics framework is, accordingly, effectiveness. On the basis of this criterion, interventions that may infringe on individual autonomy can be justified–and can

TABLE 11.1
Justificatory Conditions That Warrant Overriding Individual Autonomy

Condition	Description
Effectiveness	The proposed intervention must have a realistic chance of achieving the goal of protecting public health.
Proportionality	The public health benefits to be achieved by the proposed intervention must outweigh the infringements on individual liberty.
Necessity	In situations in which forcible intervention strategies are being proposed (such as quarantine), it must be demonstrated that other, less morally troubling interventions are not available or are incapable of adequately containing the problem.
Least infringement	Public health agents should seek to minimize the infringements on individual liberties to the greatest extent possible.
Public justification	Public health agents have a responsibility to explain why the proposed intervention that infringes on individual liberty is justified.

Note. Data from Childress et al. (2002).

only be justified–if they have a reasonable possibility of achieving the desired health outcome (e.g., reducing suicide rates). By extension, research involving high-risk populations can be justified on the grounds that it is necessary to inform the development of socially valuable programs and policies (assuming the research design is such that it will produce valid scientific evidence).

Fisher (1999) again advised that when including public good in the risk–benefit calculus for research involving members of the vulnerable groups, investigators need to approach the estimation of societal benefits with caution. The social value of the research depends on the degree of community cohesion around the topic of social import and the extent to which the prospective participants are integrated or disenfranchised from public deliberation (Fisher, 2002b; Fisher et al., 2002; Weijer & Emmanuel, 2000). Investigators need to be alert to instances in which the interests of the larger community are not congruent with the best interests or research goals of vulnerable groups within the community (Macklin, 1999).

The second, third, and fourth criteria proffered by Childress et al. (2002)—proportionality, necessity, and least infringement—are closely related and provide additional specifications of the effectiveness criterion. The justification for conducting descriptive research with high-risk populations is that without such research, society cannot fulfill the ethically desirable goal of identifying effective interventions that are proportionate to the magnitude of the problem (i.e., the benefits of reducing suicide or violence are not disproportionately outweighed by the social costs of impinging on liberty rights); that the programs and policies under consideration are necessary, if viable alternatives are lacking; and that they pose the least infringement on individual autonomy as possible. Conducting research with high-risk populations enables society to identify interventions that realize these societal values. As IRBs deliberate about the cost–benefit ratio of a protocol, the social benefits and risks of conducting the research identified in this framework must be taken into account.

The final criterion in the Childress et al. (2002) framework is that achieving the socially desirable goal of identifying and implementing effective health interventions, because of the scarcity of public resources, demands public justification, hence the rise in evidence-based medicine and evidence-based public health. In public deliberations, society needs evidence to justify the expenditure of public resources (or pooled resources, as in insurance systems) and to make informed decisions about their worth.

In combination, these five criteria may lend greater weight to the benefits of conducting research with high-risk populations. On the basis of the public health ethics framework described here, Buchanan and Miller (2005, 2006a, 2006b, 2006c) would accordingly argue for setting a high standard regarding the likelihood of harm, which lies at the crux of approving or denying approval of research in IRB deliberations.

BEST PRACTICES FOR ADDRESSING ETHICAL AND LEGAL ISSUES IN NONINTERVENTION RESEARCH

The preceding analysis provides grounds for giving greater weight to the social benefits of research with high-risk populations in balancing the need to protect participants from harm with the need to generate new knowledge to protect and promote population health. Nevertheless, researchers' obligations to minimize potential threats of harm to participants, the populations that they represent, and affiliated third parties remain important. In this section, we present an evolving set of "best practices" that we recommend for incorporation into research designs to minimize the possibility of harm to the participants, researchers, and third parties.

Understanding and Using the Law

The first recommended best practice is to review mandated reporting laws for the state in which the research is planned. Mandatory reporting laws vary by state, so it is essential to know whether a researcher is required by law to report certain threatening behaviors and the exact behaviors that the particular state law covers. It is particularly important to determine whether the law explicitly includes researchers as mandated reporters or if the mandated reporting provision could be interpreted to include researchers (chap. 2, this volume). Furthermore, researchers should consider the exceptions provided by the federal Certificate of Confidentiality (Fisher, Hoagwood, & Jensen, 1996). Researchers should not be surprised to learn that many state laws are vague about whether researchers are, or are not, mandated reporters (Liss, 1994). The issue becomes even more complicated in situations in which staff may occupy dual roles, for example, nurse and researcher, and in studies with data collected from different states (Mulvey, 2004b). In these instances, investigators and IRBs are advised to consult with their legal counsel. Proactively assessing the relevant legal environment is particularly important because case law on legal liabilities can change rapidly. Finally, knowledge of state laws may facilitate researcher access to additional stateheld data and assist in conducting certain descriptive studies (chap. 6, this volume).

Applying the Goodness-of-Fit Model

Our second recommendation is to adopt a goodness-of-fit framework to minimize the potential for harm to the research participants. Most descriptive social scientific research poses minimal risk. This book, however, has focused on the intersection between certain types of research and certain types of populations, which can create vulnerabilities not found in other types of investigations. Fisher previously developed a model of research ethics called goodness of fit that provides a framework for identifying and minimizing these research vulnerabilities (Fisher, 2002a; 2003; Fisher & Ragsdale, 2006; chaps. 1 and 9, this volume).

According to Fisher's (chap. 1, this volume) goodness-of-fit model, it is not solely the participants' characteristics that define or determine vulnerability, but also the purpose and methods of the research. Vulnerability is the result of the interaction between participant characteristics and the research design. Thus, the model calls for assessment of the risks produced by the combination of particular research goals and methods and specific participant vulnerabilities. Several inferences flow from this proposition. The first and most important implication is that vulnerability can be reduced when research procedures are fitted to participant characteristics. The second is that confidentiality and disclosure decisions need to be adapted to the specific research context and participant population. Accordingly, it is not advisable for IRBs to set rigid a priori stipulations regarding disclosure requirements for the broad category of descriptive research with high-risk populations; rather, the extent of confidentiality protections and the criteria that should trigger disclosure need to be determined in the context of the specific research focus and methodology in light of the corresponding participant characteristics.

The goodness-of-fit model poses three questions: What special life circumstances may render participants more susceptible to risks that arise in this research design? What aspects of the methodology, implementation, or dissemination may create or exacerbate such research risks? And how can research procedures be fitted to participant characteristics to best minimize risk? (Fisher, 2002a, 2003; Fisher & Masty, 2006; chap. 2, this volume). In this model, the assessment of risk is thus shifted from an exclusive focus on the characteristics of the individual alone and more appropriately determined on the basis of the interaction between the participant and the setting and circumstances in which the research is conducted. More specifically, in studies of suicide, child abuse, and violence, there are many well-known characteristics that participants are highly likely to have, such as addiction, comorbid mental health disorders, engagement in illegal behaviors, poverty, minority status, social stigma, a dangerous social network, and other problems, which increase their vulnerability; however, researchers and IRBs seldom consider the ways in which the conduct of the research itself may increase or decrease the chances of a violent episode occurring (Fisher & Ragsdale, 2006). The goodness-of-fit model takes into account the effect of external factors created by the research environment that influence the level and likelihood of risk.

During the preliminary stages of conceptualizing the investigation, not only is it imperative to know the laws of the state in which one is working, as stressed earlier, but it is also important to anticipate the most common types of risks (e.g., different kinds of substance abuse—methamphetamine versus heroin or alcohol abuse, access to handguns, rates of domestic violence) that are likely to be present in the population under investigation. This background information is critical in designing a research protocol that minimizes risk.

With this information in hand, Fisher has developed a five-step process to guide decision making about whether to disclose confidential information (Fisher, 2002b, 2003; chap. 1, this volume). The first step is to anticipate disclosure challenges. This can be operationalized by setting predefined trigger thresholds in structured interview protocols. There are a variety of mechanisms to achieve this goal. One can define positive responses to a small set of identified questions, analogous to *Diagnostic and Statistical Manual of Mental Disorders* (4th ed.; American Psychiatric Association, 1994) diagnostic criteria. One can build in skip patterns to follow up on key questions. Similarly, investigators can set up computer programs that alert the interviewers that a preset threshold has been reached or that bring up new screens for follow-up questions. A recommended best practice is to set an even lower threshold that prompts the interviewer to discuss the case at hand with the principal clinical investigator. Defined threshold triggers may consider multiple interviews together, for example, monitoring how many times a particular issue is brought up by particular subject.

Fisher's (chap. 1, this volume) second step is to investigate legal responsibilities and community resources. This includes making prearrangements with local referral sources to handle crisis situations for those problems that are most likely to be encountered in research with the particular population under investigation. Depending on the study, this may entail having qualified clinical staff on site for immediate intervention. The third step requires investigators to generate ethical alternatives and then select the best disclosure policy. This can include establishing a predetermined hierarchy of interventions in advance. If a preset trigger threshold is crossed, the field staff need to know what to do—in particular, when it is necessary to disclose (see the Staff Training section for further discussion of this point). The fourth step is to communicate the disclosure policy to research team members and participants. To do so requires making confidentiality protections and disclosure procedures and decision-making processes explicit in the informed consent document. This document should advise the participants that their consent authorizes the investigator to disclose information and other actions to be taken under the specified conditions. Researchers need to be as clear as possible in the consent process about when they will have to report situations if participants tell them about wanting to harm themselves or somebody else. Another option is to request permission in the informed consent document to speak to the participant's therapist or a family member. The fifth and final step requires that investigators monitor the implementation of the disclosure policy, encourage feedback from staff and participants, and make modifications to the process if necessary.

Case Screening

A third recommended best practice is case screening: carefully evaluating the possible interactions and outcomes that may arise between a particular research participant and investigator (Mulvey, 2004b; chap. 8, this volume). Case screening seeks to minimize the possibility of surprise and reduce the need for on-the-spot decision-making responsibility. There are several elements involved here. First, researchers need to be cognizant of assessing the match between the interviewer and interviewee, in contrast to simply assigning cases randomly. For example, it might be prudent to assign sex offenders to male interviewers. A related element is establishing guidelines about when issues arising during the course of data collection need to come back to the principal investigator for debriefing (chap. 5, this volume). Monitoring staff performance makes up a third element. At the most basic level, this may involve simply keeping counts of the number of cases that staff members bring back for discussion and debriefing, where large discrepancies—one staff member finding many instances, another none—should lead the investigator to consider the need for further training and more standardized protocols. Likewise, given that people's life situations may change, and new risks may emerge during the course of the study involving high-risk research participants, the level of risk for particular participants should be periodically reassessed to ensure that the circumstances have not significantly changed to render an earlier assessment moot (chap. 8, this volume).

Staff Training Programs

The fourth best practice is to require crisis intervention training for staff. Such training programs can be borrowed or readily adapted from police crisis intervention programs that are used for handling domestic disputes. These trainings involve several components, including responding to the crises of others as well as basic safety procedures and the creation of a safe working environment. They typically cover issues like positioning oneself; putting the person in a large, soft chair; looking for secure settings; making sure the participant is not between the interviewer and the exit door; making sure the door is not locked; pairing interviewers in the field; separating people if a situation arises; breaking eye contact; and other practical tips for protecting staff safety (chap. 8, this volume). These trainings should be tailored to the research objectives, in which, for example, a study of interpersonal violence may require different emphases than a study of suicide ideation.

Another component of best practices in staff training is to take staff through a series of case studies and discuss a range of potential responses. The purpose of these exercises is both to prepare staff for the kinds of events that they may encounter and to improve their ability to identify the ethically most salient elements in complex situations. This best practice acknowledges that it is simply impossible to provide a set of a priori procedures for responding to the full range of circumstances that staff may encounter, and so, inevitably, they will have to exercise their best judgment and need to be prepared for this possibility (chap. 5, this volume). Staff need to be trained and prepared to apply predetermined protocols flexibly and to increase their capacity to respond prudently to the virtually unlimited range of different research situations. To be clear, this does not imply that the best practices described earlier are optional; rather, this recommendation is based on the explicit recognition that novel and unanticipated events are inevitable, particularly in this type of research (chap. 10, this volume). Although such events are difficult to anticipate, staff can be trained to respond more appropriately, less rashly, less foolishly, and more prudently through case-based training exercises.

Community Collaboration

Finally, from a public health perspective, it is important to recognize an ethical standard that respects community autonomy (Buchanan, Miller, & Wallerstein, 2007; Fisher et al., 2002; Fisher & Wallace, 2000). The eighth requirement identified by Emanuel et al. (2000, 2004) is community collaboration. This standard can be achieved by requiring the use of a community advisory board (CAB). The purposes of such CABs are to protect against exploitation of vulnerable populations, to ensure fair terms of cooperation, to ratify that the methods to be used are acceptable to community members, and to minimize potential misunderstandings about the nature of the research (Castro, Rios, & Montoya, 2006; Mohatt & Thomas, 2006; Noe et al., 2006). These CABs should have responsibility for determining whether the research goals are valuable to the population of interest and the methods acceptable before the research is allowed to proceed. On the basis of the public health ethics framework outlined here, respect for communities entails a fundamental right of community members to exercise a meaningful role in determining the conduct of research that affects their lives. Respect for such rights requires that selection of CAB members reflects sensitivity to the heterogeneous nature of communities to ensure that voices of both the powerful and the powerless are considered (Fisher, 1999, 2000; Fisher et al., 2002).

This principle has important applications for minimizing the threat of harm in research with high-risk populations. Community involvement in research has changed over the decades from seeking relatively minor feedback to being truly collaborative, where community members have a stake in and a real say over the research questions to be investigated, the goals of the research, and the methods used in carrying out the research. In the evolving practice of participatory research, investigators seek to identify the questions that the population of interest thinks are most important in meeting their needs (Viswanathan et al., 2004). It is a consumer-driven approach, in which the population affected by the problem has substantive input into the type of questions that they want to have answered. Fisher's goodness-of-fit model likewise encourages participatory research that views scientists and communities as moral agents joined in partnership to construct research designs that are scientifically valid and socially responsible (Fisher & Ragsdale, 2006). This goal is best achieved through a process of "colearning" that assumes that investigators and community members bring to CABs different but equally important expertise. The investigator brings expertise about the scientific method and extant empirical knowledge about a social problem, and the community brings expertise about the validity of the social problem and the fears, hopes, and values that participants may bring to the research (Fisher, 1997, 1999, 2000, 2002b). A CAB is essential for advising researchers about the kinds of scenarios they are likely to encounter, how to handle such situations to maximize the prospects for advancing the research while protecting everyone involved, and the types of services that are available in the community.

CONCLUSION

This book has examined a critical new arena for debate and deliberation in conducting health research ethically. In the end, the numerous concerns flagged in this book do not lend themselves to simple solutions. Rather, researchers themselves need to call increased attention to the issues identified here. It is only by greater public discussion that a broader consensus can be developed and many of these issues resolved.

We would like to conclude this text with four points for further consideration. The first point is that IRBs need to seriously and honestly consider the consequences of not allowing research on these serious health problems. If the justification for prohibiting the research is the potential for harm, then this due moral consideration must be weighed and balanced against the harm that will occur if the generation of new knowledge that can lead to the development of effective interventions to prevent and reduce the currently considerable levels of harm is thwarted.

The second point is that IRBs need to recognize and be comfortable with the fact that standardized, clear-cut protocols to direct researchers about how they must respond and handle every conceivable situation have not yet been developed, nor is it likely that they will ever be finalized. Rather, the best that can be done is to use a set of best practices that have been identified over the course of the experience gained by researchers in the field. At this point in time and for the foreseeable future, it appears that rigid regulations that mandate certain inflexible and formulaic responses would be counterproductive. Researchers need to have considerable leeway in making judgments about the best way to proceed in the particular situations in which they find themselves. Because it is impossible to anticipate all of the kinds of circumstances that may arise during nonintervention research with high-risk populations, discretionary best practices are preferable to guide researchers confronting novel situations. Researcher discretion should not be significantly limited by hard-and-fast regulations. Positively, IRBs should embrace the best practices identified here as viable and proven mechanisms that can potentially reduce the threat of civil tort that put their respective institutions at risk.

The third point is that law and ethics must be viewed as complementary paradigms. What is the relationship between legal regulations and the ethical conduct of health research? Ethics has to inform regulations, and ethical decisions have to supplement regulations because regulations are meant to be broad, whereas ethical reflection and deliberation are always and inescapably necessary for the practical interpretation of regulations. In time, the development of "best practices" may move beyond merely identifying a set of guidance principles; it may also require the expansion of legal requirements, protections, and interpretations to solidify good practice. The use of law in this context, however, need not occur immediately unless specific deficiencies are identified. Although there can be little question that researchers and research subjects stand to benefit from careful and thoughtful deliberations about new possible articulations of the law, we must also recognize that a voluntary system has many advantages and may be preferable, at least for the immediate future.

Finally, we would be remiss if we did not point out that the issues examined in this book urgently need continued attention by ethical and legal scholars. It is vital to gain feedback on the public health framework put forward here and to test and modify the recommended best practices to reflect the wide range of challenging circumstances that may arise during nonintervention research with high-risk populations.

REFERENCES

Administration on Children, Youth & Families. (2007). *Child Maltreatment 2005*. Washington, DC: U.S. Government Printing Office.

American Psychiatric Association. (1994). *Diagnostic and statistical manual of mental disorders* (4th ed.). Washington, DC: Author.

Appelbaum, P. S., & Rosenbaum, E. (1989). Tarasoff and the researcher: Does the duty to protect apply in the research setting? *American Psychologist, 44*, 885–894.

Brody, B. A., McCullough, L. B., & Sharp, R. R. (2005, September 21). Consensus and controversy in clinical research ethics. *JAMA, 294*, 1411–1414.

Buchanan, D., & Miller, F. G. (2005). Principles of early stopping of randomized trials for efficacy: A critique of equipoise and an alternative ethical framework. *Kennedy Institute of Ethics Journal, 15*, 163–180.

Buchanan, D., & Miller, F. G. (2006a). Justice and fairness in the Kennedy Krieger Institute lead paint study: The ethics of public health research on less expensive, less effective interventions. *American Journal of Public Health, 96*, 781–787.

Buchanan, D., & Miller, F. G. (2006b). Justice in research on human subjects. In R. Rhodes, L. Francis, & A. Silvers (Eds.), *The Blackwell guide to medical ethics* (pp. 309–341). New York: Blackwell.

Buchanan, D., & Miller, F. G. (2006c). A public health perspective on research ethics. *Journal of Medical Ethics, 32*, 729–733.

Buchanan, D., Miller, F. G., & Wallerstein, N. (2007). Ethical issues in community based participatory research: Balancing rigorous research with community participation. *Progress in Community Health Partnerships, 2*, 153–160.

Buchanan, D., Sifunda, S., Naidoo, N., James, S., & Reddy, P. (in press). Assuring adequate protections in international health research: A principled justification and practical recommendations for the role of community oversight. *Public Health Ethics*.

Bureau of Justice Statistics. (2005). *Family violence statistics including statistics on strangers and acquaintances*. Washington, DC: U.S. Department of Justice.

Bureau of Justice Statistics. (2006). *Drug use and dependence, state and federal prisoners 2004*. Washington, DC: U.S. Department of Justice.

Castro, F. G., Rios, R., & Montoya, H. (2006). Ethical community-based research with Hispanic or Latina(o) populations: Balancing research rigor and cultural responsiveness. In J. Trimble & C. B. Fisher (Eds.), *The handbook of ethical research with ethnocultural populations and communities* (pp. 137–154). Thousand Oaks, CA: Sage.

Centers for Disease Control and Prevention. (2007). *National Center for Injury Prevention and Control: Web-based Injury Statistics Query and Reporting System (WISQARS)* [online]. Available from http://www.cdc.gov/ncipc/wisqars

Childress, J. R., Faden, R., Gaare, L., Gostin, L. O., Kahn, J., Bonnie, R. J., et al. (2002). Public health ethics: Mapping the terrain. *Journal of Law, Medicine & Ethics, 30,* 170–178.

Emanuel, E., Wendler, D., & Grady, C. (2000, May 24). What makes clinical research ethical. *JAMA, 283,* 2701–2711.

Emanuel, E. J., Wendler, D., Killen, J., & Grady, C. (2004). What makes clinical research in developing countries ethical? The benchmarks of ethical research. *Journal of Infectious Diseases, 189,* 930–937.

Fisher, C. B. (1997). A relational perspective on ethics-in-science decision making for research with vulnerable populations. *IRB: Review of Human Subjects Research, 19*(5), 1–4.

Fisher, C. B. (1999). Relational ethics and research with vulnerable populations. In *Research involving persons with mental disorders that may affect decision making capacity: Vol. II. Commissioned papers by the National Bioethics Advisory Commission* (pp. 29–49). Rockville, MD: National Bioethics Advisory Commission.

Fisher, C. B. (2000). Relational ethics in psychological research: One feminist's journey. In M. Brabeck (Ed.), *Practicing feminist ethics in psychology* (pp. 125–142). Washington, DC: American Psychological Association.

Fisher, C. B. (2002a). A goodness-of-fit ethic of informed consent. *Urban Law Journal, 30,* 159–171.

Fisher, C. B. (2002b). Participant consultation: Ethical insights into parental permission and confidentiality procedures for policy relevant research with youth. In R. M. Lerner, F. Jacobs, & D. Wertlieb (Eds.), *Handbook of applied developmental science* (Vol. 4, pp. 371–396). Thousand Oaks, CA: Sage.

Fisher, C. B. (2003). A goodness-of-fit ethic for informed consent to research involving persons with mental retardation and developmental disabilities. *Mental Retardation and Developmental Disabilities Research Reviews,* 9(1), 27–31.

Fisher, C. B., Hoagwood, K., Boyce, C., Duster, T., Frank, D. A., Grisso, T., et al. (2002). Research ethics for mental health science involving ethnic minority children and youth. *American Psychologist, 57,* 1024–1040.

Fisher, C. B., Hoagwood, K., & Jensen, P. (1996). Casebook on ethical issues in research with children and adolescents with mental disorders. In K. Hoagwood, P. Jensen, & C. B. Fisher (Eds.), *Ethical issues in research with children and adolescents with mental disorders* (pp 135–238). Hillsdale, NJ: Erlbaum.

Fisher, C. B., & Lerner, R. M. (1994). Foundations of applied developmental psychology. In C. B. Fisher & R. M. Lerner (Eds.), *Applied developmental psychology* (pp. 3–20). New York: McGraw-Hill.

Fisher, C. B. & Masty, J. K. (2006). A goodness-of-fit ethic for informed consent to pediatric cancer research. In R. T. Brown (Ed.) *Comprehensive Handbook of Childhood Cancer and Sickle Cell Disease: A biopsychosocial approach.* (205–217) New York: Oxford University Press.

Fisher, C. B., & Ragsdale, K. (2006). A goodness-of-fit ethics for multicultural research. In J. Trimble & C. B. Fisher (Eds.), *The handbook of ethical research with ethnocultural populations and communities* (pp. 3–26). Thousand Oaks, CA: Sage.

Fisher, C. B., & Wallace, S. A. (2000). Through the community looking glass: Reevaluating the ethical and policy implications of research on adolescent risk and psychopathology. *Ethics & Behavior, 10,* 99–118.

Jensen, P. S., Hoagwood, K., & Trickett, E. J. (1999). Ivory towers or earthen trenches? Community collaborations to foster real-world research. *Applied Developmental Science, 4,* 206–212.

Joffe, S., & Miller, F. G. (2006). Rethinking risk-benefit assessment for phase I cancer trials. *Journal of Clinical Oncology, 24,* 2987–2990.

Lerner, R. M., Fisher, C. B., & Weinberg, R. A. (2000). Towards a science for and of the people: Promoting civil society through the application of developmental science. *Child Development, 71,* 11–20.

Levine, R. J. (1986). *Ethics and regulation of clinical research* (2nd ed.). New Haven: Yale University Press.

Liss, M. (1994). State and federal laws governing reporting for researchers. *Ethics & Behavior, 4,* 133–146.

Macklin, R. (1999). Moral progress and ethical universalism. In *Against relativism: Cultural diversity and the search for ethical universals in medicine* (pp. 249–274). New York: Oxford University Press.

McCarthy, C. (1998). The evolving story of justice in federal research policy. In J. Kahn, A. Mastroianni, & J. Sugarman (Eds.), *Beyond consent: Seeking justice in research* (pp. 11–31). New York: Oxford University Press.

Mello, M. M., Studdert, D. M., & Brennan, T. A. (2003). The rise of litigation in human subjects research. *Annals of Internal Medicine, 139,* 40–45.

Mohatt, G. V., & Thomas, L.R. (2006). "I wonder, why would you do it that way?" Ethical dilemmas in doing participatory research with Alaska Native communities. In J. E. Trimble & C. B. Fisher (Eds.), *The handbook of ethical research with ethnocultural populations and communities* (pp. 93–116).Thousand Oaks, CA: Sage.

Mulvey, E. (2004a, September). *Ethical and legal duties in conducting research on violence: Protection for subjects, third parties, and staff.* Oral presentation at National Institute on Drug Abuse Conference on Legal and Ethical Issues in Nonintervention Studies of Suicide, Child Abuse, and Violence, Bethesda, Maryland.

Mulvey, E. (2004b, September). *Research with violent, mentally ill individuals in the community.* Oral presentation at National Institute on Drug Abuse Conference on Legal and Ethical Issues in Nonintervention Studies of Suicide, Child Abuse, and Violence, Bethesda, Maryland.

National Commission for the Protection of Human Subjects of Biomedical and Behavioral Research. (1979). *Belmont Report: Ethical principles and guidelines for the protection of human subjects of research.* Washington, DC: U.S. Government Printing Office.

National Institute on Drug Abuse. (2007). *Policy on HIV education, counseling, testing, and treatment for research subjects* (Notice Number NOT-DA-07-013). Available at the National Institute on Drug Abuse Web site, http://grants.nih.gov/grants/guide/notice-files/NOT-DA-07-013.html

Noe, T. D., Manson, S. M., Croy, C., McGough, H., Henderson, J. A., & Buchwald, D. S. (2006). In their own voices: American Indian decisions to participate in health research. In J. Trimble & C. B. Fisher (Eds.), *The handbook of ethical research with ethnocultural populations and communities* (pp. 77–92). Thousand Oaks, CA: Sage.

Powers, M. (1998). Theories of justice in the context of research. In J. Kahn, A. Mastroianni, & J. Sugarman (Eds.), *Beyond consent: Seeking justice in research* (pp. 147–165). New York: Oxford University Press.

Protection of Human Subjects, 45 C.F.R. § 46 (2005).

Public Health Service Act § 301(d), 42 U.S.C. 241(d), as amended by Pub. L. No. 100-607 § 163 (1988).

Rovi, S., Chen, P. H., & Johnson, M. S. (2004). The economic burden of hospitalizations associated with child abuse and neglect. *American Journal of Public Health, 94,* 586–590.

Seiber, J. E. (2001). Privacy and confidentiality: As related to human research in social and behavioral science. In *Ethical and policy issues in research involving human participants: Vol. II. Commissioned papers and staff analysis* (pp. N1–N50). Bethesda, MD: U.S. Government Printing Office.

Singh, J. A., Abdool Karim, S. S., Abdool Karim, Q., Mlisana, K., Williamson, C., Gray, C., et al. (2006). Enrolling adolescents in research on HIV and other sensitive issues: Lessons from South Africa. *PLoS Medicine, 3,* e180.

Strode, A. E., Slack, C. M., Wassenaar, D. R., & Singh, J. A. (2007). One step forward, two steps back—Requiring ministerial approval for all "non-therapeutic" health research involving minors. *South African Medical Journal, 97,* 200–202.

Substance Abuse & Mental Health Services Administration. (2007). *Results from the 2006 National Survey on Drug Use and Health: National findings* (Office of Applied Studies, NSDUH Series H-32, DHHS Publication No. SMA 07-4293). Rockville, MD: Author.

Tarasoff v. Regents of the University of California, 551 P.2d 334 (1976).

Thompson, M. P., Kingree, J. B., & Desai, S. (2004). Gender differences in long-term health consequences of physical abuse of children: Data from a nationally representative survey. *American Journal of Public Health, 94,* 599–604.

Viswanathan, M., Ammerman, A., Eng, E., Gartlehner, G., Lohr, K. N., Griffith, D., et al. (2004). *Community-based participatory research: Assessing the evidence* (Evidence Report/Technology Assessment No. 99, prepared by RTI–University of North Carolina Evidence-based Practice Center under Contract No. 290-02-0016, AHRQ Pub. 04-E022-2). Rockville, MD: Agency for Healthcare Research & Quality.

Weijer, C., & Emanuel, E. J. (2000, August 18). Protecting communities in biomedical research. *Science, 289*, 1142–1144.

INDEX

ABOUT THE EDITORS

David Buchanan, DrPH, is a full professor of public health, director of the Division of Community Health Studies, and director of the Institute for Global Health at the University of Massachusetts at Amherst. His primary area of research lies in analyzing the ethical foundations of public health and approaches to improving population health and quality of life. He has focused in particular on the role of public health policies and programs in promoting justice and expanding human autonomy as prerequisite to improving population-based health status indicators. In the early 2000s, he spent 3 years at the National Institutes of Health as an invited research fellow in public health ethics. He is currently a coinvestigator on a project aimed at defining ethical standards for conducting research in international settings, in conjunction with the Medical Research Council and the South African AIDS Vaccine Initiative, and the codirector of the Leadership in Global Health project now underway in the southern African region, including Mozambique, South Africa, Swaziland, Zambia, and Zimbabwe. Dr. Buchanan is the author of more than 70 articles on empirical and ethical issues in public health and of three books, including *An Ethic for Health Promotion: Rethinking the Sources of Human Well Being*. He earned his master's degree and doctorate in public health at the University of California, Berkeley.

Celia B. Fisher, PhD, Marie Ward Doty Professor of Psychology and director of the Fordham University Center for Ethics Education, is chair of the U.S. Environmental Protection Agency's Human Research Subjects Board, a past member of the U.S. Department of Health and Human Services Secretary's Advisory Committee on Human Research Protections, and a founding editor of the journal *Applied Developmental Science*. Dr. Fisher chaired the American Psychological Association's Ethics Code Task Force and the New York State Licensing Board for Psychology and served on the National

Institute of Mental Health Data Safety and Monitoring Board and the Institute of Medicine's Committee on Clinical Research Involving Children. Dr. Fisher is author of *Decoding the Ethics Code: A Practical Guide for Psychologists*, coeditor of seven books including *The Handbook of Ethical Research With Ethnocultural Populations and Communities* and *The Encyclopedia of Applied Developmental Science*, and author of more than 100 theoretical and empirical publications in the areas of ethics in medical and social science research and practice and life-span development. Her federally funded research programs focus on ethical issues and the well-being of vulnerable populations, including ethnic minority youths and families, active drug users, college students at risk of drinking problems, and adults with impaired consent capacity.

Lance Gable, JD, MPH, is an assistant professor of law at Wayne State University Law School and a scholar with the Centers for Law and the Public's Health: A Collaborative at Johns Hopkins and Georgetown Universities, a Collaborating Center of the World Health Organization and the Centers for Disease Control and Prevention. He specializes in public health law, ethics, and policy; research ethics; bioterrorism and emergency preparedness; mental health; international human rights; genetics and genomics; and information privacy. He has authored or coauthored numerous publications on topics related to public health law and policy. In addition, Dr. Gable has worked as a health law expert on projects for the World Health Organization, the World Bank, and the Pan American Health Organization. Before joining the Wayne State faculty, he was a senior fellow at the Center for Law and the Public's Health from 2004 to 2006. He also served as the project director for the Emergency System for Advance Registration of Volunteer Health Professionals—Legal and Regulatory Issues Project from 2004 to 2006. In 2004, Dr. Gable served as a professorial lecturer at the Georgetown University School of Foreign Service, where he taught a course on the politics of international health. From 2003 to 2004, he was the Alfred P. Sloan Fellow in Bioterrorism Law and Policy at the Center for Law and the Public's Health. Dr. Gable practiced health law at a major international law firm in Washington, DC, from 2001 to 2002. He received a Juris Doctor from Georgetown University Law Center and a master's in public health from the Johns Hopkins Bloomberg School of Public Health in 2001. He received a bachelor's degree with a double major in political science and biology from the Johns Hopkins University in 1995.